A Survey of

CONTEMPORARY MUSIC

A SURVEY OF CONTEMPORARY MUSIC

By CECIL GRAY

Essay Index Reprint Series

 BOOKS FOR LIBRARIES PRESS

FREEPORT, NEW YORK

First Published 1924
Reprinted 1969

STANDARD BOOK NUMBER:

8369-1294-2

LIBRARY OF CONGRESS CATALOG CARD NUMBER:

75-93341

PRINTED IN THE UNITED STATES OF AMERICA

PREFACE

IN recent years it has become customary for critics to adopt an attitude of benevolent and almost obsequious neutrality towards their contemporaries, and to avoid committing themselves to the expression of any positive opinion concerning their relative stature and significance, on the ground that modern art is as yet too near us for complete and dispassionate judgement; that a certain period of time—conveniently left unspecified—must be permitted to elapse before we can hope to be able to see it in proper perspective.

Now it is true that it is virtually impossible, or at least extremely difficult, to forecast with any degree of accuracy the *historical* importance of any living artist, or to foretell the influence which he will exercise over future generations. For in the same way that in actual history a comparative mediocrity, by virtue of the eminent position in which he has been placed by accident or birth, or in consequence of the peculiar circumstances of the time at which he lived, has often been able to exercise a more decisive and dominating influence on the course of events than many infinitely greater men possessing none of these advantages and opportunities; so it frequently happens that an artist of only second-rate importance can eventually occupy a more prominent place in the history of his art than many whose works are intrinsically better. For example, Carl Philipp Emanuel Bach plays a more conspicuous

5

Preface

role in musical history books than any of the English madrigalists at the beginning of the seventeenth century, partly because he was the son of his father, and also because he played an important part in the evolution of symphonic form. The madrigalists, on the other hand, played no part in the evolution of modern musical form, and are consequently accorded a much less prominent position in musical history. The fact remains that their actual artistic achievement was incomparably greater than that of the younger Bach ; their music remains as fresh and lovely as on the day it was written, while it is impossible to listen to his at all.

In other words, we must carefully distinguish between *historical* and *aesthetic* interest. The former is conditioned by a combination of all manner of extraneous and fortuitous circumstances which cannot be foretold ; the latter, however, exists outside time and is subject only to laws which are eternal and to conditions which are changeless. The qualities which go to make a great work of art do not intrinsically differ from one age to another ; consequently there is no more difficulty in distinguishing what is good from what is bad in the art of the present day than in that of any past day, near or remote—rather less, in fact, because artists to-day speak a living language, while those of former ages speak a comparatively unfamiliar tongue which may sometimes require a certain measure of scholarship for its adequate comprehension.

The occasional forecasts of the ultimate historical

6

significance of certain composers which are made in
the following pages are purely tentative and con-
jectural, and I am quite prepared to see them falsified
by future events of which we to-day have and can
have no knowledge. By the purely aesthetic judgements, on the other hand, I am prepared to stand or
fall. This must not be construed as arrogance.
I make no claim to infallibility, but only maintain
that my opinion concerning the music of Stravinsky
or Scriabine is as likely to be right or wrong as my
opinion on the music of Dunstable or Dufay.

Why should one be afraid of being wrong? Only
fools are always right. All positive and constructive
criticism is of value, even when it is wholly wrong-
headed. The most preposterous assertions of a Ruskin,
Tolstoi, or Nietzsche have ultimately done more for
the true appreciation of art than all the colourless
non-committal timidities of ordinary art critics.
Although his judgements were invariably wrong,
William Blake is a better art critic than Mr. Bernhard
Berenson, who is always drearily and monotonously
right. Mr. Ernest Newman's opinions are nearly
always wrong, but the fact remains that his musical
criticism is of more value than that of anyone else
in this country at the present time. No doubt it is
good to be right, but it is even better to have the
courage of one's convictions. Criticism of the negative,
discreet, and non-committal order is not merely useless
either to public or to artist, but definitely harmful to
both in permitting and encouraging a good-natured,

tolerant apathy in the one, and complacent self-satisfaction in the other. Both these things spell the death of art, and must be fought as we would fight the devil. The chaotic state of musical opinion in this country to-day is, in my opinion, largely attributable to the pusillanimous abdication of its responsible leaders, and to their voluntary assumption of the passive role of bystanders and onlookers.

No apology, then, is offered for the outspoken manner of the following studies. After all, it is only within the last generation or so that it has come to be considered almost indecent to hail a living artist as a genius, and ungentlemanly to suggest that another is an imbecile. It is only recently that the pernicious heresy has arisen which teaches that no genius is without faults, and no mediocrity without redeeming features, and that consequently we must mingle our praise of the one with blame, and leaven our censure of the other with judicious approval, until black and white are merged into a uniform level of grey. It is a heresy, not so much because it is untrue—every heresy has at its base some sound justification—but because it tends to confuse genius with talent, and consequently to destroy our only absolute standard of values. Qualities which would be faults in lesser men are often transformed by genius into something very like virtues, and mediocrities can make even the greatest qualities detestable. It may be true that in life there are no saints and no sinners, no one deserving of either eternal bliss or eternal damnation. In

8

art it is not so, for the devil is here mediocrity. There is no purgatory in the world of art, but only heaven and hell.

There has hardly ever been an age in which there have been no great and outstanding figures, and there is no reason to suppose that our age is one of the rare exceptions. On the other hand, it would be absurd to expect more than a small handful of men of genius in a single generation, and if only one out of every three composers considered in the following pages were a great master, our age would be adjudged rich beyond almost any other. In other words, the critic who sets up a high standard of values must inevitably condemn at least twice as much as he commends, and this is in itself sufficient answer to the unthinking reproach of being merely destructive which is so often made against him. If anything, I must confess to an uneasy suspicion that in the following pages I have tended rather to overpraise the objects of my sympathy and admiration than to under-estimate those of my dislike and antipathy ; for although there is only heaven and hell, there are definite grades and hierarchies in both, and it is just as much a part of the critic's business to differentiate between the degrees of salvation and damnation as merely to separate the sheep from the goats and the saints from the sinners. If I have erred in this direction, it is a fault which, while it is no less to be deprecated than the contrary tendency, can at least, I venture to think, be more readily forgiven.

9

Preface

In conclusion, it might be as well to say that the following essays are addressed to the ordinary cultured music-loving public, rather than to the professional musician. Consequently, I have endeavoured to dispense as far as is possible with terms and expressions which presuppose an advanced degree of technical knowledge on the part of the reader. If I have also reluctantly decided to do without musical illustrations altogether, it is partly for the same reason, but also because only lengthy extracts such as are given in the *Oxford History of Music* are of any value at all, either for or against a composer. Little snippets of a bar or two in length, such as appear in most books dealing with music, are not merely as useless in helping one to assess the value of a composition as the reproduction of a square inch of canvas would be in deciding the merits or faults of a painting, but are even definitely harmful, in that they are apt to encourage the already pronounced tendency on the part of musicians and the musical public generally to concentrate their attention unduly on details, instead of on the work as a whole. A musical composition must be judged, like a picture, in its entirety, and no extracts, however lengthy, can give more than a superficial impression of a composer's style.

C. G.

London, 1924.

CONTENTS

THE MUSIC OF THE
NINETEENTH CENTURY

' I am afraid I am too much of a musician not to be a romanticist.'—
Friedrich Nietzsche (letter to Georg Brandes).

BY general consent the art and literature of the first half of the nineteenth century have been designated by the adjective *Romantic*; yet it is a curious anomaly that while few words possess a greater expressive significance or evoke more powerful and vivid mental associations, there is not one that has been so loosely and indiscriminately employed, with so little regard for its true meaning, which, so far from being vague and elusive, as popularly supposed, is, on the contrary, quite definite and even precise.

Originally used by Goethe to indicate what he called the ' subjective ' as opposed to the classical or objective method of artistic treatment, it eventually came to be more particularly associated with a certain group of his younger contemporaries, such as the brothers Schlegel, Tieck, Novalis, Fouqué, Werner, and others, in whose writings certain highly characteristic elements can be discerned, notably their marked predilection for moonlit forests, enchanted castles, dragons, ogres, and various other second-hand stage properties originally belonging to the Spanish dramatists—particularly Calderon, for whom the group entertained a great admiration—and for the cult of gyneolatry affected by knight-errants and Provençal minstrels. In fact it conveyed much the same meaning then as the etymologically similar designation *romanesque* does to-day, and generally speaking can be taken to indicate

13

a deliberate and conscious reversion to the ideals of the Roman Catholic Church and of the Medieval Empire; for it was a favourite theory of the school that all great art must take its departure from mythology, that the modern artist before he could hope to achieve a great art comparable with that of the ancients, must, like them, seek inspiration in his own indigenous myths and legends, which are those of the Middle Ages. This then is the first and still perhaps the most familiar conception or definition of the romantic element in literature—the renaissance of medievalism—although actually the productions of the school possessed as little in common with genuine medieval art as the art of the sixteenth century did with that of Greece or Rome—perhaps even less.

When the word was introduced into France, however, it came to mean the very opposite—Germanic rather than Romanesque, northern rather than southern; and while a few of the earlier French Romantics were Catholic and monarchist in their sympathies (such as Chateaubriand and Lamartine), the ultimate direction of the majority was anticlerical and republican. Any leanings they may have manifested towards medievalism were purely artistic, not the outcome of religious or political conviction. They were content to exploit its picturesque possibilities and nothing more. Their sympathies were futurist, not *passéist*. And this is the second generally accepted definition of Romanticism—the revolt against convention and authority whether civil, ecclesiastical, or artistic, the vindication of personal freedom in life and in art, the pursuit of the vital and characteristic at the expense, if need be, of mere formal perfection—in a word, the artistic parallel of the French Revolution, with the famous battle of Hernani in 1830 as the storming of the Bastille of sterile convention and effete tradition, with the *gilet rouge* of

Théophile Gautier as paradoxical symbol of literary *sansculottisme*.

In England romanticism was understood to consist primarily in the feeling for nature, in the rediscovery of the beauty and strangeness of natural things, in the recognition and affirmation of man's identity with the external world. It was not revolutionary or reactionary, not occupied with ideals of the past or future, but solely concerned with the eternal present, with the immanent, unchanging realities of nature and humanity.

For others, again, the distinguishing trait of romantic art resides in the element of the bizarre, the strange, the artificial, the unfamiliar; in the search after local colour, in the pursuit of novel and picturesque emotions and abnormal sensations—in a word the cult of the exotic and unnatural, as exemplified in Poe, Hoffmann, Baudelaire, and many others.

But probably for most people to-day the word serves to denote the egoistic and introspective outpourings of Byron, de Musset, and others for whom art is an opportunity for spiritual exhibitionism and literature a confessional—the curious perpetual oscillation between the extremes of cynicism and sentiment, piety and blasphemy, lubricity and idealism, of which that race of dejected and bedraggled supermen, picturesque brigands, and amorous satanists who stalk gloomily through the pages of nineteenth-century literature—Werther, René, Jean Sbogar, Rollo, Childe Harold, Axel, Maldoror, and the rest—are perhaps the most characteristic expression.

So here we have some five or six wholly different and even contradictory definitions of what constitutes the romantic spirit in literature, and it would be easy to produce as many more again. It must be self-evident that if it does not reside in any single one of these qualities, still less can it be a synthesis of them all, for they are mutually exclusive and cancel each other out. Besides, it would be easy to show that the presence of one or all of these characteristics does not necessarily result in romantic art : for example, neither the magical paraphernalia and impossible situations of Pulci's *Morgante Maggiore*, nor the hysterical emotionalism and morbid sentimentalities of Richardson's chlorotic muse, prevent the resultant impression from being the very reverse of romantic ; conversely, Gustave Flaubert, for whom ' l'art doit s'élever audessus des affections personnelles et des susceptibilités nerveuses ', whose art is a calm, impassive, almost scientific evocation distinguished by a rigorous and pitiless suppression of subjective emotion, remains, for all that, in *Saint Antoine* and in *Salammbô*, one of the greatest of the Romantics. In the face of all this we shall be justified in assuming that the romantic element in art, whatever it may be, does not reside in community of subject-matter nor in any prescribed code of intellectual values ; that neither in identity of aim nor in a common method of artistic treatment shall we find that distinctive quality which so sharply differentiates the characteristic art of the nineteenth century from that of its predecessor, however much its separate manifestations may differ from each other superficially. It would be difficult to find a more complete antithesis than that presented by the dreamy mysticism and idealistic sentimentality of Tieck and Novalis and the emotional intensity and exuberance of Victor Hugo or Michelet ; yet we are all aware of a term common to both, transcending their many fortuitous and accidental surface differences.

It is true, of course, that we can find a common factor in the spirit of disillusion and dissatisfaction with reality which runs throughout the entire art of the century like a *leitmotiv*—a kind of spiritual malady, the *spirochaeta pallida* of the soul, variously ascribed by literary critics and historians to the collapse of the intellectual solidarity of the preceding age and the failure to realize the great ideals of the Revolution, to the destructive philosophy of Kant, to the exhaustion and apathy following the Napoleonic wars, and to the rapid growth of modern industrialism. And the art of the period, whether it takes the form of a reversion to the ideals of the past, of a prospect for the future, or of a return to nature, is all an attempt to escape from the present and actual, to build up again in art the realities or, more accurately perhaps, the illusions, of which humanity had been deprived in life. Art provides an escape from reality, a sanctuary from the forces of science and commercialism, an ark of refuge on the flood-tide of materialism and democracy. This in fact constitutes the spirit of the age, and of our own age too, for that matter—the only difference being that in the art of Laforgue, Rimbaud, Ravel, and Stravinsky, and their legitimate successors, M. Dada *et fils,* the consumptive cough becomes a drunken hiccough, the pale cheeks are concealed by a coat of paint and powder, and the folded arms and melancholy hat give place to the cap and bells and the red-hot poker. The underlying spirit remains the same in all essential respects.

But the fault of this as of all the other foregoing definitions lies in regarding the fortuitous and accidental characteristics as primary and fundamental ; it will only help us to understand the particular forms which the Romantic spirit took in one particular age. There have been many Romantic movements in art, and the element which distinguishes them all is not merely the outcome of historical events, of social or psychological conditions, neither is it the monopoly of any single age or school, but an eternal, ever-fruitful artistic principle, an attitude of mind whose presence we can infallibly discern under the most diverse

B

conditions, in the most widely dissimilar utterances. It is not even confined to the modern world, but can be found just as well in so-called 'classical' art—one whole side of Greek art and life is romantic, though it is generally ignored or passed over because it does not accord with the conventional conception of 'the Greek spirit'. It does not manifest itself suddenly, but grows steadily and imperceptibly from the beginning till it eventually predominates and finally triumphs to the exclusion of everything else. Even certain scenes in Homer exhibit the romantic tendency; for example, the parting of Hector and Andromache, and the meeting of Priam and Achilles at the end of the Iliad. Euripides and the sculptor Scopas are romantic; so too are Theocritus and the poets of the Greek Anthology, Meleager in particular. In Latin art the same element can be observed in the shorter poems of Petronius and in the lyrical interludes of his *Satyricon*, in the *Golden Ass* of Apuleius, in Ausonius: most of all, perhaps, in the exquisite swan-song of the ancient world, the *Pervigilium Veneris*, with its haunting refrain like the cadence of a fountain. The art history of every civilization viewed collectively is the progress from classic to romantic values. All romantic art is a swan-song, the final expression of a civilization, the rich autumn tints of decay, the writing on the wall, the flaming comet heralding the approach of anarchy and dissolution, known to Plato and called by him the 'rebellious principle'. And it is interesting to note that the great philosopher's penetrating observations on the nature of this rebel art (in the *Republic*) are almost identical with the confession of faith of the great romantic leader, Victor Hugo, in the famous preface to his *Cromwell*[1]. And significantly enough it is to music

[1] Plato: 'Does not the rebellious principle furnish a greater variety of materials for imitation, whereas the wise and calm tempera-

that Plato attributed the greatest power to express the specifically rebel or romantic values, 'the passionate and fitful temper'. For we shall generally find that at any given period there is one art in particular which best expresses the values of that period. In the Middle Ages, for example, the predominance of architectural conceptions and methods is immediately noticeable. The music of the Netherlanders has an architectural quality; the *Divina Commedia* is like a vast Gothic cathedral. So precise are Dante's indications and even his measurements that we could almost build his *Inferno* or *Purgatorio* from them. We are told in the latter that the breadth of each staircase is about eighteen feet; that the steps leading from one cornice to another are like those which go up to San Miniato from Florence, and that the sculptures on the floor are carven like tombstones. Beatrice herself seems not a living figure at all, but more like a carven angel with wings folded crosswise on her breast, and the grotesque evocations of the *Inferno* are more like the gargoyles on Notre-Dame than human beings.

The characteristic art-expression of the succeeding era to which all the others continually tend is painting. *The Canterbury Tales*, for example, are above all pictorial in conception and treatment, reminding us irresistibly of the sumptuous and glittering procession of Gozzoli in the Ricardi palace in Florence, winding its way through a dream-like landscape, full of wonderful living portraits and feeling for natural beauty. Similarly the *Decameron* conjures up for us the gracious,

ment being always nearly equable is not easy to imitate or to appreciate when imitated?' The artist will consequently prefer the 'passionate and fitful temper' as being more susceptible of artistic treatment and offering a wider range of possibilities.

Hugo : ' The beautiful has only one type, the ugly has a thousand.' The artist should choose for his subject-matter not the beautiful but the characteristic, &c.

flower-like men and women of Piero della Francesca or Ghirlandaio.

The following age is primarily that of literature. Mozart even, pure musician though he undoubtedly was, lives for us to-day mainly by virtue of his operas : he remains the only musician who has created living human beings, fit to rank with the creations of Cervantes, Shakespeare, Molière, or Fielding. (Wagner could only create gods, but it requires a god to create a human being.) This rare quality of Mozart must not be attributed to his librettos, which, viewed apart from the music, are wholly devoid of dramatic characterization. He achieved with notes what the great writers achieved through words. His *Don Giovanni* can be placed side by side and compared in detail with the *Don Juan* of Molière or *El Burlador de Sevilla* of Tirso de Molina.

Similarly neither the consummate literary achievements of the century nor the splendid hierarchy of the French painters, from Delacroix to Cézanne, can alter the fact that, collectively speaking, music is the art of the nineteenth century—the medium which, better than any other, realizes or embodies the characteristic aims and ideas of the time, and which alone could adequately express them. The others are local or individual phenomena, but the astonishing development of the art of music is a spiritual earthquake of a violence almost without precedent, a tidal wave which sweeps over and submerges the other arts. We have only to look at contemporary literature and painting to be immediately convinced of this. Tieck and Novalis often deliberately set out to achieve a musical effect by means of words. In *Die verkehrte Welt* the former even goes so far as to write what he calls a symphony in A major with indications of *tempo* and key-signatures for each movement : the latter proclaimed as his poetic creed that poetry should only convey a vaguely emotional and symbolical meaning like music. Hoffmann, besides writing with remarkable penetration and insight about music, was a composer of uncommon talent. His writings reveal a constant and almost morbid obsession with music and musical imagery; in his admirable story about Gluck the musical intervals are personified, and his Kreisler talks of stabbing himself with a gigantic fifth. Schiller even, in an interesting letter to a friend, declared that he always sat down to write in a musical mood: only gradually did his conception clothe itself in words. Wackenroder in his *Fantasia über die Kunst* claims music to be the greatest of the arts, infinitely superior to mere poetry. For Schopenhauer the world was ' embodied music ', and Nietzsche, alternately the greatest friend and bitterest enemy of Wagner, found in music the most significant index to the spirit of his age. His own *Zarathustra*, as he himself said, is almost music.

The musical tendency of the French and English romantic schools is equally unmistakable, though, being of a more subtle and discriminating nature, it is not at first sight so readily discernible. Their artistic limitations were less pronounced, their mental horizons less sharply circumscribed than those of the German school: it is only the ultimate phase of the movement—the so-called symbolist movement—which consciously adopted music as its aesthetic ideal and sought to evolve a theory in justification of its choice. We find Baudelaire, Villiers de L'Isle-Adam, and Mallarmé among the most zealous supporters of Wagner. Indeed, as Mr. Arthur Symons has said, ' Carry the theories of Mallarmé to a practical conclusion, multiply his powers in a direct ratio, and you have Wagner.' His poetic creed was that the greatest poem is that which in its final achievement becomes a perfect music—that of Verlaine: ' De la musique avant toute chose ... et tout le reste est littérature.'

21

The Nineteenth Century

The attitude of the earlier writers towards music, however, was less conscious and their surrender to it less complete ; yet the frequency with which their poems take their departure from some accidental effect of sound or auditory impression, not merely the outcome of a vaguely musical mood, as with Schiller, but actually of a musical or tonal stimulus, is too remarkable and significant to be passed over. Examples of this will readily occur to the reader ; it is sufficient to mention Wordsworth's *Highland Reaper*, whose song suggests to the poet ' old unhappy far-off things ', Keats's *Ode to a Nightingale*, whose voice ' charm'd magic casements opening on the foam of perilous seas in faery lands forlorn ', Browning's *Toccata of Galuppi*, evoking a picture of Venice in the eighteenth century and thoughts of the vanity and transience of mortal things, the melody of the *Carneval de Venise*, suggesting to Gautier's fancy all the well-known conventional figures of a Venetian *bal masqué*, with every note or phrase, one of them being resuscitated in an appropriate posture, the *Fantaisie* of Gérard de Nerval translating into words the verbal associations of a melody, and ' le son du cor au fond des bois ', bringing vividly before de Vigny's mind the death of Roland and Oliver at Roncesvalles. And it is a curious and arresting fact which is something more than a mere coincidence that the constantly recurring dominant *motif* of all romantic art, one of the distinctive signs by which we may at once recognize the romantic spirit wherever it may happen to be (whether it be the lamentation of the harper inscribed upon the tomb of King Entef five thousand years ago in Egypt, a Chinese lyric from the eighth century, or the *Ballade des Dames du temps jadis* of François Villon), namely, the sense of regret and melancholy for the impermanence of human things, of sorrow for the loveliness that was and is no longer—should be so often peculiarly associated with or evoked by some effect of music or of tone—the distant sound of a horn in the evening, of a woman's voice singing, the passionate ecstasy of the nightingale's lament, the music of a fountain, or the monotonous rhythm of the waves of the sea.[1]   It is because ideas and emotions such as these are part of the natural province of music, because it is the melancholy privilege of music to be able to concentrate into a bar all the yearning and sadness of human destiny—a fact of which the great dramatists were well aware.   The poignance and pathos of the last act of *Othello* or of *The Cenci* pass beyond the scope of mere words, and imperiously demand the collaboration of music, and all the tragic intensity of conflicting passions in *Measure for Measure* is resolved into the lyric :

Take, O take those lips away.

It would seem that sounds are of their very nature sad ; it is certainly very much easier to write grave music than gay.   With the exception of Bach, whose art is so often the expression of a profound tranquillity and happiness, it is difficult to think of any other composer of whom the resultant impression is not one of sadness and despair.   Even the sweetness of Mozart has a bitter core to it.

But apart from this it would be easy to show that the particular and distinctive quality which the literary romantics brought into their art was the sense of the musical values of words—the growing preoccupation with sonority, with problems of rhyme and rhythm, with trains of thought suggested by chance analogies of sound rather than conditioned by any logical necessity, which eventually grew to such

[1] And ' that vulgar and tavern musick, which makes one man merry, another mad ', heard at dusk from a distant barrel-organ, may still ' strike in one a fit of devotion '.

a pitch that in many modern writers of such wholly divergent tendencies as Swinburne and Mallarmé we find pages of almost orchestral sound signifying nothing. But even in the work of those who did not go to such extremes, words tend to lose their precise meaning and come to possess an almost symbolical signification. Grammatical structure becomes lax, moods are evoked rather than realities, things suggested rather than described, verse melts into verse like wave into wave, and its music takes precedence of its literal meaning.

Nor is this tendency confined to literature alone ; it is equally well exemplified in the plastic arts. Delacroix, the great initiator of modern painting, to quote the words of Baudelaire, ' a mieux traduit qu'aucun autre l'invisible, l'impalpable, le rêve, les nerfs, l'âme. . . . Delacroix est le plus suggestif de tous les peintres.' The sculpture of Rodin also seems often to aim directly at realizing musical conceptions. Room upon room at the Hotel Biron is filled with marble groups wholly unsculptural both in conception and in execution, hopeless attempts to render in stone the intangible abstractions and spiritual realities proper to music. All the more recent manifestations of plastic art, such as cubism, futurism, expressionism, are so many attempts to achieve the ends of music through the means of their respective arts, and are only explicable as such. In fact we may say that music is a touchstone for romanticism ; to adapt and correct the celebrated dictum of Walter Pater we might say that all *romantic* art continually aspires towards the condition of music—in other words, *romanticism is the specifically musical element in art.*

To this assertion it may be objected that when we turn to music itself we find all critics and historians unanimously agreed that the music of the nineteenth century is the expression in terms of music of the quantities of literature, that its distinctive qualities are merely a translation into tone of ideas and conceptions already expressed in words and alien to music, and that it can only be understood by reference to the literature of the period.

Apart from the very natural and pardonable *a priori* assumption that what all musical critics are agreed upon must be consequently false, the theory is *per se* insupportable. For even if it is true that these new values were first expressed in literature, it does not necessarily follow that these values were literary values. On the contrary, as I have shown, they were musical ones; in other words, the writers of the period were primarily occupied with the expression of musical ideas, and it is the literary movement which is inexplicable without reference to music—a conclusion which is not in the least impaired by the fact that in point of time the literary expression preceded the musical. Literature is always the first art in which new directions are discernible—that is all. And though it is undeniable that by far the larger proportion of the great music of the period is allied to some literary idea, a closer examination of the actual works reveals the fact that they are only retranslations into sound of what are in essence musical conceptions, or else a musical interpretation of some myth or legend of universal artistic applicability. It was Weber and Wagner who actually achieved what Tieck, Novalis, &c., so conspicuously failed to achieve; it was through Berlioz and Liszt, not through Hugo or Delacroix, that the French romantic ideals found their most consummate expression; it is Frederick Delius who at a century's distance has realized in music the essentially musical impulse of Wordsworth, Keats, and Shelley, although, needless to say, it does not necessarily follow that he is a greater artist, but only that the medium he employs is more suited than theirs to the conceptions common to them all.

The Nineteenth Century

It is in itself a significant fact that while romantic literature evokes a musical mood and almost demands music in order to complete itself, ' classical ' literature rejects it as a superfluous and even antagonistic impediment. We can very well imagine music to *Romeo and Juliet, Faust, Childe Harold,* but not to the *Ajax* of Sophocles, the *Athalie* of Racine, to *Tom Jones* or *Robinson Crusoe.* If we are so perversely daring as to attempt it, the result is the artistic equivalent of a rape—viz. Strauss's *Don Quixote.* Composers have found and will probably continue to find musical suggestiveness in Nietzsche's *Zarathustra,* but no one has yet been inspired to write a symphonic poem on the *Ethics* of Spinoza or has tried to set to music Kant's disquisition on the categorical imperative.

It is one of the commonplaces of musical criticism to dismiss the symphonic poems of Franz Liszt as ' decorative scene-painting ', as ' consisting in effects derived from a desire to illustrate ', and so on. Nothing could be farther from the truth or less in accordance with the facts. In the first of the series, based upon the poem of Victor Hugo, *Ce qu'on entend sur la montagne,* Liszt has merely sought to realize in sound the familiar conception of the contrast between the tranquillity of nature and the sadness of humanity— an idea which, though it may be realizable in any art, is more particularly suited to a musical treatment, as is shown by the actual poem itself being quite literally the description of a musical composition. In fact Hugo was guilty of a musical programme, not Liszt of a literary one. And while the *Tasso* may have been suggested to Liszt by the unhappy life and subsequent apotheosis of the great Italian poet, it might just as well, as far as the listener is concerned, bear the name of any other man who was persecuted during his lifetime and eventually immortalized—in fact of any great artist whatsoever. The work is not in any way a tonal biography of the poet ; the title bears only a symbolic relation to the music. The actual programme is contained in the sub-title, *Lamento e Trionfo*—the most elementary of all musical conceptions, and not a literary one at all. Indeed most of Liszt's works are simply variants or extensions of this simple formula. Such is the *Prometheus*, in which the composer seeks only to interpret the musical application of the myth—in his own prefixed words : ' Es genügte, in der Musik die Stimmungen aufgehen zu lassen, welche unter den verschiedenen wechselnden Formen des Mythus seine Wesenheit, gleichsam seine Seele, bilden; Kühnheit, Leiden, Ausharren, Erlösung.' *Mazeppa* again is only another thinly disguised variation of the same theme: ' Il court, il vole, il tombe—et se relève roi.' If these are to be called programme music, scene-painting, impressionism, and what not, then every other composition must necessarily be so designated which commences in a minor key, *adagio* and *piano*, and ends *fortissimo* in the major. Which is absurd.

The words of Lamartine placed at the head of *Les Préludes* convey no literary meaning whatever, and certainly contain no image susceptible of illustration. The *Hungaria Festklänge* and *Hamlet* bear no other indication of intent beyond their titles ; the three movements of the great *Faust Symphony*, called respectively *Faust*, *Gretchen*, and *Mephistopheles*, are not in any sense a tonal reconstruction of Goethe's drama or an attempt to recapitulate the sequence of its events. All these titles are purely symbolical, and it is just as legitimate to call a work *Faust* as to call it *Symphony in C minor*, to name a movement *Gretchen* instead of merely *Andante in A* : their purpose after all being only to give the listener a more precise and definite idea of what he is to expect than is afforded by the more technical expressions. They symbolize states of mind and evoke certain associations—human and psychological rather than literary or pictorial—which enable him to grasp the work more readily they are, in fact, spiritual key-signatures. Again, if these are to be considered 'programme music', then all music which shows traces of any spiritual mood or mental state must likewise be 'programme music'.

Berlioz admittedly presents greater difficulties. It would be next to impossible to deduce from his works a common formula or to discover a single direction to which they all tend to conform. Illogical, inconsistent, lacking in taste, self-restraint, self-criticism, and all the other discreet virtues, he certainly was ; but so is a volcanic eruption, and it would be as reasonable to complain of their absence from the one as from the other. Berlioz sets all our delicate and complex critical apparatus oscillating like a seismograph in an earthquake ; he is like a blind, instinctive, elemental force, as unconscious of his direction as he is unconcerned with it. But this much we can say with absolute certitude, that the habit of regarding this astonishing and bewildering genius—who, when Liszt was only a brilliant pianist, when Chopin was almost unknown, before even Meyerbeer had become famous, years before Wagner had even written *Rienzi*, had initiated and carried through single-handed, with no models but Gluck and Spontini, one of the greatest revolutions in musical art—merely as a clever and daring book-illustrator, a kind of Gustave Doré of music endeavouring to translate into sound conceptions and ideas alien to music, is one of the most signally depressing instances of the anile imbecility prevalent in musical circles. More than any of his contemporaries Berlioz was a pure musician, the spirit of music incarnate for anyone who has eyes to see, or rather ears to hear—an admittedly rare possession, but surely not sufficiently so to account for such a complete failure to appreciate one of the greatest spirits in all music. And without at all seeking to discount the frequently splendid achievement of Victor Hugo or of the other great Romantics, it is equally undeniable that it is Berlioz who is the fullest and most vital exponent of the French romantic spirit. In proportion as the greatness of Berlioz becomes more apparent year by year, so does the brightness wane and the glitter tarnish on the shield of *Hernani*. What is mere rhetoric, bombast, and exaggeration in Hugo becomes in Berlioz an irresistible torrent of eloquence, grandeur, and passion, sweeping all before it. This may be partly due to the personal equation ; with all his splendid qualities there is a strain of vulgarity apparent in Hugo which is not to be found in Berlioz. But it is even more a question of inherent artistic suitability. We condone and even approve in music things that would be intolerable in literature. If Tristan and Isolde or Salome were to behave on the stage as they do in the orchestra, the police would soon stop the performance. Music can sustain an emotional intensity which no other art can support without becoming exaggerated or hysterical—in fact literary faults are musical virtues. A very good example of this is afforded by Berlioz's *Symphonie fantastique*, and more particularly by its pendant *Lélio*, in which the literary monologue is the raving of a maniac, while the musical expression of the same sentiments and emotions is wholly satisfactory. In music there is no exaggeration, there can be no excess, because there is no possible comparison with reality, but the Damocles sword of the ridiculous is perpetually suspended above the poet's head—or, less poetically, the rotten eggs of the gallery are aimed at it. And this is in itself perhaps the best reason of all why it is in music, not in literature, sculpture, or painting, that the romantic movement attains its fullest expression.

The Nineteenth Century

Although Berlioz's works are generally associated with literary conceptions, his attitude towards them was first and last that of a musician. He appreciated in literature only that which stimulated his musical fancy. No one of genuinely literary susceptibilities could possibly have brought himself to travesty and pervert a *Faust* or *Romeo and Juliet* as he did. At every turn he violates the literary work in deference to the exigencies of some preconceived musical plan, selecting only those elements in it which suggest or demand a musical treatment. That he received as powerful a stimulus from literature as Gluck did from champagne and Wagner from satin dressing-gowns, and others in even more curious ways, may be interesting enough psychologically, but that is all; the resultant music is no more literary than Gluck's is alcoholic or Wagner's a tonal haberdashery.

Every event in Berlioz's life evoked a musical emotion and was by some alchemy transmuted into rhythm, melody, or an effect of tone colour. He seems even to have seen people as if enveloped in a musical aura; Harriet Smithson becomes a musical theme, his *idée fixe*, just as in a hashish dream our ideas are projected in the form of geometrical figures.

Now this is not programme music in the proper sense of the word, and to say that 'in a large part of the *Fantastic Symphony*, notably the *finale*, the music is sheer nonsense unless the hearer has knowledge of the programme', is wholly untrue; a knowledge of the programme tends rather to disturb and hinder its purely musical appreciation. That Berlioz himself eventually came to this conclusion is shown by a letter to a friend, in the course of which he declares that the titles alone of each movement suffice for their adequate comprehension. The object of the music is not to bring before the listener the images which may have given rise to it. The end is music, and music only,

the literary idea associated with it being not even
a means but a mere suggestion of a certain line of
thought. Real programme music, on the other hand,
in the proper sense· of the word, is that which aims
directly at the realization through music of a purpose
external to the music, in which music is only the
means to the attainment of a literary or pictorial end
(Wagner's heresy, though fortunately in actual practice
he did not act upon it), or music which strives to
represent actual happenings and ' things that you may
touch or see ' [1]. Such is the music of Strauss, who, in
a moment of expansiveness, once declared to a disciple
that he looked forward to the day when one would be
able to describe a teaspoon in music so realistically
that every one would at once recognize the intention
—or of Debussy, whose respectful solicitude for literature was so great that he refused to allow any mere
' parasitic ' musical interest to hinder the dramatic
development which *Pelléas et Mélisande* so conspicuously lacks.

More of this anon ; for the present it is only necessary to say that if we have particularly emphasized
the wholly musical intention of the great Romantic
composers in general, of Berlioz and Liszt in particular,
it is because the popular misconception of them as
absorbed by pictorial considerations and as having no
regard for the demands of form seriously militates
against their due appreciation, and is directly responsible for their present neglect, not because programme
music so called is necessarily *per se* condemnable.
Nothing could be more futile than to attempt to
limit or restrict the boundaries of an art like music,
to declare dogmatically what music can or cannot
do, should or should not do. Music is an artistic
language as much as words are, and has an equal
right to do anything it pleases. In literature the most

[1] ' As curculio, vespertilio, pugio, scipio, and papilio.'

The Nineteenth Century

dissimilar utterances are equally legitimate. We do not condemn *a priori* a lyric of Campian because there also exists the philosophy of Kant, or the plays of Racine because they are wholly at variance with the aims of Victor Hugo. Similarly the legitimacy of Bach's music does not necessarily impair that of Strauss or of Debussy.

But though the spheres of all the arts overlap, though their circumferences may be constantly extending, they are described on immutable centres. In other words, while we have no right to say that music cannot or should not do this or that, we *can* say with a fair degree of certainty what it can do better than any other mode of artistic expression, or what things it cannot do as well. And the particular conceptions which music can express better than any other art—the centre about which the musical circle is described—are those which are called Romantic. *Absolute music*, in the proper sense of the term, is not what we are accustomed to call *abstract* music, mere tonal arabesque, the element of architectonic beauty, but *romantic music*, the music of passion, emotion, and sentiment, for it is in the expression of these things that music is supreme. The romantic movement, so far from being an apostasy or a denial and rejection of the principles of musical art, was the triumphant affirmation of its intrinsic being, of its innermost aesthetic nature. Music is the romantic art; and it follows that the greatest music has been, is, and always will be, romantic, in the widest and indeed only legitimate sense of the word.

RICHARD STRAUSS

IN 1886, the year in which Richard Strauss, with his Symphonic Fantasia, *Aus Italien,* made his first decided step away from the classical tradition, to which he had hitherto been a loyal and convinced adherent, the world of music presented an interesting and at the same time problematic aspect. The long and bitter struggle which had been waged for a whole generation between the partisans of Liszt on the one hand and those of Brahms on the other had practically been decided in favour of the former. The musical campaigns of Berlioz from London to Moscow, Paris to Budapest, which he himself had likened to those of Napoleon; the dazzling career of Liszt, and the irresistible magnetism of his personality; the almost legendary existence of Wagner, with its final triumphant apotheosis—all these things had at last completely conquered the sympathy and admiration of their contemporaries. But with the death of Wagner in 1883, followed by that of Liszt three years later (Berlioz had, of course, died some time before), the movement seemed to have come to a sudden and premature close. There was no figure of sufficiently outstanding eminence to give a fresh impetus or a new direction to it, and the apostasy of von Bülow and other distinguished followers of the romantic banner seemed to have given the neo-classic school of Brahms a temporary ascendancy for the first time, from which it was not slow to profit.

It is a curiously ironical circumstance that von Bülow should have been the first to draw attention to and encourage the future leader of the movement on which

C

he himself had so decisively turned his back. But certainly he might well be excused for not having discerned a potential rebel in the quiet young man with the high ingenuous forehead, fair curly hair, baby-blue eyes, receding chin, and hesitant demeanour which the portraits of the period reveal : whose orthodoxy, amply attested by his symphony, sonatas, and quartets, must have seemed, even to the most acute and penetrating observer, beyond suspicion or reproach. Even to-day in full knowledge of his subsequent career, there is something not readily explicable in his sudden conversion. Strauss himself, surprisingly enough, attributes it to the influence of one Alexander Ritter, a nephew and enthusiastic admirer of Wagner, with whom he came into contact in the course of 1885. ' It is to Ritter alone ', he remarks, ' that I am indebted for my knowledge of Liszt and Wagner ; it was he who showed me the importance of the writings and works of these two masters in the history of art. It was he who by years of lesson and friendly counsel made me a *Zukunfts-musiker*, and set my feet on a road where now I can walk unaided and alone.'

This and similar assertions of his indebtedness to Ritter have often been quoted by Strauss's critics and biographers, but none of them seem to have realized what a very extraordinary admission it is. It is true that Strauss has recently been reproached with a lack of interest in contemporary developments, and he has perhaps been comparatively indifferent to any other music but his own ; but what are we to make of a young musician of twenty-one—i. e. at the most receptive and speculative period of his life—who, in spite of having already written a considerable number of works, was yet so little interested in the unprecedented controversy which had been raging for some twenty years or more in the musical world, that he had never even taken the trouble to make himself acquainted with either the personalities or the works which had caused it? Is there in the history of any art a recorded instance of a similar psychological development?

However that may be, Wagnerians and Lisztians alike were both so frankly delighted at his appearance that his credentials and antecedents were not too closely scrutinized. He certainly seemed to be a most eligible young man who could be relied upon to maintain the honour of his house. Consequently, his first advances in *Aus Italien* were favourably received, and the romantic orthodoxy of his next work, *Macbeth*, was so unimpeachable, so irreproachable, that without further ado the widowed muse of Liszt and Wagner bestowed her hand and estates upon him, and he was at once proclaimed as the long awaited and pre-destined successor of the great triumvirate, Berlioz, Liszt, and Wagner. But before we go on to consider his administration of the romantic estate it will first be necessary to devote a few words to a survey of its nature and extent.

Although it is no longer customary to speak of musical form in an absolute sense, there are neverthe-less two abstract principles of design, two definitely conflicting formal tendencies in music, represented concretely by the sonata and the fugue. The former evolves from diversity to unity; its essential charac-teristic is to be found in the clash of opposing forces and of sharply contrasted ideas or moods. Two themes are postulated, and the subsequent course of the movement is spent in bringing them into mutual relation and equilibrium. Fugal form, on the other hand, progresses from unity to diversity, expanding and branching out into infinite complexity from a single germ or seed, like the oak from the acorn, relentlessly, inevitably, fatally. A fugue is indeed, in

c 2

Richard Strauss

the words of Sir Thomas Browne, ' a shadowed and hieroglyphical image of the whole world '.

The main point of interest in the sonata lies in what we may term the plot, the intrigue, the action, in the picaresque adventurings of two themes through different keys, exciting situations, hairbreadth escapes, miraculous encounters, and unexpected *dénouements*—in the *pathos*, to use the language of Aristotle. There is no plot in the fugue; there we are concerned only with the revelation of implicit possibilities, with the unfolding of what is already latent in the theme itself—in a word, with the *ethos*. Given the two themes of a sonata, no one could possibly hope to be able to determine, even approximately, the course of the drama which is impending, or to foretell with any degree of accuracy the triumphant unravelling of the knot, or the solution of the problem set forth; everything is arbitrary and depends wholly on the element of the incalculable. The composer can at will change the whole current of events, can interfere despotically in the action like the *Deus ex machina* of Greek drama. But given the subject of a fugue, we can to a very great extent foresee its ultimate development if we have sufficient musicianship, because nothing can happen which is not preordained, as it were, predetermined, predestined, latent in embryo in the thematic germ. Fugue is not a problem, but a solution, a kind of square root, a deduction from evidence withheld. The composer can only develop what is there already. He is the slave of his own creation, as Frankenstein of his monster; like Wotan, he is controlled by forces greater than himself.

Now, the classical spirit, in whatever art it may happen to manifest itself, is primarily one of action, movement, and incident; consequently sonata form and its derivatives constitute the formal direction to which the classical mind inclines. The romantic spirit being essentially one of unity—of mood, subject-matter, and thematic material—lyrical rather than dramatic, contemplative rather than active, it follows inevitably that the fugue is the romantic form *par excellence*. Hence we find that the great romantic composers were impelled by the very nature of their thought towards the formal principle embodied in fugal rather than in sonata form—i.e. the principle of unity rather than that of diversity of thematic material; the Berlioz *idée fixe* and the Lisztian *representative theme* are both attempts to create a form more in accordance with their requirements than the classical form, more suited to those conceptions which we call romantic.

Now let us return to Strauss. As I have already said, he adheres closely to the formal implications of the romantic ideal in the first of his series of symphonic poems. In *Macbeth* there is nothing of the stress and dramatic conflict which characterizes the play; the whole work, with the exception of a few passing allusions to Lady Macbeth which are similar in character to the episodes of a fugue, consists in the delineation of the personality of the principal protagonist. In other words, the drama is purely psychological; the place of action is the hero's mind.

In *Don Juan*, which follows closely upon it, the tragedy is similarly enacted in the hero's soul. All the determinant factors in his downfall are to be found in his character, not in the more or less fortuitous incidents of his career. Anna, the Countess, the village maiden, the carnival scene, are all in the nature of *intermezzi*. The women are only gracious phantoms from the outside world, or, more accurately, mere projections of his own mind which flit across the surface of the work without shaping its course or exerting any influence in the final catastrophe. Nevertheless there is infinitely more diversity and action in *Don Juan* than in *Macbeth*. The episodes are of greater frequency and importance, and tend consequently to impair the unity of the work.

Tod und Verklärung, on the other hand, is again obviously modelled upon Lisztian prototypes. It is, in fact, only a thinly disguised variant of the most primitive and characteristic of that master's formal conceptions, as exemplified in *Mazeppa*, *Prometheus*, and *Tasso—Lamento e trionfo*. It is no mere coincidence that it should be, on the whole, quite apart from the question of its purely musical qualities, the most formally satisfying of all Strauss's larger orchestral works, because there is nothing in the poetic basis to interfere with the musical development which is of a quite remarkable continuity.

In *Till Eulenspiegel*, the next of the series, the Lisztian form is discarded in favour of the classical *rondo*, a choice which, it is both instructive and significant to observe, is largely dictated by the nature of the subject which Strauss has selected for treatment; indeed, it has frequently been said that one of his most noteworthy characteristics is his fine instinct for choosing the form which is best suited to his conception. Here, for example, the *rondo* form is peculiarly apposite to the nature of his programme. It is true that Till remains the central figure in the drama, but the action no longer takes place within his own consciousness, as in *Don Juan* or *Macbeth*. His personality undergoes no similar psychological change or development; the main interest of the work lies precisely in the episodes, in his exploits and adventures; consequently the romantic form would have been wholly unsuitable. This work constitutes a definite break with the old form.

In *Also sprach Zarathustra* Strauss reverts to the romantic conception. It conforms structurally to the principle of the transformation of a single theme which runs throughout the entire work, dominating it like a *leitmotiv*. This is again largely determined by the choice of subject. There is more of Faust in the character of the principal protagonist than of Nietzsche's Zarathustra.

With *Don Quixote*, however, Strauss finally abandons the romantic symphonic poem form, and adopts in its place the classical variation, which, despite its superficial similarity, is a very different thing. In the former the aim is to preserve and to emphasize the close relation between the transformations and the original theme which engenders them, and to reveal and affirm their essential underlying solidarity. In the latter, on the contrary, the object is rather to accentuate the difference between the successive variations, and to conceal, as far as possible, their common origin; and as the most remarkable characteristic of Don Quixote was the discrepancy between his fundamental sanity and his fantastic delusions, so the most striking feature of Strauss's work consists in the ingenious and extravagant distortions to which the theme, naturally so grave and knightly, is subjected.

Ein Heldenleben, although called a symphonic poem by the composer, is really nothing of the kind. Both in form and programme it is more in the nature of the first movement of a symphony, magnified and distended out of all proportion, and consists in strongly contrasted sections and in the conflict of opposing forces. The first three parts constitute the exposition, the battle section is the working-out, and the final sections are a recapitulation, not only of the work, but also of the hero's—i.e. his own—life and achievements.

Finally, the *Sinfonia domestica*, which follows at a distance of five years, is wholly classical both in form and programmatic intention, while the *Alpine Symphony* is again, like *Heldenleben*, a kind of gigantic first movement.

Richard Strauss

This necessarily brief exposition of Strauss's purely formal career reveals, first, a fluctuating alternation between the classic and the romantic forms, and a steady recession from the latter, ending in the complete triumph of the former; secondly, a definite relation between this progression and his constantly growing predilection for pictorial and literary suggestions. It will be noted that the works in which they predominate are the farthest removed from the symphonic poem. This is no mere coincidence either, as we shall see if we reflect a little. The best symphonic poems will invariably be found to be those which contain the least amount of illustrative intention, and, as was shown in the preceding chapter, Liszt was very well aware of this. The reason is, of course, that the romantic form must evolve out of itself, must unfold itself by the force of its initial momentum. It cannot develop satisfactorily in accordance with the dictates of some extraneous literary intention. The symphony, on the other hand, can very much more easily be mapped out in accordance with some preconceived scheme; it is a far more architectural form, and as the architect is largely governed in his work by external considerations, such as the amount of space at his disposal and so forth, so the symphony lends itself much more readily to the realization of some preconceived literary scheme than does the symphonic poem. Consequently, Strauss's increasing tendency to sacrifice musical continuity and organic development to some illustrative purpose inevitably led him away from the romantic back to the old classic form. In his later works he builds in sections, according to some ground-plan, which he then brings into co-ordination and balance; the music does not grow spontaneously from bar to bar.

In short—and this is the point I wish particularly to make—Strauss, so far from being, in his orchestral works, as most critics suppose, the successor of Berlioz and Liszt, the master who extended and perfected their formal innovations, giving satisfactory shape to what were only, in their hands, tentative and imperfect experiments, was, on the contrary, directly opposed to them and their ideals ; so far from continuing and perfecting their achievement, he turned his back upon it.

His operatic sequence presents analogous features. The first opera, *Guntram*, which falls between *Tod und Verklärung* and *Till Eulenspiegel*, is, like *Macbeth*, essentially romantic in tendency and derivation, full of long soliloquies and entirely lacking in dramatic interest. *Feuersnot*, written some ten years later, after *Heldenleben*, is in the nature of a transition work. The action is much swifter, and is no longer, as in *Guntram*, held up in order to give vent to a purely musical impulse.

But it is not until we reach *Salome*, after his virtual abandonment of the concert hall for the theatre— i.e. after the *Sinfonia domestica*—that Strauss finally attains the goal towards which he had all the time been perceptibly striving. The pictorial element in his music which had been gradually assuming greater importance with each successive work had now finally gained the upper hand. The music is completely unintelligible without reference to the text ; no opportunities are taken for the purposes of purely musical development. Not merely is the music illustrative of the action, but every bar is crowded with the most minute and graphic word-painting. Hardly an image contained in the text is allowed to pass without its musical equivalent, the texture of the score being made up almost entirely of a rapid and unending succession of literary images transposed into musical synonyms. In this work and in *Elektra* Strauss reached a terminal point beyond which it was

41

manifestly impossible for anyone to go. They are
the logical conclusion towards which all his works,
from *Aus Italien* onwards, inevitably tend.

It is a curious and instructive paradox that the composer who most insistently proclaimed the aesthetic
falsity of the symphonic poem as a form, and the
inability of programme music to make itself intelligible
without the elucidatory aid of stage action, namely,
Richard Wagner, should have achieved his most complete and homogeneous artistic success with a work
which is to all intents and purposes a symphonic poem
to which voice parts have been not too skilfully
added ; while Strauss, who had always upheld the
legitimacy of the symphonic poem and had always
been a convinced believer in the power of music, alone
and unaided, to express practically anything, came
ultimately to the music-drama as the most appropriate
form for the realization of his artistic aims. *Salome*
and *Elektra* are the logical outcome of Wagner's
theories ; *Tristan* is the most eloquent vindication of
the Lisztian ideals. The theories of both Wagner and
Strauss are diametrically opposed to their practice.

And so we find that in the end Strauss is no more
the successor of Wagner than of Liszt and Berlioz,
and although he did unquestionably fall heir to the
romantic heritage as regards orchestral technique,
harmonic vocabulary, and idiom generally, he applied
them to wholly different ends. His avowed object of
bringing music into direct relation with daily life, and
of developing its descriptive scope to such a pitch that
it would be possible to depict a teaspoon in music, is
at the opposite pole from the aim of the romantic
composers, who sought to depict vague intangible
moods and ideas rather than concrete realities, and are
more attracted to the exotic, the strange, and the
remote than to the commonplace actualities of every-
day existence.

But, singularly enough, it is not this aspect of Strauss's art that has caused most controversy, but his endeavour to extend the graphic capacity of music to include abstract ideas as well. For example, a great deal of ink has been spilt over *Zarathustra* and the alleged inability of music to express philosophical conceptions. It is all the more curious because there is less actual illustration in this work than in almost any of his others. The misunderstanding probably originates in the mistaken idea that Nietzsche's work is an abstruse and highly recondite essay in metaphysics. Actually Nietzsche was not a philosopher at all, and only a very superficial though brilliant thinker. On the other hand, he was a great poet, and *Zarathustra* is really nothing but a magnificent prose poem. In what, one would like to know, does the inherent unsuitability for musical treatment of such suggestions as 'Religious Ideas', 'Joys and Passions', 'Of Knowledge', 'Dance Song', &c., consist? Ideas such as these—if indeed we can dignify them by the name of ideas—are the very stuff of which music has always been made, and probably always will be made. It is strange to find a critic of Mr. Newman's gifts swallowing whole Strauss's representations of windmills and bleating sheep, and yet objecting to his attempts at expressing abstract emotions. For example he instances a theme which Strauss introduces in *Zarathustra*, complaining that 'It no more suggests disgust than it does the toothache; and when at a later stage he (Strauss) brings in the theme in diminution and asks us to see in this the partly convalescent Zarathustra making sport of his previous depression of spirits we can only say that we are unable to oblige him'. This is very naïve and illogical. After all, does the aggregation of the seven letters in the word disgust convey any idea of the sensation of disgust, or does even the sound of the word? On the contrary the word only suggests it to us by virtue of our tacit acceptance of an association. Ultimately, no words express their meaning in the strict sense except onomatopoeics such as ' hiss ' or ' hush ', but that is no reason why we should restrict our literature to the limited sphere of action to which they give access. All art depends on our acceptance of certain conventions. Their artificiality does not necessarily invalidate the use which we make of them. In the Moscow Art Theatre, we are told, a strip of hanging drapery was employed to represent the tower in *Pelléas et Mélisande*. It is beside the point to complain that it does not look in the least like a tower ; we are only asked to suppose for a moment that it is a tower, for the purposes of the play. Euclid would have been the first to admit that AB no more suggests a straight line than it does an able-bodied seaman, but without such elementary assumptions he is unable to prove his propositions. The fact that Strauss's theme might represent toothache just as well as disgust is wholly irrelevant.

The point is that once you admit the capacity of music to represent actualities and are prepared to justify its employment for the purpose, it becomes impossible to draw the line at any definite place and say, ' This cannot be allowed '. In the same way that language originated in the formation and employment of words imitative of natural sounds and writing in pictorial representations of the object which was to be denoted, so the earliest and most primitive employment of music as a means of description is naturally to be found in the representation of more or less readily identifiable phenomena, such as the sound of running water, the rustle of leaves in the forest, or the songs of birds. It would be difficult to find any one to-day who was prepared to deny the power of music to suggest such things or to dispute the legitimacy of using it for that purpose. Yet it would be at least a logical position to take up, since in actual practice Mozart is probably the only composer of the highest rank who seems never to have exploited this resource of his art. But once you admit the validity of the procedure, you must accept its logical implications. For as there are only a very limited number of phenomena which lend themselves to such direct and recognizable transcription, a convention or symbolic representation is employed in language and ideographic writing to correspond to a second group of concepts. In the Mexican pictographic writing, for example, the idea of famine or starvation was represented by a human figure with protruding ribs, eternity by a serpent with its tail in its mouth, and so forth. Similarly one can find in music innumerable attempts at giving a symbolic rendering of such ideas, particularly in the work of Wagner, whose sword, swan, and ring motives belong to this category.

Finally, there is the ideographic stage, in which there is no definite relation between the idea expressed and the characters which are used to express it. The connexion is purely arbitrary. It is this that Strauss has so often attempted to do, and in associating a more or less arbitrary sequence of notes with some particular idea he is not necessarily making music perform a task of which it is fundamentally incapable, or one which is outside its legitimate sphere of action. It is as well to remember that Bach, in his setting of the *Credo* in the great *B minor Mass*, has clearly shown —to quote the admirable words of Schweitzer—that the dogma of the Trinity ' can be expressed much more clearly and satisfactorily in music than in verbal formulae. His exegesis of these passages in the Nicene Creed has resolved the disputes that excited the Eastern world for generations and finally delivered it over to Islam ; his presentation of the dogma even

Richard Strauss

makes it acceptable and comprehensible to minds for whom dogma has no attraction.' In view of this and many similar instances in the work of the master, who would be bold enough to challenge the ability of music to express, with a mathematical precision surpassing even that of Spinoza, even the most abstract and metaphysical conceptions in philosophic thought? There is nothing music cannot be made to do in the hands of a man of genius; the fact that Strauss frequently, perhaps generally, fails to convince us, is not a consequence of the inherent disability of music to express his ideas, but simply because the majority of his ideas are not worth expressing, his intentions not worth realizing. Moreover, he is perpetually seeking to express in terms of music ideas which have already received complete and satisfactory expression in some other medium. The music of *Salome* and *Elektra* is largely a mere reduplication of what has already received dramatic and literary form, and these works are, in fact, a kind of artistic Rosetta stone expressing identical thoughts in two languages, literary and musical. Strauss does not, as Bach nearly always does, achieve something which could not just as well be achieved in any other artistic medium. It is the fault of Strauss, not of music; in a word, he has not sufficient genius.

The sudden *volte-face* which Strauss executed after *Elektra* has mystified and disconcerted many people, although in reality there is nothing at all extraordinary in it—indeed, it was only to be expected. The explanation of it is that Strauss never was a revolutionary artist or an innovator, either of the kind of Berlioz or Moussorgsky, who were instinctively and fundamentally in opposition to existing traditions from the very outset of their respective careers, nor of the type of which Wagner and Schönberg are examples, who only attain to their end after years of ceaseless endeavour to express themselves, and after countless doubts and hesitations. Psychologically Strauss is the very type of the conventional musician ; in a less stormy and critical period the chances are that he would have continued to work contentedly and unquestioningly in the traditional forms of his time. His sudden and dramatic conversion to the aims and ideals of the romantic faith was due to circumstances and to environment rather than to natural inclination or inward conviction ; besides, it was always more apparent than real.

Once this simple fact is grasped there is no mystery about Strauss ; it explains him and everything about him entirely. It explains, in the first place, the suspicious alacrity with which he suddenly became a *Zukunftsmusiker* after having been a docile follower of Brahms. For immature as the early works of a man of genius may be, one can always trace some kind of mental development or at least some kind of artistic connexion between them and the works of his maturity. This one cannot do in the music of Strauss. They seem, and are, totally unrelated to each other. It is only at the end of his career that the *Kapellmeister* shows himself again unmistakably.

It explains too the complete lack of sincerity which every intelligent or sensitive student of his work cannot fail to recognize. He may sweep us off our feet for a moment, but he never convinces us. More than that even ; we feel that he is perpetually offering violence to his artistic conscience. In his heart of hearts he probably rather dislikes modern music, dislikes even his own, in the same way that Byron despised his own poetry, preferring that of Pope and Dryden. One finds in both musician and poet the same almost insulting insouciance and perversity, the same insatiable desire to startle and shock—always a sure symptom of spiritual discord and inner conflict.

47

Richard Strauss

Strauss's admiration of Mozart has often been regarded as a mere pose; it never seems to have occurred to anyone to suspect that in reality it is his ' modernity ' that is the pose, his love of Mozart the only genuine and sincere thing about him.

Above all does this explain the undercurrent of weariness and disgust, of satiety and disillusion which runs throughout his entire work like the *idée fixe* in the *Symphonie fantastique* of Berlioz. As M. Romain Rolland has said so admirably in his essay on Strauss, ' Guntram kills Robert, and immediately lets fall his sword. The frenzied laugh of Zarathustra ends in an avowal of discouraged impotence. The delirious passion of Don Juan dies away in nothingness. Don Quixote in dying forswears his illusions. Even the hero himself admits the futility of his work and seeks oblivion in an indifferent Nature.'

The ancient Greek dramatists were fond of depicting their heroes triumphing even in adversity, maintaining their spiritual integrity in the face of overwhelming disaster and irremediable defeat; Strauss's heroes invariably prevail over their adversaries, but are defeated through some fatal weakness, some spiritual flaw within themselves. And so with Strauss himself; he has gained the whole world, but he has lost his soul. His whole career is symbolically mirrored in his own *Don Juan*—in the splendid vitality and high promise of the beginning, the subsequent period of cold and reckless perversity, the gradual oncoming of the inevitable nemesis of weariness and disillusion, until at last, in the words of Lenau, on whose poem the work is ostensibly based, ' ergreift ihn der Ekel, und der ist der Teufel der ihn holt '; and the theme of disgust that is blared out triumphantly in *Don Juan* reappears in *Zarathustra*. In place of the arrogant triumphant figure conceived and portrayed by Nietzsche we are shown a man tormented by doubts and disillusion, desperately seeking relief in religion, passion, science, and intellectual ecstasy, and finally ending up where he began, in doubt and disillusion. Strauss's Zarathustra is, in fact, only an intellectual Don Juan—himself. A strange kind of a Superman, this ; one wonders what Nietzsche would have to say to it.

Finally, what could be more natural, more under-standable, than that this artistic Don Juan, this intellectual Faust, satiated with the exotic charms of Salome, and nauseated by the hate-drunken ravings of Elektra—his Donna Elvira, his Countess—should at the last turn back to the little country maid—his Mozart? ' I have always wanted to write an opera like Mozart's,' he is reported to have said after the first performance of *Der Rosenkavalier*, ' and now I have done it.' Never was a man more pathetically, grotesquely mistaken. One cannot spend most of one's life in a kind of spiritual debauchery, in pursuit of a false or unworthy ideal, as Strauss has done, even with the intention of ultimately achieving the work for which one is fitted, without fatally, inevitably killing something within oneself. Unfortunately, one only finds it out too late, and Strauss, in trying to achieve his long-deferred, long cherished, and secret ambition, failed hopelessly, miserably, tragically even. He was no longer capable of it. The divinely innocent and virginal Mozartean muse cannot be wooed and won like an Elektra or a Salome ; all we find in *Der Rosenkavalier* is a worn-out, dissipated *demi-mondaine*, with powdered face, rouged lips, false hair, and a hideous leer. Strauss's muse has lost her chastity. Does he himself actually believe that *Der Rosenkavalier* is like *Figaro*? Are we to regard this declaration as a pathetic self-deception, or as the last crowning perversity? It would be difficult to say, and it is perhaps more charitable to infer the former.

It is unnecessary to devote much space to the

consideration of Strauss's subsequent works. It is sufficient to say that they bear witness to the gradual degeneration and final extinction of his creative powers. There are still many happy moments in *Der Rosenkavalier*, but there are fewer and fewer in each successive work. Such as they are, it is the craftsman and not the artist who is responsible for them. From being a man of possibly unequal genius he has become a man of second-rate talent. His faculty of artistic discernment, though never his strong point, has completely deserted him. The impurity of style and juxtaposition of dissimilar idioms which was always one of his outstanding faults is carried to a disconcerting extreme in *Ariadne auf Naxos* and *Die Frau ohne Schatten*. In the first, Mozart dances a minuet with Mascagni, and Handel with Offenbach; in the second, Wagner is reconciled to Brahms, and Mendelssohn to Meyerbeer. Needless to say, this admixture of styles is not effected with any deliberate satirical intention, but from sheer lack of taste, and cynical indifference. He has manifestly no longer the desire to write a fine work, let alone the capacity. Even the workmanship in his later period is no longer distinguished, but slipshod, flaccid, and slovenly. Not only is the artist in Strauss dead, but even the craftsman has lost his conscience and integrity.

Music, it has often been said, is more subject to the law of change and to the caprices of fortune than any other art; the idiom of to-day is obsolete to-morrow, and the popular idol of one generation is almost invariably a subject of execration to the next. To become a leader of musical opinion is almost as invidious a distinction as to be elected president of a South American republic; more poetically, each composer, like the priest of Nemi in Sir James Frazer's *Golden Bough*, slays his predecessor, and is fated to be himself in his turn slain by his successor.

Richard Strauss

It would be difficult to find a more striking example of this than Richard Strauss. Hailed on his appearance as the successor of Wagner—Richard the Second—only some ten years ago still, for most people, the most commanding figure in modern music, he is to-day, apart from Germany and Austria, almost ignored by the leaders of progressive musical opinion. No composer of such formerly unquestioned eminence has ever suffered such a startling change of fortune, such a sudden and decisive reversal of a favourable verdict.

That this is not due merely to the progressive deterioration of his talents—a fact readily admitted even by the rapidly dwindling and wellnigh extinct race of his admirers—is certain, although it may have helped to accelerate his downfall. For in this respect Strauss is by no means an isolated instance. Lack of staying power, inability to develop steadily from strength to strength, is one of the most familiar and alarming characteristics of the modern composer, who, to all intents and purposes, might just as well be dead after his fortieth year for all that he subsequently achieves artistically. But with Debussy, whose falling-off is no less painfully evident than that of Strauss, the comparative inferiority of his later work only serves to accentuate and to bring into higher relief the finer qualities of his earlier period. Strauss's decline, on the contrary, has thrown a searchlight upon the defects and failings of even his best work.

Again, it may be true that every artist who has achieved some degree of eminence must inevitably pass through a transition period of temporary neglect, indifference, and even contumely, preliminary to his final definitive assumption into the ranks of the immortals, but the sudden and dramatic eclipse of Strauss is of a very different order. Mortification has already set in before death, so to speak. His work is

Richard Strauss

dead beyond the hope of any ultimate rehabilitation or triumphant resurrection. It has suddenly gone grey from the breath of a few brief years and even what had formerly seemed to be his most brilliant and radiant pages are already spotted by the phosphorescence of decay. In spite of his many great qualities, in spite even of a strain of real genius, he seems clearly fated to survive as a figure of only historical interest or significance, as a mummy artificially conserved in the museum of musical history—a melancholy prospect which should give pause to the more impassioned and unreflecting adherents of more recent idols, for whom, in all probability, the same fate is in store.

There are a few other specimens similarly embalmed to whom he bears a distinct resemblance—Spontini, for example, and Meyerbeer perhaps even more. It is curious to note incidentally that their careers present several striking analogies. All three, for example, held the same official post of Court Kapellmeister at Berlin, and were alike the musical dictators of their respective periods. Meyerbeer, it is interesting to note, was hailed as the successor of Beethoven in precisely the same way that Strauss was regarded as the heir of Wagner, and with as little justification. It was the megalomaniac and exorbitant mechanical requirements of Spontini and the revelation of the simpler, purer art of Weber that was the immediate cause of the former's downfall—strikingly analogous in its suddenness and completeness to that of Strauss—and there is little doubt that the primary reason for Strauss's lapse from enlightened favour is to be sought in the recognition of the delicacy, subtlety, and economy of means which characterize the art of Debussy. The art of Strauss, whatever its qualities, is essentially, like that of Spontini and Meyerbeer, a synthesis of previously existing terms, a regrouping and reconstruction, however skilfully or carefully concealed, of elements previously exploited by others. The art of both Weber and Debussy, on the other hand, with all its limitations and serious defects, contains the element of novelty, the powerful enchantment of new horizons, the suggestion of a whole world of infinite and fascinating possibilities.

Meyerbeer has often been wrongly reproached with insincerity ; he simply lacked entirely any very strong or definite convictions. He was an artistic opportunist from want of a clear sense of direction rather than from a lack of moral integrity or conscience. One does not feel that he was in any way sacrificing his ideals and convictions by writing the kind of music which the public wanted him to write. But with Strauss, as we have already observed, one always feels the inner conflict between his conscience and his ambition, between his aspiration and his achievement. The source of all Strauss's perversity is to be found in the fact that whenever he has written a thoroughly sincere and deeply felt work, unspoilt by bravado and the wish to *épater le bourgeois*, he has invariably failed to achieve a popular success ; the more rein he gave to his perversity, the more he was appreciated. ' One should hear him speak in cold disdain of the public ', writes Romain Rolland in the essay from which I have already quoted, ' to know the sore that this triumphant artist hides.' We can well believe it ; but unfortunately the only result of the failure of *Guntram* and *Macbeth* was to make him court by sensationalism the favour and appreciation which had been denied to his more musicianly qualities. For Strauss achievement had never been a sufficient reward in itself. With all his scorn for the public he has not hesitated to become its abject slave in return for applause and recognition.

Wagner undoubtedly loved riches, luxury, fame, applause, the homage and admiration of the public as

Richard Strauss

much as any man, perhaps more than most. But these things were always incidental; they did not constitute the motive power behind his art. With all his faults as a man, with all his shortcomings as an artist, he worked *ad majorem Dei gloriam*. Ultimately nothing else matters; it is the final test of an artist's greatness. And with all his great gifts Strauss fails in this test. For it would be idle to deny him the possession of many, even of most, of the highest qualities we demand in a musician, and certainly of more than almost any of his contemporaries. He is one of the very few composers of to-day who have shown themselves capable of constructing works on a monumental scale, of holding our attention for long stretches at a time. There is a nervous energy and exuberance, particularly in his earlier work, a vitality and fertility of invention, which one may seek in vain elsewhere at the moment, and he is admittedly unsurpassed in the art of handling the modern orchestra. It is true, of course, that with such resources at one's disposal, anyone with only a very small modicum of talent can frequently achieve effects of quite surprising beauty. But Strauss has much more than that; he has, or rather he had, real genius. The tragedy lies precisely in the fact that he might have been a very great artist. But as it is, one can only speculate as to which works, if any, stand any chance of surviving him. Always a difficult problem, it is more than usually so with Strauss, whose most interesting and characteristic achievements are nearly always the least satisfactory as whole works; when they are irreproachable from the point of view of form and are not spoilt by lapses of good taste, they are generally somewhat uninteresting. However much we may dislike *Don Quixote*, we would rather go to hear it than *Macbeth*; we would rather put up with the aesthetic monstrosities of *Elektra* than be compelled

54

to sit out a performance of *Guntram*. But this is probably only because *Don Quixote* and *Elektra* still sound comparatively novel and unfamiliar to us ; their manifest imperfections must inevitably tell against them in the long run, and posterity will in all probability solve the problem by performing none of them. The same remarks apply equally to all the early and late works ; they are either undistinguished or imperfect. But if one had to make a choice, it would be of *Feuersnot* and *Salome* before any of the other stage works and before all the symphonic poems. The former is singularly free from any blemishes without being immature or commonplace. It possesses great charm and great vitality, and is more expressive of the *echt deutsch* aspect of Strauss than any other of the larger works—it is in fact the real Strauss. It is just possible that it may in time return to the stage from which it has been banished by the more flamboyant charms of its successors.

But on the whole it is *Salome* which, despite all its faults, stands the best chance of ultimate survival. In the first place, one's critical sense is neither so alert nor so exacting in the theatre as in the concert-hall. On account of their dramatic felicity, we tolerate faults in *Salome* which we would condemn in the symphonic poems, and minor errors of taste disappear from sight in the magnificent continuity, nervous energy, and onward sweep of the whole. No one who walks down Unter den Linden can fail to be struck by the impressive effect of the street as a whole ; when he examines each building separately, however, he is repelled by the blatant vulgarity of the individual conceptions and the tastelessness of the detail. It is the same with the music of Strauss. The music of most other modern composers, whether good or bad, is generally more satisfactory in detail than in mass ; the part is greater than the whole. In the music of Strauss, on the

55

other hand, the work as a whole is better than any of its constituent parts viewed separately. Almost alone to-day Strauss possesses the architectonic quality of mind.

In this and in many other things besides there is a more than superficial resemblance between him and the French novelist Zola. The latter's architectural power is remarkably impressive, his detail tasteless and vulgar. His style also, like that of Strauss, is a jumble of the most heterogeneous and dissimilar elements, from Chateaubriand to the de Goncourts. Both artists excel in the delineation of the horrible and the repulsive, and both similarly fail when they attempt the sublime, the tender, or the passionate. Strauss is at his best in portraying the ravings of Klytemnestra, the death agonies of Aegistheus, or the amorous perversities of the daughter of Herodias. In such things there is a sinister grandeur which is both convincing and impressive ; but when he has instead to depict the tender womanliness of Chrysothemis or the love of Elektra for her brother the result is very little different from what one would expect from Puccini or Mascagni. In *Tod und Verklärung* the first section is admirable ; it is full of the very stench of death and the menace of approaching dissolution. The transfiguration section, on the other hand, is cold, sophisticated, effusive, shameless, reminding one irresistibly of the *café* in Montmartre representing Heaven, in which one is served by waiters dressed as angels in white robes and holding harps. *Zarathustra* is one of his weakest works, mainly because the conceptions which he has set himself to realize in music are of great sublimity. The world of religious aspirations is represented by a sanctimonious passage reminding one of the worst effusions of the Rev. John Bacchus Dykes in *Hymns Ancient and Modern* ; the idea of science suggests nothing more original to him than an arid fugue; the ecstatic Dionysian dance of the Superman is the kind of thing one would expect to hear in a Viennese night-club.

Salome, on the other hand, is his masterpiece, because he has very few opportunities of perpetrating such offences, and the music assigned to the prophet is the only blot of this kind on the work. In it he has come nearer than any other artist to realizing that strangely fascinating and repulsive conception which has haunted modern art and possessed the thoughts of so many painters, musicians, and writers, like a succubus; far more than Wilde or Gustave Moreau has he succeeded in portraying in *Salome*—to quote the words of Huysmans in *A Rebours* : ' the symbolical deity of indestructible Lust, the goddess of immortal Hysteria, the accursed Beauty, chosen among many by the catalepsy that has stiffened her limbs, that has hardened her muscles; the monstrous, indifferent, irresponsible Beast, poisoning like Helen of old all that go near her, all that she touches.'

' In these pages of *A Rebours* ', writes Mr. Arthur Symons, ' the art of Moreau culminates, achieves itself, passes into literature.' And so one may say that in Strauss's score the cold, mechanical preciosity of Wilde's prose culminates, achieves itself, passes into music.

FREDERICK DELIUS

IT is with considerable diffidence that one approaches
the task of writing an essay on the music of Delius,
for it has already been so ably discharged by
Mr. Philip Heseltine as to make the present attempt
seem at best superfluous. Nevertheless the attempt
must be made, since a book which is intended to be
a more or less complete survey of contemporary musical
activity would be something very like Hamlet without
the Prince of Denmark if Delius were passed over,
even in respectful silence. And if in the following
pages there may seem to be many things which look
like unacknowledged quotations or at least paraphrases
of what Mr. Heseltine has probably said much better,
I would only say in self-extenuation that the greater
part of the essay was completed before the appearance
of his book. But in any case the reproach of plagiarism
which such striking coincidences may possibly call
forth cannot diminish the pleasure one experiences in
finding one's conclusions so strikingly confirmed and
supported by a critic who has probably a more intimate
knowledge of the music of Delius than anyone else at
the present time in this country.

But apart from this single exception it would be
difficult to find in all that has been written about
Delius a true sense of his significance and importance.
And yet he is not only a very much older man than
many composers who are prominent in musical life
to-day, but is actually the senior of many whose
reputation is already on the wane, whose day seems
already over, such as Richard Strauss. Not that he
has been ignored or neglected, by any means, but
simply that the measure of attention he has received

Frederick Delius

has always been of that unflattering, indiscriminate variety which is paid to a large number of comparatively, sometimes superlatively, unimportant figures.

Perhaps this is inevitable. True genius is never conspicuous or spectacular in its manifestations ; the artist who encounters violent antagonism or provokes wild and immoderate enthusiasm is seldom of the first rank, despite the popular prejudice to the contrary. Admittedly, there are exceptions, but they will generally be found to be the result of some extraneous or personal circumstances. Looking at Everest, we are told, no one would for a moment suspect that it was the highest mountain in the world. It is only in comparatively recent years that its pre-eminence has been conclusively established. Its symmetry and calm repose had always attracted less attention and commanded less respect than the more immediately picturesque and melodramatic appearance of lesser peaks. And similarly, we know, old Bach, the lordly Himalayan giant of music, seemed markedly inferior to Telemann, and other composers of even less importance, in the eyes of his undiscerning contemporaries and successors for a hundred years and more. In every age we shall find the most outstanding figures, in their varying degrees, confounded with small talents, exciting neither enthusiasm nor hostility, but merely a kind of listless, good-natured, half-hearted tolerance. Such has been the fate of Delius up to the present time, as it has been the fate also, until fairly recently, of his great contemporary in the world of letters, Joseph Conrad, with whom, incidentally, he has much else in common.

It is of course easy to understand and to forgive this apathy and indifference in the general public. After all, it only asks to be led, preferably by the nose, and if Delius has not up to the present succeeded in attracting its attention, the reason is simply that he

Frederick Delius

has never made any effort to do so. There are very few artists of any age—least of all the present one, in which self-advertisement has almost come to be a necessary condition of artistic existence—who have made less effort to bring themselves into public notice.

The attitude of reserve on the part of musicians towards Delius is not so easily explained. No doubt there is in it something of the feeling which a trade-unionist entertains towards a blackleg. In the words of Mr. Heseltine, he is a man 'who holds no official position in the musical life of his country, who does not teach in any of the academies, who is not even an honorary doctor of music; who, moreover, gives no concerts, makes no propaganda for his music, plays no instruments, nor even conducts an orchestra'. In fact Delius stands quite outside the musical world; he hardly seems to be a musician at all. But there is more in it than this; for whether it is that music lacks the more or less direct contact with life and nature which the other arts enjoy, or whether it is simply the outcome of the vicious system of musical education which prevails in our academies and conservatoires, the fact remains that the majority of our composers, whatever they themselves may affirm to the contrary, tend to regard music more as a craft than an art, and to believe, unconsciously perhaps, in the existence of technique in the abstract, as something apart from the particular conception to be realized; as a kind of arsenal of ready-made weapons, the use of which can be learned as one might learn carpentry or needlework. In this respect the so-called revolutionary composer is often just as bad as, and sometimes even worse than, his conservative colleague. The only difference between them is that the one desires to retain the time-honoured traditions, while the other seeks to extend or even abolish them, only in order to establish a new convention in place of the old.

Frederick Delius

Delius, on the other hand, is an artist before he is a musician ; for him music is not merely a decorative craft, the skilful weaving together of a pleasant pattern of sounds, signifying nothing, but a creative art and the means to the apprehension and the expression of the supreme realities of life. For him there are no such things as technical or formal problems ; he would agree with Baudelaire that the only enduring satisfaction an artist can experience is to achieve precisely that which he set out to achieve—that and nothing more, nothing less. The craftsman's characteristic penchant for seeking out obstacles merely for the sake of overcoming them is entirely foreign to Delius's nature. He is not one of those Alpine mountaineers of art who spend all their time and energy in climbing inaccessible pinnacles and negotiating difficult ' chimneys ', only to break their necks in the end. When he climbs mountains it is solely in order to reach his destination ; he neither goes out of his way to encounter difficulties nor does he execute wide detours in order to avoid them.

It is quite natural, therefore, that this complete indifference to craftsmanship and technique, combined with his aloofness and detachment from musical life in general, should have earned for Delius the reputation of being a dilettante or amateur—the two most opprobrious epithets in the musician's vocabulary. Moussorgsky, for example, has with remarkable tenacity been called an amateur for the last fifty years, though in what way his work could be improved upon by a professional musician it would be extremely difficult to say. He achieved what he set out to achieve ; what more does anyone ask, provided that object was worth achieving, which none of his critics seem to deny ?

Similarly, the occasional bareness and apparent clumsiness of a good deal of Delius's music have often

61

Frederick Delius

misled superficial critics into the assumption that they are the outcome of a faulty technique and insufficient training. But few composers of the present day have worked harder or more unremittingly at the problems of his art. I myself have seen the manuscripts of quite twenty early works, all in the larger forms, and including several operas, written in the course of a very few years. In them Delius reveals as sound a technical training and as complete a mastery of conventional conservatoire musicianship as any academy professor could desire. The seeming bareness and uncouthness to which I have alluded only appears as the real Delius emerges, comparatively late in life. They are deliberate, conscious, dictated by his expressive purpose. Where other and lesser composers would summon to their rescue all the resources of dexterous craftsmanship in order to conceal the occasional deficiency of inspiration to which even the very greatest are subject, Delius steadfastly refuses to avail himself of such adventitious aids. It is possible that with a little more insincerity he might have been a more perfect artist, but there can be little doubt that he would also have been a lesser one. One cannot have it both ways. Delius's faults, in other words, are positive. They do not proceed from a lack of certain qualities, but rather from the possession of others more important.

Delius is not by any means one of those artists who succeed in finding themselves quickly and in expressing their personalities with great ease. On the other hand, his complete maturity, when it did come, came very suddenly. A few passages in his earlier work sound a prophetic note, but even in such a comparatively late work as *Paris*, written in 1899, there are few traces of the mature Delius of the *Village Romeo and Juliet*, a music-drama based on the story of Gottfried Keller begun only a year later. This sudden magnificent efflorescence of his talent is a most remarkable phenomenon. Unlike that of Strauss, it was the outcome of some internal transformation. Any stimulus which came from outside can only have been the single crystal dropped into a super-saturated solution.

This work, besides being one of its composer's most consummate achievements from a purely musical standpoint, is also a very important landmark in the history of opera. Before we can hope to understand precisely what it was that Delius was trying to do in this work, it will be necessary to devote a few words to a consideration of the aesthetic problems involved, although like the fabulous Sphinx of ancient mythology—with the head and breasts of a woman, the body of a dog, the tail of a serpent, the wings of a bird, the paws of a lion, and a human voice—this curious artistic hybrid, consisting of music, poetry, drama, the plastic arts, and frequently even metaphysics and other equally imponderable ingredients, is in the habit of slaying those unfortunate and audacious mortals who are unable to divine the correct answers to the inscrutable riddles which she propounds. On the other hand, the Sphinx, as soon as the right answer was returned by Oedipus, dashed her head against a rock and immediately expired. If this were likewise the fate of opera as it is at present conceived, the risk would seem to be well worth taking.

The history of music in the theatre is not unlike that of music in the church. Literary men have always been in the habit of regarding the theatre as part of their domain, and under their exclusive jurisdiction; the other arts are only permitted to enter the sacred precincts on sufferance and on the explicit understanding that they must be content to play a humble and wholly subordinate role, and to conform strictly to the rules and regulations which have been laid down for them. In leaving the church for the

Frederick Delius

theatre at the beginning of the seventeenth century, so far from attaining freedom, music was only in reality exchanging one taskmaster for another; papal anathemas and remonstrances gave place to the equally intolerant bulls of excommunication which emanated from the literary pontiffs whenever she attempted to assert herself or to claim a greater degree of attention than they were willing to countenance. Under these circumstances it is not surprising to find that musicians —never at any time distinguished for the daring or independence of their intellectual activities— should tend to approach operatic problems with a predominantly literary bias. For example, the Florentine initiators were avowedly only attempting to put into practice the theories of the Humanists concerning the nature of the Greek drama, in which music played only a very small and subsidiary part, and, as Mr. Newman has shown in his study of *Gluck and the Opera*, all Gluck's reforms were nothing more or less than the realization of the theories entertained by the literary men and philosophers of the period concerning the function of music in the theatre. His aesthetic creed might be summed up in the single sentence, ' I sought to reduce music to its true function, that of supporting the poetry ', a principle which was reaffirmed a century later by Wagner in his famous dictum that music, so far from being the end of opera, should only be the means to a dramatic end. In *Pelléas* Debussy's intention of dispensing with any parasitic musical development—to quote his own words—is only a restatement of the same doctrine.

Such, in brief outline, is the history of operatic theory. In actual practice it has always been observed that the greatest operas are those in which the music plays the dominant role and the dramatic interest is a mere accessory. The reason why we generally make ourselves acquainted with the plot of an opera before

64

going to see it is that we are then in a position to listen to the music without having to attempt to follow or pay attention to the action ; and secondly, because the music hampers the dramatic development to such an extent that it is frequently impossible to understand what it is all about. Ultimately we go to opera for music, and music alone, and this applies just as much to the operas or music-dramas of the so-called reformers as to those of Mozart or Rossini. In the same way we listen to a song of Schubert or Brahms for the music, not for the poem.

Now, it will always be found that the moments in opera which are most satisfactory are those in which the music is free to unfold itself undisturbed by dramatic exigencies. When action appears the musical interest diminishes and sometimes vanishes altogether. We automatically cease to listen to the music. The problem which confronts the composer of an opera is consequently how to eliminate or reduce to a minimum the dramatic action. There have been two satis-factory solutions, and two only. The first is the old classical opera in which the necessary action is developed in recitative, and the main musical interest reserved for the set numbers. Secondly, there is the solution of the romantic music-drama in which the action is practically eliminated, such as *Tristan*, which, as we observed in the preceding essay, is little more than a symphonic poem. These are both true musical forms, as much as the symphony, the fugue, the song, or the dance; but the monstrous and unholy hybrid, begotten upon music by drama, which is the opera of Strauss, Puccini, and most other writers of to-day, is not a form at all. It is neither drama, music, nor any-thing whatsoever. So now let it dash its head on a rock and trouble us no more !

Delius is perhaps the first composer since Mozart to recognize and accept the implications of what had

E

Frederick Delius

been arrived at empirically, and to set himself in the *Village Romeo and Juliet* to write an opera in which the dramatic element of the stage representation only serves to interpret and elucidate the musical action ; in which the stage action is only the realization of the drama which is already embodied in the music, as the programme in the symphonic poem. In fact, the *Village Romeo* might be called a symphonic poem with the implicit programme made explicit upon the stage.

That the composer's intentions should have been wholly misconceived is not at all surprising, for Delius has always shown a distaste as laudable as it is rare in these days for theorizing about his work and attempting to explain himself in lengthy manifestoes. The result has been that producers have always tried to make the work dramatic and realistic, and both critics and audiences have judged it from the standpoint of Puccini and Mascagni. But even making all due allowances for this, one cannot help feeling that there are slight faults in the work itself which are to some extent responsible for the unsatisfactory impression which one receives in performance. The composer has not always been completely successful in subordinating the dramatic action to the exigencies of the music. Here and there it intrudes itself forcibly, and the operatic conventions have not been entirely eliminated. The work seems at times to hover exasperatingly on the border of two worlds. It is certainly not a work which should be presented in a realistic manner, yet a wholly symbolic rendering might not be satisfactory either. There is at once too much realism for the one and not enough for the other.

This at least is the impression which the *Village Romeo* makes upon one after careful study and a couple of unsatisfactory performances ; nevertheless it would be necessary to see it presented according to the composer's intentions before committing oneself to

66

a definite judgement of its merits as a stage work. But there can be no two opinions concerning the beauty of the music, which is of the best that Delius has ever given us. He has occasionally equalled but certainly never surpassed it. The only criticism one might make is against the voice parts, which strike one occasionally—particularly in the part of the Black Fiddler—as needlessly angular and unvocal. This is also true of *Tristan*, and one might therefore be reasonably led to suppose that it was an unavoidable defect of the romantic symphonic opera, were it not for the fact that it is a defect shared by all modern composers of the most opposite tendencies. The vocal parts of Delius and Wagner may often be awkward, but they are at least more interesting than those of the French school. If the former are instrumental, those of Debussy and Ravel are merely declamatory, approaching speech in fact—having no justification save in a mistaken aesthetic. Delius's subordination of vocal interest to the demands of the orchestra at least brings with it great compensations of a purely musical order.

After the *Village Romeo and Juliet* follows the magnificent series of choral and orchestral works—*Appalachia*, *Sea-Drift*, the *Mass of Life*, the *Songs of Sunset*—in which rather than in the purely orchestral works, or even the operas, Delius's greatest strength lies. In my opinion Delius stands unsurpassed by any composer since Beethoven in this medium. Wagner and Verdi may be better writers for the stage, Berlioz and Liszt may be greater symphonists, Mendelssohn and Brahms may have written more perfect *concertos*, and Schubert and Schumann finer songs, but there is nothing in the whole of the last century which can be placed above Delius's achievement in the larger choral forms. The *Requiem* and *Te Deum* of Berlioz are the only works one could put on the same level

Frederick Delius

with it. In the works above mentioned the romantic spirit expresses itself fully in the only form in which it had not already done so. They complete the cycle, as it were.

Appalachia is one of the most surprising and original works of modern times. On paper, and particularly in the extremely inadequate published piano score, it seems entirely ineffectual; a mere sequence of trite and commonplace variations on a trivial and uninteresting theme; yet in performance few works are more profoundly moving, in a quite indefinable and inexplicable way. One might almost suppose that one's appreciation of it was due to some curious idiosyncrasy in oneself, to some involuntary association of ideas, were it not for the fact that one was by no means alone in experiencing that same emotion. Nevertheless it is quite impossible to say in what precisely resides the extraordinary appeal and fascination of such a passage as, for example, that in which the baritone enters with the words, ' Oh, Honey, I am going down the river in the morning'. Criticism, when confronted by such mysteries, must perforce hang its head in silence. The passage is so simple; there is really nothing there—and yet so much, everything, in fact.

Sea-Drift, curiously enough, makes exactly the opposite impression. On paper and at the piano it is overwhelmingly beautiful. Not only is it one of the most intimate and intensely moving works that Delius has ever written, but it is also one of the most wholly satisfying from the formal point of view. Yet it never seems to ' come off ' in performance quite as well as it ought to. This is probably in large part due to the somewhat exacting and not altogether effective part for solo voice. On the other hand it may very well be that the peculiarly intimate quality of its appeal fails, through no fault of the work, to

make itself felt in the cold and unsympathetic surroundings of the average concert-hall. Nevertheless,
it is a great work.

The *Mass of Life*, based on excerpts from
Nietzsche's *Also sprach Zarathustra*, is the largest
and most ambitious of all the choral works—possibly
even the most ambitious of all Delius's works, without
exception. Unfortunately I have not had the privilege
of hearing a performance of it, and in view of the
danger of trying to judge the music of Delius from
a study, however diligent, of the score alone—as
shown by one's experiences with the two foregoing
works—it would be a sheer impertinence for me to
attempt to estimate the place which it occupies in
relation to his other works. It is considered by many
to be his greatest achievement, and, it is interesting
to learn, the composer himself inclines to this view.
One is all the time conscious that he is putting forth
his full strength. There is in it none of the almost
nonchalant confidence and unconventionality of *Appalachia*, for example. The composer is taking no risks
here. There is more solid craftsmanship in it than
one generally associates with Delius's music, and in
consequence it is perhaps not such an intensely personal utterance all through as other works are. Not
that this is in any sense a defect. Rather the opposite,
in fact ; the theme and general conception demand
a large and somewhat impersonal accent. In the same
way that the Roman Catholic priest, when officiating
at the Mass, is no longer a mere mortal, with ordinary
human desires and passions, so Delius in the *Mass of
Life* lays aside, to a certain extent, his individuality
and his personal outlook. Nevertheless they reveal
themselves here and there, notably in the third section
of the first part—one of the loveliest things Delius
has ever written.

It seems a long way from the heights of the

mountains where the Nietzschean superman dwells, to the enervating and sultry valley where Cynara, the superwoman of Ernest Dowson, languidly reclines upon a bed of roses. After the mystical and esoteric Midnight Song of Zarathustra, the sensuous and exotic *Songs of Sunset*. This work stands at the very opposite pole to the *Mass of Life*. In absolute contrast to the latter, it is supremely personal throughout ; not a bar in it from beginning to end could have been written by anyone but Delius. The constraint and discipline of the preceding work seem, by a natural law of reaction, to have led the composer to the opposite extreme of human experience. Nothing less Nietzschean could possibly be imagined. It is full of the nostalgia of autumn and the sense of transience and decay, the bitterness of ' unfulfilled desires and vain regrets ' ; more than any other of Delius's works the *Songs of Sunset* express ' that haunting sense of sadness and regret for days gone by which the Portuguese call *Saudades*—a word which has no equivalent in the English language '.[1] Like *Sea-Drift*, it has no determinable form and practically dispenses with recurring themes. Nevertheless, it achieves a remarkable impression of unity.

In many ways it is a matter of regret that such works as the four above mentioned should be heard so seldom, and yet, when one comes to think of it, would one willingly have it otherwise? Is it not more fitting that such works as these should have a place apart in our musical life, like the composer himself, and should only be performed upon rare occasions? Snobbish though it may be, one does not care to think of them being mauled about by amateur choral societies—the inevitable penalty of popularity. Fortunately, the almost prohibitive cost of giving these works adequately will preserve their inviolability

[1] L. Cranmer Byng, in a note to his translations of Chinese poets.

and their remote, secret charm for some time to come.

It will be convenient to consider Delius's three remaining choral works here, although other important works intervene. The *Arabesk*, based upon a poem of Jacobsen, a Danish writer little known in this country though famous on the Continent, does not strike one as being a particularly characteristic specimen of Delius's art ; like the poem, it is a somewhat enigmatic production, and difficult to enter into. It is possible, though doubtful, that greater familiarity might enable one to appreciate it more than one does. A curious and, to my thinking, unsatisfactory feature of the work is the large number of alternative notes provided for the solo singer, by means of which three or four separate renderings are not only possible at moments, but, it would seem, equally desirable. It is difficult to see the reason for this, as in many instances the alternative notes are both well within the natural compass of the voice.

The *Song of the High Hills* impresses one at first as being a very powerful but slightly unequal work ; with increasing familiarity, however, one has the somewhat unusual experience of finding the weaker moments pass almost unnoticed. Its imperfections are those which only a great work can have ; they hardly seem to matter. As in *Appalachia,* the restrained and sparing employment of the chorus is more than compensated for by the tremendous sense of climax which the composer ultimately achieves thereby. It is music of epic breadth and virility, in striking contrast to the intimate lyricism of the *Songs of Sunset* and *Sea-Drift.* In my opinion it is by far the finest work of Delius's latest period. It was written in 1912.

Of the large choral works the last of all, namely the *Pagan Requiem*, is by general consent the weakest. It possesses all Delius's most characteristic faults

Frederick Delius

without their compensating virtues. The texture of the work lacks continuity and organic design without achieving that spiritual unity which *Sea-Drift*, for example, does achieve. The best moments in the work are, on the whole, variations upon ideas and conceptions already better realized elsewhere ; such as, for example, the serene close, recalling so many similar endings in his works.

The principal interest of the period which follows the *Songs of Sunset* consists in a series of purely orchestral compositions : *Brigg Fair*, the first *Dance Rhapsody*, *In a Summer Garden*, and the two pieces for small orchestra, ' On hearing the first Cuckoo in Spring ' and ' Summer night on the River '. It is particularly interesting to note that in the two first named the composer's treatment of variation form bears a striking resemblance to that of the early English virginal composers, which is the more surprising because it must have been entirely unconscious, for at the time when Delius wrote the works in which these similarities occur he was undoubtedly unacquainted with the music of his forerunners. The form as they conceived it is very different from that of Bach, which consists in the subjection of a characteristic harmonic progression to every possible variety of melodic and rhythmic experience, the theme being chosen less on account of its intrinsic beauty than for its infinite potentialities and its sharply defined and easily recognizable character : neither is it that of Beethoven as best exemplified in the Diabelli variations—that pocket manual of hints on how to become a magician, by means of which mice are transformed into prancing steeds and pumpkins into gorgeous coaches—in which the theme selected for treatment is purposely insignificant, a Cinderella among melodies, a little slut at whom no one would look twice, so that our wonder at its subsequent transformations may thereby be the greater. The procedure of Delius and the Elizabethans is different from both these. The subjects of such works as *Brigg Fair* and the *Dance Rhapsody* (No. 1) are at once highly organized and distinguished for their melodic beauty, offering in consequence little opportunity for either development or metamorphosis. On the contrary, they are distinctly unpromising and intractable for these purposes, and therefore remain fundamentally unaltered throughout the course of the works, the principal interest consisting in the enhancement of their natural beauty by means of elaborate and diversified harmonic treatment and instrumental decoration.

Needless to say, this formal analogy between certain works of Delius and those of the Elizabethans is not a mere coincidence, but is the consequence of a definite spiritual affinity. National characteristics are proverbially difficult to define; but on the other hand they are readily felt, and nothing could be more unmistakably English than such things as the *Dance Rhapsody* (No. 1) or *In a Summer Garden*, or the two lovely pieces for small orchestra—in spite of the fact that the first of these two latter happens, quite irrelevantly, to be based on a Norwegian folk-song. How magically too do the first few pages of *Brigg Fair* evoke the atmosphere of an early summer morning in the English country, with its suggestion of a faint mist veiling the horizon, and the fragrant scent of the dawn in the air! What art could be more fitly described as 'simple, sensuous, and passionate'?

Delius, like Keats before him, has often been unthinkingly reproached for the almost excessive sweetness and over-ripeness of his music. This is so largely a matter of personal taste that it is impossible to argue about it. It can at least be pointed out that his sensuousness can never be qualified as sickly or effeminate, and the fact that the possession of this quality

73

does not exclude the possession of great strength and virility is amply testified by such works as the *Mass of Life* and the *Song of the High Hills*. Keats's *Hyperion* provides an interesting and instructive parallel. It is as well to bear in mind that this very sweetness and sensuousness is perhaps the most noteworthy characteristic of English art. The purist who would condemn it in the music of Delius is at the same time condemning a great part of Shakespeare, particularly the early works—Marlowe, Beaumont and Fletcher, Ford, Herrick, Campian, Dowland, Purcell even, and indeed, most of the greatest writers and all the greatest musicians England has ever produced. It is the very quintessence of the English spirit in art.

This is one aspect of Delius's music, but there is another one, equally important, revealed in the more than striking resemblances between many of Delius's most characteristic and personal themes and Celtic folk-song, particularly the Hebridean melodies in the now well-known collection of Mrs. Kennedy Fraser. Needless to say there can be no question here of influence, conscious or unconscious, since innumerable examples of it can be found in his work even at a time when these songs were not only unpublished but uncollected and totally unknown, their very existence unsuspected. Neither is the phenomenon to be accounted for by the fact that the pentatonic scale, which is the essential feature common to both, is to be found elsewhere, in other folk-music and in the work of many other modern composers. There is no real similarity between Celtic and Hungarian, Chinese, African, or Scandinavian folk-song and the pentatonic element in the music of Debussy, Ravel, Stravinsky, or Bartók is of a very different nature from that which we find in the work of Delius. Perhaps the most arresting examples of this affinity are to be found in the *North Country Sketches* and in a setting of a poem of

Frederick Delius

Fiona Macleod, called *Hy Brasil*—the name given in Celtic mythology to the land of eternal youth. That Delius, an Englishman of Dutch extraction, should without being aware of it have arrived at almost identically the same melodic formulas as the nameless singers of the mysterious western islands, in expressing the same conception, is only one more proof—if indeed such were needed—of the truth that nationality is a purely spiritual thing, that whenever two artists give expression to the same order of ideas or emotions, their utterances will inevitably resemble each other, however far apart their racial origins and traditions may happen to be.

And so we find in the art of Delius the reconciliation of qualities generally, though wrongly, conceived as opposites; the union of the two different fundamental aspects of the national mind—the Anglo-Saxon and the Celtic.

This discovery is all the more piquant in that Delius has always been reproached by the more ardent nationalists on account of his alleged cosmopolitanism —a misconception which has arisen largely from the fact that he is of foreign extraction, though of English birth, and has lived the greater part of his life abroad. Besides, he has never claimed to be a nationalist composer, and his Anglicism has never been consciously and deliberately cultivated as it has been by many of his less successful compatriots. Most piquant of all, Delius is probably completely unaware of it himself.

The whole artistic aim and purpose of Delius being expression, it follows naturally and inevitably that his least successful works are those in which he handles forms which have been consecrated by centuries of gradual evolution: in which the expressive aspect is, if not a minor consideration, at least only commensurate in importance with problems of design and

75

Frederick Delius

téxture, and with the decorative treatment of particular instruments. Such are the works of the last
period, the concertos, violin sonatas, 'cello sonata, and
the string quartet especially, one of Delius's few complete failures. This is not to say that these works do
not contain a great deal of very beautiful music ;
they certainly do, notably the lovely violin concerto ;
but one feels that this aspect of his work does not
reveal him at his very greatest. In so far as Delius
accepts conventions, his music tends to become less
characteristic, and to aspire towards an artistic ideal
which is foreign to its innermost spirit.

But although Delius's outlook is always intensely
personal, his art is never in any way autobiographic like
that of most romantic artists. He has often been called
introspective, which implies a certain self-conscious-
ness and a tendency to self-analysis which is wholly
alien to his nature. The tender melancholy of so
much of his music conveys a sense of detachment ; it
is the emotion which is felt by the spectator rather
than by the actor in the tragedy. The element of
personal experience, the note of self-pity, which are so
repulsive in the music of Tchaikovsky, are entirely
lacking in that of Delius. He seems always to stand
outside and above his own creation, like the chorus
in Greek tragedy—sympathetic, understanding, but
always aloof and impersonal. It is this sense of detachment combined with sympathy, reminding one of
Wordsworth, which imparts such poignance to works
like *Sea-Drift* and the *Village Romeo and Juliet*.

The music of Delius belongs essentially to the same
phase of romanticism as the art of Flaubert, Gauguin,
Verlaine, and Baudelaire. They are all alike possessed
by the nostalgia of the infinite and the unappeasable
longing for an impossible bliss. Flaubert sought refuge
from reality in the desert with St. Anthony, and in
ancient and barbaric civilizations ; Gauguin sought for

Frederick Delius

a material paradise in the islands of the South Seas, inhabited by the last remnants of a primitive and virginal humanity; Baudelaire found an artificial paradise in opium and hashish dreams, Verlaine in the absinthe of the cafés of Paris and Brussels; Delius sought a material paradise in Florida, and a spiritual one in the Celtic Hy Brasil or Land of Heart's Desire, hidden far away in the western ocean beyond the setting sun, a land where all the trees of the forest drip with wild honey, where all the year the flowers are in bloom, and no death is.

There is a Celtic legend which tells how Oisin (or Ossian as he is more familiarly known to us) went to dwell in the land of the immortals. One day, after much feasting and revelry, they called upon him to sing to them a song of human joys. And Oisin did as he was asked, but what he sang seemed to his listeners the saddest thing they had ever heard. So it is with Delius; despite the tranquillity and serenity which pervade his music one hears always as its burden or undercurrent ' the still sad music of humanity ', the sorrow that lies at the heart of all mortal joys, the sense of happiness irrevocably past, the bitterness at the core of all great sweetness. His music is not the song of the immortal ones, the Danaan or the Sidhe, who sing of a region far beyond all human joys and sorrows; it has rather all the frailties and imperfections of mortal things, and perhaps for that very reason seems sometimes to possess an intimacy and a depth of appeal to which they cannot, from their very nature, attain. There may be greater musicians, completer artists than Frederick Delius, but there are very few indeed for whom one entertains a more personal regard or a warmer affection.

EDWARD ELGAR

IN a recent critical study, Mr. Harold Nicolson drew a sharp distinction between the poet and the bard in Tennyson; between the writer of 'In Memoriam' and many exquisite lyrics, and the Poet Laureate who was responsible for 'The Charge of the Light Brigade' and similar patriotic and occasional effusions. Similarly, Mr. Bernard Shaw in *Back to Methusaleh* makes his Elderly Gentleman of the year A.D. 3000 refer to two writers of the name of Kipling who lived in our time: 'The one was an eastern and a writer of merit; the other was a western and only an amusing barbarian.' In order to do justice to Elgar it is equally necessary to distinguish clearly between the composer of the symphonies and the self-appointed Musician Laureate of the British Empire, always ready to hymn rapturously the glories of our blood and state on the slightest provocation. The one is a musician of merit; the other is only a barbarian, and not even an amusing one.

If I refrain from taking into consideration a third Elgar, the composer of *Salut d'Amour* and innumerable equally negligible trifles, it is because it can legitimately be pleaded on his behalf that these productions have been the means of enabling him to devote himself to the composition of other and better works, undisturbed by material considerations. The Muse looks with a tolerant and indulgent eye upon such harmless misdemeanours and infidelities. Like a true woman, she is generally kindest to those who treat her with least respect, and she probably regards with wondering pity and amused contempt those artists, so dear to the heart of the writers of penny novelettes, who would rather starve in garrets than write an unworthy page. At any rate she certainly withholds her favours from them with quite remarkable consistency, for they have never been known to write a good work. Indeed it would be difficult to name any artist of eminence who has not at some time or another perpetrated a bad work with the openly avowed intention of making money, and even more difficult to find one to whom it had done any visible harm. In fact one may safely conclude that such things have nothing whatever to do with art, and do not affect it one way or another, for better or for worse.

Unfortunately, the same cannot be said of works such as the *Imperial March*, the *Banner of Saint George*, the *Coronation Ode*, the *Pomp and Circumstance Marches*, the *Fringes of the Fleet*, or the *Crown of India* (undoubtedly the worst of the lot)—all of them perfect specimens of that exotic growth called Jingoism which flourished with such tropical luxuriance in this country a quarter of a century ago, and is now, fortunately, almost extinct. It seems to be only too horribly true that Elgar takes this aspect of his art as seriously as any other, and not merely for the purse of gold or even in the hope of receiving the butt of Canary sack which is one of the traditional emoluments of Poets Laureate. In the *Music-makers*, for example, the whole intention of the work is obviously to give one clearly to understand, by means of elaborate quotations from his own works in the style of Strauss's *Heldenleben*, coupled with a reference to *Rule Britannia*, that he regards himself as one of those artists who, in the words of the poem on which the music is based, 'build up the world's great cities' by means of 'wonderful deathless ditties'. Now it is quite possible that the immortal 'Land of Hope and Glory' tune may at some time or other have aroused such patriotic

79

enthusiasm in the breast of a rubber planter in the tropics as to have led him to kick his negro servant slightly harder than he would have done if he had never heard it, and served to strengthen his already profound conviction of belonging to the chosen race ; but however admirable and praiseworthy such a result may be from the point of view of empire building, it has no meaning whatever from the point of view of art, which, in so far as it is worthy of the name, is eternally dedicated *ad majorem Dei gloriam,* and not to the greater glory of John Bull or any similar tribal fetish. It is at least an indisputable and highly significant fact that while nationalism has always been one of the most powerful of all external incentives to artistic creation, imperialism never has been, whether in France under Napoleon, in Germany under the Hohenzollerns, or in England during the last seventy years or more. The reason for this is simply that national feeling has its roots in the very soil, quite apart from racial origins or historical associations ; it is part of ourselves, of the air we breathe, of the food we eat. We cannot escape it even if we would. Imperialism, on the other hand, has no such basis in reality. It is not even any longer a political, but only a commercial reality. As Mr. G. K. Chesterton has so admirably put it :

> Our principal exports, all labelled and packed,
> At the ends of the earth are delivered intact :
> Our soap or our salmon can travel in tins
> Between the two poles and as like as two pins :
> So that Lancashire merchants, whenever they like,
> Can water the beer of a man in Klondike
> Or poison the meat of a man in Bombay :
> And that is the meaning of Empire Day.

A critic has said of Elgar's work that it is ' parcelled out into water-tight compartments filled with liquids of varying density, and suited to all occasions of life. The homely plebeian mild and bitter of the *Cockaigne Overture*, the champagne of the *Enigma Variations*, the pungent sack of *Falstaff*, the consecrated wine of the oratorios, all are drawn upon at the appropriate moment.' This may be all very true, but unfortunately it is also true that the mild and bitter of the *Cockaigne Overture* has been watered, like that of Mr. Chesterton's man of Klondike; the champagne and the sack alike have been tainted by the phylloxera germ of Imperialism which has battened on the national vine; and even the consecrated wine of the oratorios has often a most suspicious resemblance to Australian burgundy in accordance with the doctrines of Imperial Preference. In other words, this aspect of Elgar's art is not merely negligible like *Salut d'Amour* and its fellows, but has definitely exercised a pernicious and subtly contaminating influence over his whole work. For example, he concludes a work like *Caractacus*, which, with all its faults and in spite of its somewhat depressing choir-festival atmosphere, has much to commend it, with a chorus in which we are invited to brood on the glorious day which is coming when

> The nations all shall stand
> And hymn the praise of Britain
> Like brothers, hand in hand:

and many similar examples of the intrusion of this bombastic spirit, even into purely instrumental works, can easily be found. The final number of the *Enigma Variations*, for example, is undiluted jingoism.

There is a considerable diversity of opinion among critics concerning the merits and demerits of what are perhaps Elgar's most ambitious works, namely, the oratorios—*The Dream of Gerontius*, *The Kingdom*, and *The Apostles*; the reason being that one's attitude towards them must inevitably be largely conditioned by temperamental considerations. There is a particular quality about this music which makes it quite impossible, even if it were desirable, to dissociate the intrinsic worth of the music from the conceptions and emotions of which it is the expression, or to regard it from a purely objective and wholly detached point of view. One must either like it or dislike it, that is all.

The atmosphere of *Gerontius*, in particular, demands a certain temperamental affinity in the listener before he can hope to enjoy it, and I must reluctantly confess that I lack this qualification entirely. The air is too heavy with the odour of clerical sanctity and the faint and sickly aroma of stale incense, and the little light there is filters dimly through stained glass windows. After a time one begins to long for a breath of fresh air or a glimpse of sunshine. With all its spirituality and undoubted sincerity the atmosphere is sanctimonious rather than saintly, pious rather than fervid. This music has neither the radiant candour and innocence of Palestrina, nor the unearthly ecstasy of the Spaniard Vittoria—only the emotional mysticism of Newman. *Gerontius* is essentially the musical counterpart of the Oxford Movement.

But while one can at least say that *Gerontius* is a well-constructed work as a whole, partly because it is counter-drawn, as it were, upon a poem possessing a certain organic unity and logic of its own, and may for that reason at least succeed in making an appeal to those for whom the underlying spirit holds no attraction, this can hardly be said of *The Apostles* or *The Kingdom*. They seem to have been primarily conceived as successions of separate scenes and detached episodes presented in sequence, like early Italian frescoes ; on the other hand, an attempt has been made at the same time to impart some kind of formal unity by stringing them together on a thread of leading themes, associated with certain literary or dogmatic conceptions, as in the music of Strauss. One feels that the composer has failed to reap the advantages of either method ; the repetition of thematic material throughout robs the individual scenes of their freshness and spontaneity, and at the same time fails to knit them together into a whole. He achieves monotony without unity. This is greatly to be regretted, for the episodes are frequently admirable in isolation, except where a theme is dragged in by the scruff of the neck for some literary purpose and then as ignominiously thrown out again. The workmanship is in detail nearer perfection and more musicianly than in *Gerontius*, yet all the many fine qualities in these works cannot conceal the fact that they are complete failures, even for those who are most sympathetically disposed to their underlying spirit.

One cannot help thinking that the cause of this is largely to be sought and found in a certain narrowness of outlook and emotional scope in the composer, exemplified in his characteristic inability to conceive or depict anything in the nature of sin or evil. As Mr. Newman has observed, ' If Mary Magdalene (in *The Apostles*) has never done anything worse than is suggested in these kittenish strains, she really had not much for her conscience to reproach her with. A Dorcas meeting is riotous in comparison.' Even Judas has to be represented as an English gentleman labouring under a mistaken sense of duty, and Elgar's one attempt to depict the powers of evil, in the chorus of demons from Gerontius—they also do duty as Germans in the *Spirit of England*—might conceivably frighten small children under seven years of age at a Christmas pantomime.

' In this respect one is strongly reminded of César Franck, whose *Béatitudes* and *Rédemption* reveal precisely the same failing. The faithful M. Vincent d'Indy has endeavoured to excuse this failing by observing that his master's nature was so lofty and noble that it was impossible for him to conceive, much less adequately represent, anything so foreign to his thoughts and actions as evil; the implication being, of course, that Franck is the greater for this failing. With all due respect to everybody concerned—Franck, d'Indy, and Elgar—this will not do. This nobility of soul, this saintly inability to understand evil, is no doubt highly creditable to them as human beings, good citizens, and family men; but in an artist who sets out to depict episodes in what is perhaps the greatest, the most tremendous drama in human history, it is a grave defect. Was the life or character of Dante or of Milton any less noble for their ability to depict evil? Surely not; the greatest artists, and the greatest men, are those who possess the widest and most universal understanding of life in its entirety, and not merely certain aspects of it. Anatole France has said, ' Les plus grands pécheurs sont l'étoffe des plus grands saints', and it is no idle cynicism, but a profound truth. The contrary is also true, that the greatest saints are potentially the greatest sinners, as Dostoevsky has often shown. The murderer and pickpocket, François Villon, attains to a greater height of spirituality than the saintly and irreproachable César Franck, and in precisely the same way that Elgar fails to understand or conceive evil, he fails equally to rise to the greatest heights of his subject. He is simply unequal to the task which he has undertaken, and only achieves a somewhat pallid and refined spirituality which soon becomes exceedingly monotonous.

There are several other points of close resemblance between the sacred works of Franck and Elgar, though whether they are the result of a direct influence or

merely of a natural mental affinity, it would be difficult to say. Not only is their harmonic style very
similar, but their melodic invention also. For example,
the theme in Franck's *Béatitudes* to which Christ
sings, ' Heureux ceux qui pleurent, car ils seront
consolés ', is almost identical with one of the principal
themes of *The Apostles.* The one is in three, the
other in four, time ; otherwise there is virtually no
difference.

The lack of spiritual breadth and understanding to
which we have referred, runs throughout Elgar's
entire work, and is often in striking disharmony with
the conceptions which he sets himself to realize. His
Falstaff, for example, though a merry gentleman,
would never say anything that might possibly bring
a blush to the cheeks of a delicately nurtured young
Englishwoman. He is not the Falstaff of Shakespeare,
but of his celebrated editor, Mr. Bowdler. Again, the
overture *In the South* is Italy seen through the eyes
of a specially conducted Cook's tourist. Consequently,
in the same way that Franck's best work is contained
in the *Prelude, Chorale, and Fugue*, the *Prelude, Aria,
and Finale*, and similar works, so Elgar's best achievements are the two Symphonies, the *Variations*, the
string quartet, the *Introduction and Allegro* for strings.
In them his consummate musicianship and amazing
fertility of resource are given full play, unimpeded by
literary and imaginative associations demanding a
spiritual breadth and insight which, like the Belgian
master, he conspicuously lacks.

The symphonies of Elgar have often, and wrongly,
been compared to those of Brahms. There is really
very little resemblance between them. Their methods,
in fact, are fundamentally opposed to each other. It
has already been pointed out in the essay on Strauss
that the essential characteristic of the classical symphony consists in the interaction of two strongly

contrasted themes, while the symphonic poem, on the other hand, is generally evolved from a single thematic germ. The symphonies of Brahms are essentially an attempt to renew and revivify the old classical form ; Elgar, again to a certain extent like Franck, sought to apply to the symphony the methods of construction of the symphonic poem. But while the general course of the movements in his symphonies is carefully mapped out and planned on the traditional lines, Brahms seldom succeeds in conceiving themes sufficiently contrasted to generate the action, so to speak. His themes are never properly first and second subjects, neither masculine nor feminine, but rather like the symbolic figures of Michael Angelo—too robust and muscular to be women, too graceful and effeminate to be men. They are in fact hermaphroditic. Similarly Elgar is equally incapable of conceiving themes which are susceptible of spontaneous generation, of giving birth to the whole movement as in a fugue of Bach or the *Fifth Symphony* of Beethoven. His most characteristic subjects, such as the first theme of the E flat Symphony, generate by splitting themselves up into several separate organisms, each bar or phrase becoming a theme in itself, according to the method of parturition which biologists call binary fission.

Brahms, by virtue of his fine architectural sense, is generally able to achieve a satisfactory balance and proportion in his movements. The ground-plan is always admirably laid out, but he seldom succeeds in linking together the various constituent sections of his building ; his joins and flexures are invariably the weakest parts of his movements. Elgar, on the other hand, has an equally fine sense of continuity and flow. Having no preconceived ground-plan, he does not irritate us, as Brahms so often does, by an arbitrary return to a subject in order to impart logic and balance to the whole. Where he fails, however, is precisely where Brahms succeeds. Despite the continuity and flow of his movements, they seldom give one a sense of equipoise and harmonious balance. He is like an orator to whom one train of thought suggests another, which in its turn suggests a third, and so on indefinitely; he passes from one point to another with great appropriateness and without any sudden divagations or transitions, but generally loses himself in the maze which he has constructed. He is weakest when he lamely comes back without apparent reason to the theme from which he has strayed. Brahms is like an orator who always knows what he is going to say next, but is never able to make satisfactory transitions from one point to another. On the other hand, he is always quite at home when he returns to his subject; he has had that moment firmly fixed in his mind all along.

Both the virtues and defects of Elgar's symphonic style, his power of passing from one point to another with perfect logic and of holding our attention all the time and his inability to establish a final impression of coherence and proportion, are due to the fact that he never seems to have an absolutely clear idea of what he wants to do and of what he wishes to say when he starts to write a work. He is a born *improvvisatore* of the old school, of the type who will sit down and extemporize a work out of any theme one cares to give him. His attitude is characteristically summed up in the words recorded by a biographer: ' My idea is that there is music in the air—music all around us ; the world is full of it, and you simply take as much of it as you require.' And so he simply takes the first handful that presents itself, seeming to write from bar to bar without any very clear idea of what he is going to do next. The frequent triviality and tawdriness of his material is due not so much to any inherent lack of critical discrimination—he is probably as well aware of its intrinsic shortcomings as anyone else—as to a mistaken interpretation of the familiar and incontrovertible truth that fine feathers do not make fine birds, or fine themes fine works; that the greatest masterpieces seem often to be constructed out of the most insignificant materials. He has learnt from experience that in the course of his working he will often light quite unexpectedly and almost accidentally upon some line of thought which will open up to him a whole world of enchanting possibilities of which he has never dreamed. In the handling of the material alone the unanalysable and incommunicable magic resides, and he knows that, once he has started, the work will probably be taken out of his hands, as it were, and will shape itself. If this happens, the chances are that the result will be a good work; if not, a bad one. He can never tell beforehand which it will be. As Maeterlinck has said, ' The poet enters with his lamp the treasure-house of darkness and the ineffable, but woe to him if he knows to a jot and tittle with what booty he returns, and if the best part of his glory is not the jewel he has won by mistake. Woe to him if he has divined all its secrets, and if he has been able for an instant to hold his work in control between his two hands.'

Now this is all very true, but it is only one part of the truth. It is true that no artist knows precisely what his work will be in the end, but he must have some definite direction, some definite object in view all the time, even if he should never find it. Otherwise he can never be one of the greatest. The type of artist to which Elgar conforms is like a knight-errant who rides out seeking for any adventure that may cross his path; whether it is a wicked magician, a beautiful maiden in distress, a hoary dragon, or only a wild boar, it is all the same to him. Whatever he finds will content him. The greatest artists, on the other hand, are knights of the Grail who will spend their whole life, if needs be, in an eternal quest, seeking tirelessly, endlessly, for the vision which eludes them ; whom neither beautiful maidens in distress, nor dragons, nor all the Klingsor allurements of *houris* and magic flower-gardens can seduce from their unalterable and inviolable purpose. To them alone are the greatest mysteries revealed, for them alone the greatest experiences reserved. With all his admirable qualities, Elgar is not of them.

It is a most remarkable circumstance that, after centuries of almost complete musical sterility, England should suddenly produce simultaneously two composers of such stature and rank as Delius and Elgar ; it is no less surprising that they should be so entirely different from each other. It would indeed be exceedingly difficult to find, in any art or at any time, an example of a more complete antithesis, unless it is that of Delacroix and Ingres in painting. They do not seem to possess a single quality in common. They excel in different spheres, and the virtues which the one possesses the other conspicuously lacks. The style and method of Delius is simple to an extreme degree, almost primitive ; the quality of his thought generally extremely subtle and refined. Elgar's technique is complex and highly organized, his thought often undistinguished to the point of banality. It is impossible not to admire unreservedly the consummate ability of the composer of such works as the violin or the 'cello concerto ; it is equally impossible not to dislike extremely the vulgarity and tawdriness of a great part of the material out of which they are constructed. A Delius score often seems surprisingly clumsy and incompetent, but nevertheless it seldom fails to convince one in performance. A score of Elgar, on the other hand, is a thing of joy to study on account of the inexhaustible wealth of technical invention which it reveals in every bar, and the cunning resource and subtlety with which it is employed; yet the dominant impression left by its performance is frequently one of dissatisfaction and disappointment.

In their instrumental predilections, too, they are strikingly opposed to each other. To think of Delius at his most characteristic is to think of passages like the opening bars of *Brigg Fair* or the *Dance Rhapsody*, in which the strings, however delicate and sensitive his writing for them may be, are employed as a kind of massed harmonic background against which the melodic voices of the wood-wind are projected and displayed. No composer has ever written with such an intimate understanding of this department of the orchestra. On the other hand, it is probably the sole defect of Elgar's admirable sense of tone-colour that he is inclined to treat the wood-wind rather as if they were stops on the organ, without much perception or consideration of their individualities ; the main weight of his musical argument is confided to the strings, in accordance with the classical tradition. While Delius's writing for the trumpets and trombones is often coarse and insensitive, especially in *fortissimo*, there is probably no composer living who can write more effectively for the brass than Elgar ; his trombone parts in particular are unsurpassable models of brilliance and refinement. Delius's main strength lies in the amazing richness and variety of his harmonic resources ; Elgar's harmonic palette is timid and restricted in comparison, his contrapuntal skill being his most valuable and characteristic asset.

These are only a few of the more obvious points of divergence between the two masters, and it would be easy to adduce many others, for there is not a single aspect of their art in which they could be said to coincide. The reason for this is that they approach their art from two entirely different angles. Delius is first and foremost a creative artist for whom music is the means to the expression of spiritual realities. Elgar, on the contrary, is primarily a craftsman. He is more preoccupied with making a finely constructed piece of work than with giving expression to any very profound or strikingly individual conceptions. Indeed, as far as mentality and outlook are concerned, when we have given to César the things which are César's, and to Brahms the things which are Brahms's, there is singularly little left except unimportant mannerisms and the self-consciously Tennysonian *nobilmente*. Delius, as we have already seen, is not at his best in handling traditional forms, but only in his more imaginative and wholly personal conceptions. Elgar is at his best in the traditional forms of symphony, concerto, and variation, while he is correspondingly deficient in the more imaginative qualities of mind. In the music of Delius the qualities one appreciates most are those which are to some extent common to all the arts ; in other words, he is an artist before he is a musician. What one admires in the work of Elgar is rather those ideas and conceptions which are specifically musical and indissolubly bound up with the employment of a particular medium or form, and the successful solution of the problems to which this choice gives rise. While Elgar's personality and mentality are in many ways more readily accessible to the mind of the average audience than those of Delius, his music nevertheless possesses an esoteric quality resulting from the medium which only the initiate is capable of recognizing and appreciating. Hence the discrepancy between the great popularity of certain of his works and the neglect of others. Delius appeals more to the cultured and imaginative section of an audience whose interest in art is not confined to and bounded by music alone. The difference between them is, in fact, much the same as that which obtains, on the highest plane, between Beethoven and Mozart, between Michael Angelo and Raphael.

It is not surprising, therefore, to find that very few people are capable of appreciating both to an equal degree. But even if it should be impossible to possess an equal sympathy and temperamental affinity for both, there is no reason why one should not be willing to admit their eminence in their respective spheres. The praise we give to the one detracts nothing from the other; they are not antagonistic, but rather complementary to each other, not merely in that they both represent separate halves of one whole, from a purely musical point of view, but also in what they express, as far as one can separate the two things. They are both profoundly English; and while Delius reveals a strikingly close affinity to the Elizabethans as well as to the poets of the romantic movement, Elgar is more representative of the England of to-day, or, more accurately, perhaps, of yesterday. The music of Elgar is essentially the musical counterpart of the literature and art of the Victorian era. This is probably the reason why it inspires such an extraordinarily violent antipathy and animosity in many of the present generation. Every age tends to react most violently against its immediate predecessor, and consequently the qualities which are most characteristic of the Victorian age are those which are most despised at the present time. On the other hand, while it is true that every artist must to some extent express his age, he is only a great artist in so far as he is able to rise above it; and it must be admitted that in the greater part of his output, Elgar does not rise above it. He never gets entirely away from the atmosphere of pale, cultured idealism, and the unconsciously hypocritical, self-righteous, complacent, Pharisaical gentlemanliness which is so characteristic of British art in the last

century. Very few artists during that period escaped
it, however great they may have been. Ruskin,
Tennyson, Matthew Arnold, Walter Pater, Burne-
Jones, Thackeray even—these are only a few names
taken at random—were all tainted with this spirit,
and unfortunately Elgar has not escaped from it
either. This it is which, more than anything else
just prevents Elgar from being a great artist. He
might have been a great composer if he had not been
such a perfect gentleman.

It is an interesting and significant fact that the
artists who during this same period have most completely escaped from this pervading, subtly insinuating
atmosphere of gentility, such as Byron, Shelley, Landor,
Delius, have passed the greater part of their actively
creative life abroad. It has often been said by Elgar's
admirers that it was a fortunate thing for his individuality that he was unable, for material reasons, to study
music abroad. On the contrary, it was the one thing
which might have saved him. Swinburne is a melancholy example of the effect which this atmosphere of
smug respectability can exercise over an artist of the
highest rank. His best work was all done when he
was a wild and disreputable *enfant terrible*; when he
went to Putney with Watts-Dunton he lost every
vestige of the genius he once had. Much the same
thing has happened to Elgar, though in a less sudden
and spectacular manner. The pity of it is that it was
by no means inevitable; the quality of mind to which
allusion is made was not innate in him any more than
it was innate in Swinburne, for there are many passages
in his works which reveal more than a mere presage
of a reckless, angry intolerance and a proud strength
which serve to remind us of what Elgar might have
been under more favourable circumstances. It is
entirely the outcome of environment, a kind of
encrustation of the soul, like the barnacles on a ship's

keel. As it is a complaint to which only English artists are subject, one can only suppose that it is one of the more disagreeable penalties of ruling the waves; English artists must have their souls scraped periodically, or they are lost. In spite of this, however, it seems safe to say that the two symphonies, the *Introduction and Allegro*, the *Enigma Variations*, and possibly also the string quartet, will continue to occupy an honoured place in English art for many years to come.

CLAUDE DEBUSSY

IT is a self-evident truth which does not stand in need of demonstration that our appreciation of a work of art depends largely upon the degree of understanding and insight which we ourselves bring to bear on it. But while our ability to enter into, let us say, the art of Bach is almost entirely conditioned by the scope of our purely musical intelligence, there are many other artists, less magnificently impersonal in their outlook, less universal in their appeal, whose art relies in great measure for its effect upon a kind of intimate collaboration on the part of its listener or contemplator ; mere passive receptivity, even when it is accompanied by a high level of insight, is not in itself sufficient to enable us to enter into the spirit of it.

The music of Debussy, to a greater extent than that of anyone else, seems to demand an almost personal understanding between composer and audience for its proper appreciation. It possesses to a marked degree the power of suggesting much more to a sympathetically disposed mind than to others it seems to contain ; on the other hand, it often leaves entirely unmoved and indifferent those who have no such personal relation or temperamental affinity to it. In order to appreciate this music we must meet it half-way, as it were, and contribute a kind of active sympathy of our own, otherwise it will certainly not yield up its secret to us. It does not impose itself brutally upon us or extract our unwilling admiration, as does the art of Wagner, for example, however much we may sincerely detest it and rage against it ; Debussy's muse must be wooed like a woman, for she only gives herself to those who love her. Sometimes a phrase of Debussy, of which the actual intrinsic musical interest seems, viewed objectively, to be so exceedingly slight and tenuous as to be almost non-existent, will have a direct appeal, as if to oneself alone. No one else, one imagines, could possibly feel it in quite the same way. Is it justifiable to assume that this intimate appeal is definitely latent in the music, though only accessible to those who are temperamentally able to respond to it, or is it a mere projection of one's own individuality, similar to that which leads one to endow a person one loves with all kinds of attributes and perfections which he or she does not in reality possess?

This it is which makes it so difficult to arrive at an impersonal and judicial estimate of Debussy's achievement. Purely objective criticism of this music seems entirely out of the question, for, apart from this subtle spiritual appeal, there is singularly little to interest us in it.

It is precisely the same difficulty which we encounter in many artists and writers of the same period as Debussy, who had very similar ideals in their respective arts. Mr. Arthur Symons, in his *Studies in Seven Arts*, writes:

'In the nineteenth century, as in every century, there have been painters who have deliberately turned backwards, or aside, haters of reality, dreamers who have wanted to gather in some corner of unlimited space. Poets rather than painters, the visible world has seemed too narrow for them, and one like Monticelli has tried to paint in terms of music, and another like Rossetti has tried to put the spiritual mysteries of passion, or like Watts, the bodily form of great emotion and high duties, literally upon the canvas—Gustave Moreau, Puvis de Chavannes, Burne-Jones, Rops, Beardsley, are others. Most of them are not perfectly equipped as painters, but may seem to escape at least

96

from some of their limitations by this commerce with another world. All have an interest beyond their mere skill as painters, with various kinds of appeal to those who go to art for something which is certainly not the art of it.'

Debussy occupies much the same place in music that these painters occupy in painting. He is not, as he has so often been called, an impressionist; for although his method and manner may sometimes seem to be analogous to those of the impressionist school of painting, his ultimate intention is wholly opposed to theirs. In the first place, it is clear that genuine tonal impressionism would consist in the direct notation and transcription of natural sounds, and would not concern itself, as so-called impressionist music does, with the subject-matter of an alien art, such as goldfish, moonlight effects, reflections in the water, and so forth. In the same way that Courbet said, ' On ne doit peindre que ce que les yeux peuvent voir,' the musician would similarly say that one should only put into his music the sounds which are to be heard in nature and in daily life.

Such an art, it is not difficult to see, is only theoretically possible, and could never hope to rival that of the painters, since it is based on a wholly artificial analogy, and has no roots in the intrinsic nature of music as an art. For while it is true that the impressionist painter is certainly creating, and not merely imitating natural effects, he is creating by means of selected natural forms; music, on the other hand, does not possess a fixed body of material fact external to itself which is capable of affording the data or subject-matter for direct observation and transcription comparable to that which is afforded to the writer by human nature and social institutions, or to the painter by nature animate or inanimate. There is no musical parallel to the inexhaustibility of suggestion and external stimulus contained in the subject-matter of literature and painting. There is no inherent logic or inner necessity in natural sounds, independent of the artist ; they serve no vital purpose, and possess no implicit significance of their own, neither are they susceptible of reproduction in terms of art. In other words, there is no direct relation between, say, the sound of running water, or the rustling of leaves in a forest, and musical art as we know it. The musician can only effect a highly conventionalized transposition by analogy, as in Wagner's Rhine music or the Forest Murmurs in *Siegfried*, which is precisely the opposite of what the impressionists achieved in painting. This is only natural ; for while the impressionist ideal of observing nature directly and objectively transcribing it, to the exclusion, as far as possible, of sentiment and emotion (which appertain particularly to music) and of philosophic or psychological interest (which belong essentially to literature), is in absolute accordance with the aesthetic nature of painting, it is wholly irreconcilable with the aesthetic nature of music, which is not impressionist, but expressionist.

But quite apart from whether impressionism is even possible in music, it is at least certain that the ideal of the direct transcription of nature to the exclusion of the element of personal sensibility and emotion, is the opposite of what Debussy sets out to do. Strauss, in fact, is the real musical impressionist, with his bleating sheep and squealing babies. Debussy's tone-painting, like that of Weber and Wagner, is essentially subjective ; in his own words it is ' Une transposition sentimentale de ce qui est invisible dans la nature '. It is the music of nature, certainly, but it is not descriptive ; its purpose is not to evoke a definite picture, but to suggest the mood or emotion which the particular image in question aroused in the artist's mind. His conception of nature is, indeed, wholly anthropomorphic; to quote his own words again, his art seeks to establish a ' Rapport entre l'âme innombrable de la nature et l'âme d'un personnage '. In a word, Debussy belongs to the school of writers and artists called Symbolists ; he is the musician of the Symbolist movement. As was observed in the first chapter, Mr. Arthur Symons, in his admirable study of the literary side of the movement, wrote as follows concerning Mallarmé, the high priest and legislator of the school, ' Carry the theories of Mallarmé to a practical conclusion, multiply his powers in a direct ratio, and you have Wagner.' If he were now to re-write his book in the light of subsequent developments—it was written some twenty-five years ago—he would possibly put the name of Debussy in place of that of Wagner. His statement would then be correct, for Debussy is the practical outcome of Mallarmé's aesthetic pronouncements, and it is no mere coincidence that the first, and in many ways the best of his mature works, *l'Après-midi d'un Faune*, should be a tonal transcription of Mallarmé's most satisfactory achievement.

There can be little doubt that music possesses an infinitely greater aptitude for embodying and expressing this order of vague but intimate suggestion and association of ideas than any other art. In the familiar and classic instance of the old man of Khartoum in the limerick, who, it may be remembered,

> Kept a tame sheep in his room ;
> ' To remind me ', he said,
> ' Of some one who 's dead,
> Though I cannot quite recollect whom ',

the old man's conduct is quite inexplicable and his emotion incommunicable. But if he had been a musician instead of being a poet, he would have

Claude Debussy

experienced no difficulty in imparting to us his elegiac emotion without the necessity of having to mention the somewhat disconcerting association of ideas which gave rise to it. And too often, like the old man of Khartoum, the literary symbolist fails in his attempt to find the eternal in the transitory, or at any rate to communicate his discovery to others and to enable them to share in his emotion, because he is compelled, by the unalterable nature of his literary medium, to attempt the evocation of his emotion by means of the reconstruction of the frequently trivial and always fortuitous occasion of it, and by its expression through more or less concrete images.

In other words, literature and the plastic arts are essentially and primarily concerned with the concrete and the actual; their nature abhors purely abstract, disembodied emotion. Writers and painters are condemned to labour under the ineluctable necessity of creating living realities, which can only ultimately and secondarily become symbols of universal application. They can only arrive at the fundamental implication by way of the particular instance, at the general theorem through the individual problem. Music, on the contrary, resents the concrete and the actual; she can only breathe freely in the rarefied atmosphere of the abstract and the disembodied emotion. Consequently we find that a literary or pictorial work almost inevitably takes rise from a definite, external, concrete stimulus or suggestion; the initial conception of a musical work, on the other hand, is generally a vague and intangible mood which only receives precise and particular form from the composer afterwards. Symbolism is, in fact, essentially a province of music, and this explains how it is that Debussy in such works as the *Nocturnes, La Mer, l'Après-midi,* and *Pelléas,* achieves on the whole what painters like Rossetti and Gustave Moreau, and writers like Mallarmé and Maeterlinck, entirely failed to achieve. The characters in the latter's plays, it will be observed, speak and behave in precisely the same fashion as our friend the old man of Khartoum. And in the same way that music, as I sought to show in the first essay, is the art in which the romantic ideals attained their most perfect form and expression, so symbolism, which is only a continuation, or rather second wave, of romanticism, after the backwash of impressionism, found in music its fullest realization. Just as Weber was the musician of German romanticism and Berlioz the musician of French romanticism, so Debussy is the musician of the Symbolist movement, and it is as such that we shall best understand him. It is this fact more than anything else which explains the curiously subtle and indefinite appeal his music has for those who are in personal sympathy with it.

Debussy is not one of those artists who only find themselves after years of incessant striving and innumerable failures and disappointments. He seems always to have been singularly sure of himself and his artistic purpose, for already in the *Ariettes oubliées* of 1888 we find ourselves in the presence of a wholly personal, fully developed, and self-assured art. Properly speaking, there are no early works, unless we except the cantatas *l'Enfant prodigue* and *La Damoiselle élue*, and anyhow the second of the two already shows, in the choice of subject and in some of the music, the direction in which his artistic affinities lay. Consequently, a chronological survey of his work lacks entirely that element of fascination and wonder which we experience in watching the gradual growth of an organism from a seed to its final triumphant efflorescence. There is no process of gestation to observe; as Minerva sprang fully armed and grown up from the brain of Jupiter, so the art of Debussy was produced fully matured without the agency of an artistic

Claude Debussy

mother. Like Minerva too, she remained a virgin, and any attempt which has been made to approach her has only ended, like the attempt of Vulcan, in the production of an Erechthonian monster of exceeding deformity and hideousness. Debussy's art is unique, intangible, inviolable, without ancestors or descendants. It can have no influence on the future of music; and this is at once its strength and its weakness.

The influence of Moussorgsky on Debussy has always been greatly exaggerated by writers on music; it was more an affinity than a direct influence, and even then it was rather an affinity of method than of mentality or artistic aim. There is ultimately very little in common between them. Moussorgsky, one cannot help thinking, like Cézanne, whose secret ambition it was to receive official recognition and to see his pictures hung in the Salon side by side with those of Bouguereau and other painters whom he similarly despised, harboured a certain reluctant respect, not altogether unmixed with envy, for the qualities he most affected to despise in others. It would be difficult otherwise to explain his frequent and sudden lapses into conventionality. He had not always the courage of his convictions, as Debussy always had. Moreover, Moussorgsky is always a Scythian; he has no part in the rich musical heritage of the western world. Like Alaric the Visigoth, gazing in bewilderment at the sacred and legendary city lying defenceless at his feet, torn between reverential awe and the lust for destruction; or like a medieval monk, suddenly confronted with a Greek statue, undecided whether to spare or destroy it: so Moussorgsky, in face of the musical tradition of centuries, alternately covets and disdains it. Debussy, on the other hand, is hypercivilized and over-refined, a Roman of the decadence. His contempt for, or, more accurately, his indifference to, the traditional legacy of musical civilization is the outcome of close contact and of too great a familiarity. His cult of the primitive, like that of Rossetti, Morris, and Burne-Jones, results from a deliberate choice; in the same way that they called themselves Pre-Raphaelite artists, so we might call Debussy a Pre-Mozartean musician.

Symbolism in all the arts is distinguished by the deliberate avoidance of all accepted means of expression, of all merely mechanical procedures, of all purely decorative adjuncts, and by the reversion to a simpler and more primitive method of working. So it is with the music of Debussy. His predilection for melodic formulas based upon the so-called pentatonic scale is one of the most obvious examples of this tendency in his music. Some aestheticians, observing the dominant role which this scale plays in the folk-music of many, perhaps even of most, primitive races or nations in an early stage of cultural development, have been led to hazard the conjecture that it represents the root language of music, the universal scale from which all others have evolved. It is, of course, a theory which is too purely speculative for either acceptance or rejection, but there is no questioning the fact that the pentatonic scale is peculiarly adapted to and habitually associated with the expression of that particular variety of primitive though subtle emotions and associations of ideas which we call symbolic; and it is not too fanciful to suggest that Debussy's constant employment of melodies based upon it can be traced to a desire to appeal to a kind of subconscious racial memory, and is essentially a kind of musical atavism recalling a more primitive state of aesthetic consciousness.

Similarly it could be pointed out that his characteristic love of modal melody and harmony can be traced to the same source, and his constant employment of common chords in strict parallelism is only a reversion to the most primitive form of harmonic writing. It is in fact nothing more or less than the medieval practice of *faux bourdon*, which is really not harmonic at all, but only a doubling of the melody in the third and fifth. Conscious harmonic thinking only dates from the moment at which parallel motion is abandoned in favour of contrary and oblique motion, and the same is true of counterpoint, a striking confirmation of the truth that these two elements of musical syntax, which are always spoken of and written about as if they were not merely two separate but two wholly opposite things, are in reality inseparable and interdependent. And it is, to say the least, remarkable that the composer who is popularly supposed to be above all things a harmonist, and to have contributed more than anyone else to the alleged enormous advance in modern harmonic thought, is in reality not a harmonist at all. No composer of eminence, with the possible exception of Berlioz, has ever possessed so little true harmonic sense as Debussy. This may seem to some a mere paradox, but a moment's reflection will show that it is an actual truth. Few indeed among modern composers have actually progressed further than the earliest tentative experiments of medieval musicians; the principle on which their harmonic writing is based is, almost without exception, nothing but that of organum and its offspring *faux bourdon*—for it obviously makes little difference if seconds, sevenths, and ninths are thrown in with, or instead of, mere thirds and sixths. Debussy often uses harmony as Bach used instrumental colour in his writing for the orchestra; whole passages and sometimes even whole pieces such as the *Voiles* from the first book of *Préludes* are harmonized almost throughout on one single chord, and *Pelléas* has with justice been called 'the land of ninths'. Indeed, in his harmony, Debussy is as curiously limited, monotonous, and restricted as in his melody.

His rhythms too are singularly lifeless and torpid as a general rule, and this fault is generally admitted by his greatest admirers ; such exceptions as there are in his work, like the *Fêtes* and the finale of *Ibéria*, strike one as being either not altogether successful or not particularly characteristic of the composer. Debussy lacks entirely the leaping pulse and vitality which constitute Strauss's greatest asset, and even the factitious vitality and machine-like energy of Stravinsky.

In short, it cannot be too emphatically insisted upon that the objectively musical interest of Debussy's music is almost as slender and tenuous as Hans Andersen's Emperor's clothes. He consistently sacrificed every constituent element of musical language to the expression of a particularly restricted order of sensations and emotions. He achieved his purpose by means of a narrowing and not a broadening of artistic scope. The fact remains, however, that he did in many works achieve it, and ultimately nothing else matters very much, provided always that what he had to say was worth saying. And on the whole one can safely say that it was ; the world would be the poorer without such works as the *Nocturnes*, *l'Après-midi*, the string quartet, *La Mer*, and a small handful of songs and piano pieces.

I am far from sharing the general opinion that *Pelléas* is Debussy's masterpiece, or even that it is, as a whole, to be included in the foregoing enumeration of what seem to me to be his most significant works. In the first place, there can be little doubt that it is too long. It has been said that the opera, as Debussy originally conceived it, was very much shorter, but that Maeterlinck, to whom it was submitted for the necessary approval preliminary to publication and performance, asserted that the many cuts which had

Claude Debussy

been made in the play destroyed its meaning entirely, and insisted on the composer setting to music several scenes which he had omitted. The probabilities are that this is true; it is certainly the impression that the work makes in both study and performance.

It is interesting to observe that *Pelléas* was conceived and written at precisely the same period as Delius's great opera, the *Village Romeo and Juliet.* The subjects have much in common with each other, and both works are attempts to arrive at a satisfactory solution of the perennial problems aroused by the union of music and the drama. Yet it would be difficult to imagine two works more completely opposed to each other, both in theory and in practice. *Pelléas* has been referred to as a new departure in the history of opera, and fundamentally opposed to the Wagnerian conception of music-drama; but actually Debussy's intention of dispensing with any merely parasitic development of the music is only a variation and restatement of Wagner's theory that music should be subordinated to the interests of the drama, to say nothing of the theories of Gluck and the early Florentines. On the other hand, Wagner, as we have seen, fortunately did not act upon it, while Debussy did; he is the first musician to follow to their logical conclusion the principles laid down by the literary theorists of the eighteenth century. He has so thoroughly succeeded in subordinating the musical interest to dramatic exigencies that there is practically nothing left of the music. It is a *reductio ad absurdum* which demonstrates the utter aesthetic falsity of the literary ideal in music. Even if this ideal were realizable, if it were possible to achieve a satisfactory result by reducing music to the task of underlining and elucidating the words and nothing else, the particular choice of a text proved very unfortunate. For in the same way that the writers of the romantic period, as

106

Claude Debussy

I sought to show earlier in the book, were primarily occupied with the expression of musical ideas in terms of literature, so the writers of the Symbolist movement were similarly endeavouring to make words perform the task of music. Maeterlinck's play is not merely musical in conception, but every phrase is chosen for its musical suggestiveness rather than for its literal sense. In fact, considered purely as literature, a great part of the play is sheer nonsense, a mere accompaniment to melodies unheard which Debussy, with an almost heroically perverse self-abnegation, refuses to provide, preferring to creep along timidly in the footsteps of the poet instead of providing the musical wings which the latter perpetually demands, and even implores.

Although there is no process of gradual development to be found in the music of Debussy, a very definite decline is perceptible, beginning about 1905, after *La Mer*, one of his best works. The cause of it is only too clear and understandable, for the determination to achieve a wholly personal expression by means of restriction and exclusion led, as it always must, to a condition of premature exhaustion and sterility. By the time Debussy had reached his fullest maturity he had no longer anything left to say. The particular kind of originality which Debussy and so many modern artists possess is a talisman which enables them to accomplish great things for a time, but like the *peau de chagrin* of Balzac it automatically dwindles away with use until in the end there is nothing left of it. To create only out of one's personality and to disdain the rich traditional legacy of the past is the artistic equivalent of living on one's capital. Sooner or later there must come an end to its resources. It has no means of renewal or replenishment. It is not a fresh, ever-living source welling up spontaneously from the soul of music, but a pool of still water, which tends to become stagnant and unwholesome even before it is wholly depleted. And when Debussy had come to an end of his natural resources, and had exhausted all the limited possibilities afforded by the narrow and restricted circle of conceptions to which he had chosen to confine his talents, he was confronted with the alternative of either repeating himself and writing variations on what he had already done, or of reverting to some form of traditionalism. For a time he chose the former, and in the works which succeed *Pelléas*, such as *Ibéria*, although they are far more accomplished than many of his earlier works, the old elusive appeal and subtle charm have almost entirely disappeared. They all reveal a growing preoccupation with the outward manner, a lack of spontaneity, an ever-increasing tendency towards stereotyped formulas and mere pattern weaving. But worse was to come. By this time Debussy was not merely recognized and accepted ; he had actually become a cult, a popular fashion. ' Savez-vous une émotion plus belle qu'un homme resté inconnu le long des siècles, dont on déchiffre par hasard le secret ? ' he had written in his earlier days. ' Avoir été un de ces hommes—voilà la seule forme valable de la gloire.' Yet the sensitive, aristocratic artist who had once written these words, with their fine distaste for fame and notoriety, lived to see himself a *chef d'école* with a horde of parasitic admirers and imitators. Such is the irony of fate. It might almost be supremely comic if it were not so pathetic. ' Écoute, Claude,' said a friend to him one day, ' les debussystes m'agacent.' ' Moi, ils me tuent,' replied Debussy bitterly. And again in a letter to a friend, ' Si je pouvais vous prier de me trouver un petit coin . . . pour secouer cette atmosphère de fausse grandeur qui, quoi qu'on fasse pour y échapper, . . . finit toujours par passer sous notre porte.' But the tragedy was that it had not merely crept under his door, but into his very soul. Fame had found him wholly unprepared and defenceless, and he only made a half-hearted resistance to it.

The results of it were immediately and fatally apparent. As in France freethinkers have a disconcerting habit of repenting of their sins and being received into the Church on their death-bed; as anarchists and pacifists hasten into uniform in time of war, singing the *Marseillaise*; as the revolutionary artists, *Indépendants* and *Fauves*, one after another, as soon as they achieve popular fame or official recognition, subside with almost indecent alacrity on to the matronly bosom of *la tradition française*, vowing eternal faithfulness ; so even with Debussy, the proud aloof individualist, the symbolist, the worshipper of strange and exotic gods, the collaborator of Rossetti, Maeterlinck, and d'Annunzio. His last works, the *Sonates pour divers instruments*, appear with the astonishing inscription, ' par Claude Debussy, *musicien français*', and they are by a long way the worst things he ever wrote. Debussy is the least French of musicians. How is it possible not to see this ? His best work is that which is most exotic and least French ; his greatest quality, his only quality, lies in the wholly personal and entirely original nature of his art, owing very little, and giving nothing, to anyone. And yet he, of all musicians who have ever lived, has been made the object of a Chauvinist cult, and genealogies have been elaborately constructed in order to show that he is descended from Rameau and Couperin. They are obvious forgeries. In so far as Debussy is French at all his descent is very different, and not nearly so distinguished. *L'Enfant prodigue* and *La Damoiselle élue* are not the offspring of the ancient lineage of Rameau and Couperin, but the guilty fruit of liaisons with the Manon Lescaut and Marie-Magdalene of Jules Massenet. The influence of

Claude Debussy

Massenet is the only French element in the music of Debussy, and it is an influence which he never succeeded in throwing off. It is apparent even in the last of his good works, the *Martyre de Saint Sébastien*. Who was it who said that in every Frenchman there was 'un fond de Massenet'? Was it Debussy himself? Whoever it was, it is a profoundly true statement. While smug gentility and hypocrisy are the curse of English art, and facile sentimentality and *Schwärmerei* that of German art, so this soft, enervating, female, boudoir prettiness has always been the disease against which French artists have had to fight. Very few of them have escaped the infection; even the work of such great artists as Renoir and Rodin is permeated with it.

So much for Claude Debussy, *musicien français*; and incidentally, is there not something shameless and undignified in this anxiety to be recognized as such? Was there ever a great traditional artist who so consciously claimed to be so? Has Anatole France, for example, ever inscribed his books with the legend, *écrivain français*? Since when has it become customary for aristocrats to go about reciting their genealogical trees in public? Such practices, so far from convincing us of the justice of the claims, tend rather to induce us to regard the pretensions with doubt and suspicion.

The steady decline in the quality of Debussy's work in the last years, although it was only the natural consequence of his self-imposed limitations, was undoubtedly accelerated and intensified by the inroads of the terrible illness from which he suffered. He was not cast in the heroic mould of a Beethoven, or even a Wagner, to whom illness and suffering, if it did not act as an incentive to creation, brought at least a depth of sympathy and human understanding to which they might not otherwise have attained. With

110

Debussy it certainly does not seem to have checked or impaired the capacity or the will to create; as a matter of fact he wrote much more in the last years than ever before. What it did was very much subtler and far more fatal. It blunted the fine edge of his critical faculty and relentlessly undermined the absolute rectitude of his sense of artistic fitness; above all, it insidiously invaded the innermost sanctuary, the ivory tower of his imagination, chilling and blighting all its delicate charm and wayward fantasy. A great constructive artist, or one whose strength primarily resides in solid or brilliant workmanship, suffers far less in this respect than one like Debussy or Rossetti—on whose work illness had similar results—their chief asset being precisely their keen sensibility, and their field of action lying in the more subtle half-shades of thought and execution. In the last works these qualities disappeared, leaving behind only an outer shell of empty convention and irritating mannerism. One work alone stands out from among all the rest, namely, the *Martyre de Saint Sébastien*. Allowing for the difference in scale, one might say that *Pelléas* is Debussy's *Tristan*, but *Sébastien* is his *Parsifal*. For it, like *Parsifal*, is full of the spirit of death, written, as it were, with death standing at the composer's elbow, not only inspiring the thought, but guiding also the hand that wrote. There is no more of pain and suffering in the music of Amfortas than in the section of Debussy's work called ' le Laurier blessé ', and in both works there is the same curious blend of mysticism and sensuality, the same peculiar zest in the portrayal of the infliction and endurance of pain. *Sébastien* may legitimately be called decadent; the fact remains that it is one of the highest points to which Debussy ever attained. It will never achieve the popularity of many of his works; it is not even appreciated at its true value by his most enthusiastic admirers. One

Claude Debussy

greatly regrets that Debussy was never able to give effect to his intention of transforming it into a lyric drama. As incidental music it is not completely suited to either theatre or concert-hall, and this is perhaps sufficient reason to account for the unmerited neglect into which it has fallen. With this music Debussy's genius shines out brightly for the last time; henceforward he was but the shadow of his former self.

Debussy stands, on the whole, in much the same relation to us to-day as that in which Wagner stood to our immediate predecessors. He is essentially the musical representative of a certain definite cultural moment, the embodiment and personification of a certain attitude of mind, a phase of thought and feeling through which we have all of us at some time or other passed. We inevitably feel towards him as towards an old and valued friend whom we have perhaps outgrown, but to whom we owe much. It seems almost an act of treachery or sacrilege to speak harshly or slightingly of one who has meant so much to us as Debussy; it is impossible to forget those early days of our youth when he seemed to represent our innermost and dearest ideals, to express our most intimate thoughts and most personal experiences. And though these days have long since departed, and with them all the glamour and youthful illusions in which we had involuntarily clothed him, we can still feel at times, in listening to his music, those emotions which Rousseau has so marvellously described in that passage of his *Confessions* in which he revisits in imagination the scenes of his childhood and re-lives the dead past.

Whatever our attitude may be towards Wagner at the present day, it is impossible to deny the great and enduring influence which he has exercised and will continue to exercise in the future; whatever the intrinsic value of his work he remains an historical figure of the first importance, and at one time one felt with regard to Debussy that, however much one's personal attitude concerning him might be modified in the future, he would likewise exercise a dominating and lasting influence on succeeding generations of musicians; that he too, though undeniably of lesser stature, was a great innovator who had opened up new roads by which many would in future travel. But time has robbed us even of that illusion; the new continent which we had supposed him to have discovered has turned out to be only a remote and hitherto un-exploited region of the known world, the possibilities of which he has himself fully exhausted. His music belongs to a world of dreams and shadows, inhabited by frail and evanescent phantoms which know neither joy nor sorrow, grief nor rapture, nor any earthly emotion; a land where neither sun nor moon shines, nor any darkness falls, where the only light is a mysterious and unending twilight, ' the light which never was on sea or land '.

It is pleasant to linger there awhile, lulled into oblivion and forgetfulness by the drowsy scent of lotus flowers and poppies, but sooner or later we must arise and depart, and seek once more the world of men and women, the sunshine, the busy streets, and the multitudinous sounds of human endeavour. And though, once departed, we may often think of it and of the time we spent there with feelings of wistful regret and tender affection, and in imagination hear again the sirens singing and the waves of a tideless sea gently and monotonously lapping on the shore of that most distant and lonely of islands, we can never again return there. It is the music of dreams, not of life.

MAURICE RAVEL

ALL art criticism which aims at being anything more than a mere expression of personal opinion must, to a certain extent at least, proceed by means of the Euclidian methods of deduction and demonstration. In other words, the artist presents us with a certain figure or construction, and it is not enough simply to comment upon the attributes and properties we perceive in it, any more than it is enough to state that the angles at the base of an isosceles triangle are equal without showing why they are and why they must be. Very little art criticism gets beyond the equivalent of showing empirically that the angles are equal by the simple process of measuring them; it seldom, if ever, gets down to the fundamental principles and aesthetic reasons which explain why, how, and wherefore. This is not to suggest that criticism is an exact science like geometry. But just as every discovery of value in the realm of science is simply the systematic verification of what had originally been arrived at by pure intuition, and the reduction to a generally applicable abstract principle or theory of facts which had hitherto only been known empirically, so in criticism, if our opinions are to be of value to anyone but ourselves, we must take the trouble to support them by means of logical reasoning, and show them to have a more solid basis than personal prejudice. It may be a fact that no speech ever made in the sacred precincts of the Mother of Parliaments, however impressive, has yet succeeded in inducing any member to vote in a different way from that in which he would have voted if he had never heard it, and

114

probably no intelligent lover of art is likely to be convinced by mere argument, however cogent and conclusive, that what he had thought to be a good work was in reality a very bad one, or vice versa ; but the fact remains that the critic who can bring forward sound reasons for his beliefs and for the conclusions he has arrived at concerning an artist's work, even if he is not altogether right in his premisses—or his head—will inevitably carry more weight than the critic who merely gives his opinion for what it is worth, however subtly discriminating and sensitive his taste may happen to be.

It is a remarkable fact that in all that has been written about the music of Ravel it is virtually impossible to find anything more than mere expressions of personal opinion. The only study of any length devoted to him which I know is that of M. Roland Manuel, an enthusiastic follower and disciple, who has achieved the remarkable feat of writing some fifty pages concerning the object of his admiration without saying anything at all beyond the fact that he thinks it is all very good. Why and in what way it is good he evidently finds difficult to express.

The reason for this and similar failures is due, not so much to the fact that M. Roland Manuel is an incompetent critic, but to the fact that it actually is exceedingly difficult to say why we like or dislike the music of Ravel. Some artists lend themselves more generously to the rigorous application of critical methods than others. If I may be allowed for a moment to revert to my simile, the properties and characteristics which their figures present are easily discernible and demonstrable at a glance. With the work of others, on the contrary, we must produce lines and construct elaborate figures on the original before we can hope to prove our point, or to substantiate the conclusions at which we had arrived intuitively. Ravel belongs to this latter category. The proposition which we are called upon to consider in his work is not susceptible of demonstration without our resigning ourselves to the preliminary task of raising ponderous and seemingly purposeless constructions on and around the very simple and straightforward figure that it presents. The data are too few, and in themselves suggest very little. To put it in another way, the smooth, polished surface of his work gives us no purchase, no secure foothold. We must first erect scaffoldings in order to examine it closely or to penetrate into the interior.

What, in the first place, are the most notable characteristics of the music of Ravel; what are the qualities in it that one either admires or dislikes? They are refinement, delicacy, restraint, clarity, according to some; preciosity, effeminacy, bloodlessness, insipidity, according to others. From whichever point of view we regard it, however, one certain fact emerges, on which all are agreed, namely, in the words of M. Manuel—one of the few definite statements which he permits himself—Ravel ' s'efforce vers un idéal qui est la négation de tout romantisme '. Now, it will be remembered that in the introductory essay I set out to show that what is generally called Romanticism is essentially the spirit of music; and the corollary, that ' the particular conceptions which music can express better than any other art, the aesthetic centre about which the romantic circle is described, are those which are called romantic '. If this is true, it follows that in so far as Ravel is pursuing an ideal which is the negation of romanticism he is moving away to the circumference of the musical circle, if not beyond it. It is at least certain that the qualities which we are wont to call ' classic ', such as restraint, clarity, formal perfection, and emotional reticence, have produced singularly little great music. They may be positive qualities in other arts, but on the whole they are negative qualities in music.

To this statement it may be objected that it fails to take account of Mozart. This is absolutely true. Mozart is the one ' classic ' composer in the history of music who is at the same time one of the greatest of all composers. But the fact that my argument does not apply to Mozart no more implies that it is unsound than the miracles of the saints imply that there are no laws of gravity. No natural principles, no fundamental laws of existence are applicable to him. There can be little doubt in the mind of any sane person that Mozart was a divine changeling, a love-child of the god Apollo. Only a fool could possibly believe that an ordinary mortal child of seven could have written the works which he is known to have written at that age. That would constitute an infinitely more flagrant breach of natural laws than the tacit admission of his divinity, and his consequent emancipation from the laws to which ordinary mortals are subject.

But for the sake of those readers who are too sceptically minded and incredulous to admit this wholly rational and simple explanation, one might as well state here once and for all that no kind of critical method, no aesthetic system of weights or measures, are applicable to the work of the greatest masters. One cannot systematize the eternal and unchanging, weigh the imponderable, or measure the infinite. Bach, Beethoven, Mozart inhabit worlds of their own and obey only their own mysterious and indeterminable laws. It is true, on the other hand, that even they occasionally descend to earth, and when they do it will be found that they conform as strictly to the ineluctable conditions of the ordinary world as any one else. There are many works of Mozart which illustrate my contention as thoroughly as those of any other composer. And however that may be, not even Ravel's greatest admirers would go so far as to place him with the greatest masters of all time.

There is a second statement of M. Manuel which will also be admitted by both friendly and hostile critics to be substantially if not adjectivally true, namely that ' Toutes ces manifestations ridicules, . . . presque impudiques . . . de passions grandiloquentes et vaines, sont éloignées autant qu'il est possible du génie français'. Very true indeed. All those ridiculous and almost indecent manifestations such as the *Sanctus* in Bach's B minor Mass, all those grandiloquent passions such as we find in the Fifth or Ninth Symphonies of Beethoven, are certainly not to be found in French music. This very profound remark explains how it is that the greatest of all French musicians, the only great composer, in fact, that France has ever produced, Hector Berlioz, is a romantic of the most extreme type. The typically French spirit in art, at its purest and best, is essentially classic in tendency. It is impossible to doubt this ; as another musical critic, Mr. Paul Rosenberg, has said : ' So repeatedly have temperaments of this (i.e. the classic) character appeared in France that it is difficult not to hold theirs the centrally, essentially French tradition, and not to see in men like Rabelais only the Frank, and in men like Berlioz only the atavism to Gallo-Roman times.'

The French are, as a race, the Greeks of modern times. And Greece too, it may appropriately be observed, similarly produced no music of the same significance as her achievement in the other arts. In fact it may be said without fear of contradiction that neither the Greek nor the French genius finds its fullest expression in music. They were neither of them musical races. The only idea the former had of music was in alliance with a literary text. For them it was only a subdivision of literature; they had no conception of purely instrumental music. Similarly, it is interesting to note, the little the French have achieved in music has been almost entirely, certainly overwhelmingly, in the domain of dramatic music. In what we call pure music their contribution has been small and ineffectual in comparison.

And if, as I have sought to show, the centre about which the musical circle is described consists in the romantic values, it necessarily follows that wit and humour are only on its circumference: the reason being, of course, that the sense of the ridiculous, existing as it does only in relation to actuality, and immutably based upon some comparison or contrast with human frailties or existing social institutions, is essentially a literary thing. Even in painting and sculpture, and particularly in architecture, there is little or no wit. Such instances of it as exist can all, without exception, be referred back to literary and human associations. It is not the abstract curve of a particular line in an engraving of Hogarth or Goya which makes us smile, but the object which it serves to depict. It follows that music, of all the arts, is most at a disadvantage in endeavouring to express witty conceptions, because it has less direct contact with reality than any other, except perhaps architecture. This, as we have seen, constitutes the strength of music in expressing romantic conceptions.

Consequently, we find that music can only be witty by virtue of its association with some literary or dramatic idea. The wit in *L'Heure espagnole* of Ravel, for instance, is wholly literary, except in so far as it is attained by means of the artificial deterioration of tone quality, or by making instruments play passages unsuited to their character, and so forth.[1]

[1] In the same way the only architecture which makes one laugh is bad architecture.

Maurice Ravel

But this is, of course, not wit at all, but merely horseplay or slap-stick. It is the musical equivalent of Charlie Chaplin. It is remarkable to observe what an extraordinarily primitive sense of humour most musicians and musical audiences possess. A composer has only to write a low note for the bassoon *fortissimo*, for no apparent reason—for obviously if it occurred logically at the end of a descending phrase it would not be amusing at all—and the whole audience will lean back in its collective chair and rock with inextinguishable laughter, while the literary equivalent of it, in the pages of *Comic Cuts*, would assuredly fail to bring even a wan smile to the face of a District Messenger boy.

On the whole, however, Ravel is very rarely guilty of this sort of thing. His temperament is too fastidious, aristocratic, and sophisticated to permit him to play the clown for the entertainment of the lowest section of the musical public. He prefers to leave this highly profitable occupation to barbarians like Stravinsky, who have not the same scruples.

In spite of Ravel's great reputation as a wit and retailer of musical *bons mots*, one does not feel that his laughter rings altogether true. His irony and cynicism are very much akin to those of Jules Laforgue, that disillusioned dandy, immaculate and outwardly imperturbable, and are only a mask which serves to conceal, somewhat ineffectually as all masks do, if not the pageant of a bleeding heart, at least an almost morbid, quivering, nervous sensibility. Indeed, it is very difficult to understand how the popular conception originated of Ravel as an artist, 'à qui l'absence de sensibilité fait encore une personnalité'. He is actually an extremely sentimental little person who is only rather too ashamed to show it. Most professional cynics and ironists are like that, as a matter of fact.

And so, in conclusion, we find, as we should expect

to do, that whenever Ravel tries to be most French, as in the *Tombeau de Couperin* or *L'Heure espagnole*, he is most arid, sterile, and uninspired. On the other hand, when he has chosen to exploit his *petite sensibilité*, and in his more tender and sentimental vein, he has produced a few very charming works. This side of him is more in evidence in his earlier years and in works such as the *Pavane pour une Infante défunte*, and the string quartet in F ; with all their charm and delicacy, however, they are limited in scope, and entirely lacking in breadth and vitality. If Ravel had done nothing more than this he would be a very minor poet indeed, but fortunately he was able to achieve a work in which he succeeded in giving his talent a larger and more vital expression. This is the ballet *Daphnis et Chloé*.

I have said that there is a distinct parallel between the French and the Greek spirit, and the analogy is as true in the art of their decadence as in that of their prime. There is a definite similarity between later Greek art and that of the eighteenth century in France, when the polished elegance and epigrammatic brilliance of Voltaire, Montesquieu, and other representatives of their age dissolved into the soft and sentimental art of Rousseau and Bernardin de Saint-Pierre. The dominant spirit in the music of Ravel, when he allows himself to be himself and does not pretend to be Couperin *redivivus*, belongs essentially to the *fin du dix-huitième siècle*, and consequently it is no mere coincidence that he should have been attracted to the charming idyll of Longus, and should have made it the literary basis of what is by a long way his best work. In *Daphnis et Chloé* Ravel said once and for all, and said it well, everything that he had to say. In the work of no other living composer, except perhaps Schönberg, is there such a disproportionate distance between his masterpiece and the rest of his work. In *Daphnis* he for once gets right away from the patchouli-scented atmosphere of the Salon which clings to almost all the rest of his music. The insipidity and preciosity which one finds so irritating in him as a rule give place to an almost full-blooded vitality and exuberance. He has escaped momentarily from his hitherto inveterate limitations. To be sure, Daphnis and Chloé are not quite the charmingly frank and unashamed little animals of the Greek original, some of whose behaviour, in an English translation, has to be veiled in the decent obscurity of Latin, as the saying is, but they are certainly not the Dresden china shepherds and shepherdesses that the rest of his music might have led one to expect. They are only slightly Gallicized into a kind of *Paul et Virginie*, in the same way that even Racine was compelled to take out naturalization certificates for Hippolytus and Phaedra before they were allowed to cross the carefully guarded frontier of the French tradition. And although Pan is obliged to lay aside some of the more arcane symbols of his divinity in order to appear on the French stage, it is nevertheless his cult and no other which is celebrated in the pages of this brilliant and fascinating score.

It was hardly to be expected that Ravel would quickly repeat such an admirable performance, but one was not prepared for the rapid decline which subsequently manifested itself in his art. It seems as if, like his own Chloé, he had been forcibly abducted by M. Diaghilev and his pirate band, and made to dance for their pleasure against his will. One such experience was enough for him. After this one tremendous adventure he speedily retired to the salon from which he had momentarily emerged and in which he has since remained. He is like a man who has had one great experience, one moment in which he lived fully and intensely, but who is content to dwell upon it in memory, making no attempt to recapture it or equal it. He has settled down to a comfortable artistic middle age, surrounded by cats and blue china, and has returned to the 'plaisir délicieux et toujours nouveau d'une occupation inutile'—the motto from Henri de Régnier which is inscribed on the title-page of Ravel's *Valses nobles et sentimentales.* Something seems to have happened to Ravel, as to most modern composers. Perhaps his Muse, always rather delicate, has never quite recovered from the effects of over-indulgence in vodka. Perhaps her constitution will not stand the strain of leading such a fast life. However that may be, she certainly seems to have developed agoraphobia, and has no longer sufficient courage to cross the narrow threshold of the artist's personality or to come out into the world. Whether she will ever do so again becomes increasingly doubtful every year.

In each successive work since *Daphnis*, Ravel seems to reveal a constantly growing obsession with purely stylistic considerations, leading, as it always does and always must do, to aridity and premature sterility. The Trio, despite its comparative virility and its undoubted effectiveness, does not bear the test of keen scrutiny and repeated hearing; the later sonata for violin and 'cello is only a piece of elegant and accomplished trifling; and at the time when Ravel should by rights have reached his fullest maturity he seems to have become incapable of anything more than elaborate and artificial *pastiches* like *La Valse*—a weariness to the flesh—and hackwork like the orchestration of the *Pictures from an Exhibition* of Moussorgsky. Even his vein of wistful and tender sentimentality has become narrower and more restricted with each new work. His talent resembles those Arabian torrents which, instead of growing larger as they progress, steadily diminish in volume until they finally disappear in the desert sands. It has no generous source of replenishment in lofty mountains, no tributaries of enrichment in the influence of other composers, and it fears to merge itself in the limitless ocean of impersonality. Ravel has preferred sterility to the possible dilution or diminution of his individuality.

It was otherwise with the great romantic composers, who owed the greater part of their strength to their admirable eclecticism and catholicity and to their incomparable breadth of vision, resulting in an extension of artistic scope, an enrichment of resources without parallel in musical history. Modern composers, on the other hand, such as Debussy and Ravel, have sought to attain to individuality through exclusion. They tend to emphasize and accentuate those qualities of mind which differentiate them from the rest of the world, rather than those which they share with the rest of humanity. In other words, mannerism and idiosyncrasy usurp the place of true individuality, which is not a surface quality, but an attribute of mind that can transform and impart significance to the most ordinary and even commonplace conceptions.

Turgenev has observed somewhere that it may be a scientific fact that all the leaves on a tree are different from each other, but what struck him as being much more remarkable was how much alike they all are. And it may be true that we are all different from each other, but these differences are accidental, unimportant, and unessential, and should be suppressed rather than cultivated. It is certainly undeniable that the bulk of contemporary artists by deliberately avoiding all these ideas and conceptions which are common to all, and by restricting themselves to the expression of those which belong to themselves alone, are simply committing artistic suicide. For the most part one finds that they produce one or two good works and then spend the rest of their lives in writing or painting variations on them. The cult of originality has become a sterilizing obsession, and in no artist of the present day is it more apparent than in Ravel. Only the very greatest could live upon themselves in this fashion without exhausting themselves prematurely, and he is assuredly not one of them.

Although Debussy's talent similarly came to a premature grave, this deliberate circumscription on his part was largely justified. He was always greatest when he was most personal in his utterance. It constituted his strength, not his weakness. Precisely the opposite is true of Ravel. His best work, as we have seen, was achieved on the solitary occasion on which he came out of the hothouse of his own individuality. His outlook is not comparable to the intensely subjective outlook of Debussy. The latter certainly did create and people a little world of his own imagining, while Ravel's originality consists rather in looking at the ordinary world from a personal angle. He has no such intensely personal message to deliver as the older master had. His personality has always been a very modest and restricted one, and even from a purely stylistic point of view, in spite of his preoccupation with it, he has invented very little, if anything. His melodic invention is extremely limited in scope; his themes, though graceful and refined, are short-winded and lacking in vitality, and seem always to be variations on each other. Despite a certain piquancy of a somewhat precious and *recherché* order, his harmonic style is timid and unoriginal, and lacks resource and variety, largely because, like that of Debussy, it consists of chords whose constituent parts move entirely by similar motion. Rhythmically, on the other hand, he is more original, and infinitely superior to Debussy, and on the whole one can say

Maurice Ravel

that the criticism of him as only an imitator of the latter is without foundation. Rather the opposite, in fact ; it is more than probable that Debussy in his later years was influenced by Ravel, particularly in his desire to become a *musicien français.*

The element which one most dislikes in Ravel's music, however, is his orchestration, which reveals the influence of the Russians, and of Rimsky-Korsakov in particular, in the constant preoccupation with external brilliance and meretricious glitter. He relies to a quite disproportionate extent on what one might call the confectionery department of the orchestra—harp *glissandi,* glockenspiel, and celesta, the last of which has not yet succeeded, and probably never will succeed, in living down its association with Tchaikovsky's sugarplum fairy. Nothing palls so quickly on the palette as this cloying sweetness. The *Rapsodie espagnole* is perhaps the most extreme example of this tendency.

In conclusion, it seems as if *Daphnis et Chloé* is the only work of Ravel which stands much chance of surviving him. It is unfortunate that it is cast in such an ephemeral form as that of the modern ballet, whose butterfly existence is not likely to be prolonged much further. Nevertheless the work will probably survive in the concert-hall in some form or another.

IGOR STRAVINSKY

SINCE the time of the eminent French critics Sainte-Beuve and Taine it has become the fashion to regard the artist as being primarily the product of his age and environment, and his work as the expression of the ideas and conceptions which are current in his time, in forms which he has inherited from his predecessors. This is one of these plausible half-truths which are more pernicious and misleading than many fallacies. The history of any and every art conclusively shows that the artists who most completely express the spirit of their respective ages are not by any means the greatest, but, on the contrary, are nearly always of the second rank. It is true that the artist may, and to a certain extent probably must, reflect his age, but he is only great in so far as he is able to transcend it. On the other hand, it must be admitted that the artist who only expresses what everyone round about him is thinking or feeling will attain a more immediate recognition and popularity than he who does not. It is this simple fact that explains the extraordinary and overwhelming popularity of Stravinsky to-day and the prominent position which, by almost universal consent, he occupies among modern composers. For whatever one's personal opinion may be concerning the intrinsic value and ultimate significance of his music, it must be admitted that he is to a greater extent than any other living composer the embodiment of the artistic ideals and aesthetic convictions which are most characteristic of our age. Indeed, he is so entirely the product of his age and environment that he hardly seems to be an

Igor Stravinsky

individual at all; and this is only natural, for if he were a strongly individual artist it would unavoidably prevent him from reflecting them faithfully. Stravinsky is simply an impersonal sum-total of pre-existing terms, a synthesis of all the separate and frequently conflicting tendencies which constitute that complex phenomenon we call the spirit of the age. His name is only a convenient shorthand for a complicated mathematical equation or chemical formula. He is not a man, but an idea; in the language of Kant he is an historical postulate. If one might be permitted to adapt a famous epigram to suit the occasion, it could be said that if he had not existed it would have been necessary to invent him.

Not even in his early work does one find any signs of originality. This may seem to be a paradox to those good people who imagine that originality is a quality which one only acquires after ceaseless effort, towards the end of one's life, and not, as it really is, an innate quality of mind which informs every thought and act of a person from his earliest years. It is of course true that its expression may be immature, but it is nevertheless latent and clearly perceptible all the time. In many instances the earlier work of a composer is more original than his later work; Schumann, Berlioz, and Mendelssohn are examples of this. Sometimes the earlier works are a truer index to the composer's personality than those by which he is commonly judged, as we have already seen in the music of Strauss; and even in those composers who might at first sight seem to be exceptions to our rule, such as Beethoven, Wagner, or Schönberg, a closer examination will reveal the fact that their mature utterance is only the final realization of what was already latent, although only potential, in even their crudest and most imperfect attempts—that their artistic progress and development is less a growth or

128

change in their personality than a gradual and frequently painful discovery of those methods and procedures which are best suited to its expression. But it is difficult to find an individuality in either the early or late works of Stravinsky. Not even his most fanatical admirers can find much to say for the facile and Chopinesque *Études* for piano, the sentimental and undistinguished songs, or the *Scherzo* for orchestra, recently metamorphosed into a ballet dealing with the domestic life of bees. They are just what one would expect from any pupil of Rimsky-Korsakov, neither more nor less; even his first ballet, *l'Oiseau de Feu*, is palpably a descendant of *Le Coq d'Or*, though it must be conceded that he already far outshines his sire in the brilliant rainbow hues of his plumage and tail-feathers.

This brings us to the second and perhaps most important of all the influences which have determined Stravinsky's artistic development, namely his association with the *impresario* M. Serge Diaghilev, and his Russian ballet. Indeed, it would be difficult to imagine what his career would have been without it, or conversely, what the Russian ballet would have been without Stravinsky. One cannot think of the one apart from the other; they are like the Siamese twins, indissolubly bound together, both in life and in death. On the other hand, it is impossible to doubt that Stravinsky is largely the creation of Diaghilev, for one finds a precisely similar type in the person of Diaghilev's leading scene-painter and designer Bakst. There is no difference between Bakst and Stravinsky; they are both expressions of the same terms in their different arts : both are projections of ideas in the mind of Diaghilev; apart from him they have no more existence than the puppets in *Pétrouchka* have apart from the old Charlatan. It is Diaghilev who animates these little figures and pulls the wires and

gives them the fictitious life they have. In reality
they are only lay figures stuffed with sawdust. Diaghilev
is undoubtedly a remarkable man ; he is the real artist
behind the Russian ballet, expressing himself through
the medium of innumerable personalities which are all
subordinated to him. And it is a remarkable fact that
neither Bakst nor Stravinsky has ever had any success
apart from him.

Pétrouchka is the ideal ballet, and to one who has
had a good dinner with wine, liqueur, and cigar
provides a very pleasant evening's entertainment. But
that it should be considered an important landmark
in the history of music, or of art generally, is a critical
aberration which, it is fairly safe to say, will occasion
considerable hilarity in the course of a very few years.
One can only account for it by making generous
allowance for the conditions under which it is performed. For it is both curious and instructive to
observe how the atmosphere of the theatre will betray
even the finest and most discriminating judgement,
and will excite even the coldest and most unimaginative
listener. The very moment a man enters the audi-
torium he may observe, if he takes the trouble to
analyse his sensations, that his psyche undergoes a
subtle yet profound change. He is no longer the same
as he was five minutes before.

More especially is this true of the ballet. The
simultaneous appeal to different senses—the beauty of
the stage-setting, the sensuously attractive rhythms
and the glowing colour of the music, the elegance of
gesture and the primitive sexual appeal of the dancing
—all conspire irresistibly to rob us of any sense of
criticism which we might otherwise possess. But all
this has very little to do with art. The serious objection to the ballet considered as an art-form is that its
appeal is too primitive, too purely physical and
emotional. In the words of one of the greatest living

critics, whom we have already had occasion to quote several times in the course of this book, namely Mr. Arthur Symons: 'Look at the dance, on the stage, a mere spectator. Here are all these young bodies, made more alluring by an artificial heightening of whites and reds on the face, displaying, employing, all their natural beauty, themselves full of the sense of joy in motion, or affecting that enjoyment, offered to our eyes like a bouquet of flowers, a bouquet of living flowers, which have all the glitter of artificial ones. As they dance, under the changing lights, so human, so remote, so desirable, so evasive, coming and going to the sound of a thin, heady music which marks the rhythm of their movements like a kind of clinging drapery, they seem to sum up in themselves the appeal of everything in the world that is passing, and coloured, and to be enjoyed, everything that bids us take no thought for the morrow, and dissolve the will into slumber, and give way luxuriously to the delightful present.' It would be impossible to find a more exact and penetrating analysis of the emotions one experiences at the performance of a Stravinsky ballet. These emotions are not aesthetic emotions; they are the emotions of life, not of art. The appeal of the Russian ballet has nothing to do with music; one had only to look at the audiences which thronged the Alhambra theatre nightly during the Russian ballet season of a few years ago, to be convinced of this. It was not a musical audience, to say the least. It is true that this is a reproach which has often been made against the typical Wagner audience, but while that is composed chiefly of people of a certain level of general culture and intelligence with an interest in the other arts, the Stravinsky audience consists primarily of people who have not the faintest interest in or understanding of music, and even very little appreciation of art in any shape or form. They come,

Igor Stravinsky

quite frankly and avowedly, for the erotic appeal of the whole performance. In the 'nineties Wilde and others sought to realize their aesthetic impulses in their lives, to make their lives into works of art ; the devotees of the Russian ballet, the Stravinskyites, seek the satisfaction of normal human activities in art, and try to make art into a form of life. Both are wrong. Art cannot be identified with life in either of these two ways. Art is a part of life, perhaps the most important part, but the ideas and emotions it expresses are not common to other human activities. Its sole *raison d'être* lies simply in this differentiation. It is impossible to live aesthetically, and it is an abuse of art to employ it as a substitute for normal, or abnormal, human activities, to seek in it the satisfaction of natural desires and passions. The Russian ballet is an aesthetic monstrosity, neither life nor art, but a kind of substitute for both.

The music of *Pétrouchka* is undoubtedly effective theatre-music, if we use the word theatre in its conventional sense and not in that of Mr. Gordon Craig —i. e. not the theatre in the mind of God, to speak Platonically, but the theatre in the mind of the ' gods '. It is not music which, at any time and in any place, under any circumstances, whether performed in the theatre, the concert-hall, or in the tranquil seclusion of one's own home, continues to exercise its fascination over us. Like the dancers and actors, it is made up for the stage, and in the concert-hall it is like an actress in her dressing-room after the performance ; what had seemed so charming and alluring in the harsh, unnatural glare of the footlights is seen to be only a combination of false hair, painted cheeks, rouged lips, and violet-lidded eyes. It no more stands the test of the concert-hall than Bakst's flamboyant and pretentious decorations stand the test of exhibition in a picture gallery. Divorced from the acting, dancing, and elaborate *mise en scène* which are its necessary concomitants, it stands revealed in all its high-sounding emptiness and shameless vulgarity.

It may be objected that this is precisely the effect which the composer intended to realize, that the tinsel and *bric-à-brac* of the music is only the reproduction of the spirit of the play. But unfortunately Stravinsky has so often given it to be understood that his music is to be considered solely as music, without reference to the action with which it is associated, that this argument is inadmissible. Even if one were to admit the objection, it does not follow that a composer has written a good work merely because he has achieved his purpose. It behoves us to inquire whether his purpose is worthy of achievement. If a man commits a murder, it is not as a rule considered an extenuating circumstance that he intended to commit it, and the fact that a composer has realized a trivial and tasteless conception with considerable skill does not entitle him to our gratitude and reverent admiration. Hell may be paved with good intentions; it does not necessarily follow that Heaven is paved with bad ones.

A great deal has been made of Stravinsky's biting wit and irony, as exemplified particularly in *Pétrouchka*, but they are wholly negative. The savage satire of Swift, Velasquez, or Goya, the pitiless mockery of Voltaire, the kindly irony of Anatole France, the transcendental buffoonery of Villiers de l'Isle-Adam, are all in their way positive and proceed from some definite conception of life, or some outraged ideal, moral or aesthetic. Even the cynicism of Laforgue is based on a despairing recognition of his own futility, and the futility of all earthly existence; it is the cry of a disillusioned spirit, scorched and lacerated by life. The ghastly inhuman laughter of Schönberg's *Pierrot Lunaire* similarly has its roots in human experience, in a metaphysical conception of life. But Stravinsky's

Igor Stravinsky

irony is purely negative. One is not conscious of any intellectual power behind it ; it is truly cynicism, in the original Greek sense of the word—a meaningless dog-laugh, a baring of the teeth in a senseless grin, expressing nothing.

Being himself lacking in intellect and emotion Stravinsky has elevated his deficiency to the rank of a virtue ; according to him, the artist should no longer think or feel, but must become purely objective. Hence his predilection for puppets, marionettes, and automata in general, first exemplified in *Pétrouchka*. He conceives human beings as mechanical dolls, pulled hither and thither by the strings of their physical needs and desires. In this he is really not objective at all. He is merely attributing subjectively to others his own emptiness.

His opera *Le Rossignol* is a curiously significant illustration of this. It is not a successful work by any means. The first part was written before *l'Oiseau de Feu*, the second part after the *Sacre du Printemps*, and the whole work shows only too clearly the discrepancy between the two. It falls between two styles, so to speak, the one belonging to the romantic fairy-tale manner of *Le Coq d'Or*, the other to the satirical manner of the later works. In the first part Stravinsky attempts to realize the profound conception of Hans Andersen's tale, and fails ; in the second he unconsciously depicts and satirizes himself in the form of the artificial bird, who, in the story, supplants the real bird and wins the favour of the Emperor. According to the allegorical meaning of Hans Andersen's tale, the nightingale is, of course, the genuine artist, and the mechanical singing bird the sham artist. No one has ever satirized himself so cruelly and withal so unawaredly as Stravinsky has here. And this at least disposes of his objectivity ; in all his works he depicts nothing but himself, as every artist must. There is really no such thing as pure objectivity. As Anatole France says, 'Tous ceux qui se flattent de mettre autre chose qu'eux-mêmes dans leurs œuvres sont dupes de la plus fallacieuse illusion—on ne sort jamais de soi-même.' It is possible that some day, like his old Charlatan in *Pétrouchka*, Stravinsky will discover, to his infinite bewilderment and consternation, that the orchestra is not a mere mechanical toy, but has a soul, and will be haunted by the reproachful little ghosts of the instruments which he has so cynically prostituted for the amusement of the gaping crowd.

The great popularity of *Pétrouchka* and *l'Oiseau de Feu* has always been a source of irritation to the devout Stravinskyites, who are loth to admit that their idol could ever appeal to the public at large, or to any but themselves. They are afflicted by a kind of persecution mania, a consuming passion for martyrdom, which, however, has always been doomed to disappointment. The more esoteric and abstruse they proclaim his work to be, the more eagerly it is received. This has been the melancholy fate of even the *Sacre du Printemps*, which can always be relied upon to fill the house whenever a performance of it is given, in spite of the quite impressive attempts on the part of its admirers to represent it as a work which can only appeal to the highest order of musical intelligence. On the other hand, a few critics consider *Pétrouchka* to be his best work and the *Sacre* to be markedly inferior. This has always seemed to me a grave error of judgement, for quite apart from whether one considers either of them to be masterpieces, there can be little doubt that the latter work represents the final stage in a certain clearly defined line of thought, in which *Pétrouchka* is merely a middle term or half-way house. The *Sacre* embodies a definite ideal, a conception of art which has been ruthlessly pushed to its

135

Igor Stravinsky

ultimate and wholly logical conclusion; the earlier work is both stylistically and in general conception a comparatively timid and conventional thing. The highest compliment one can pay to the *Sacre* is to admit frankly that it challenges one's innermost aesthetic convictions in a most peremptory fashion, and demands an immediate answer to the recurring questions concerning the nature of music, its scope and its function. It is the final stage of a long process of evolution; one cannot write or speak about it without being compelled to envisage fundamental artistic problems. In order to know what any man thinks about music one has only to ascertain his attitude towards the *Sacre*. With that evidence one can easily fill in the rest for one's self. Either it is, as its greatest admirers claim, one of the summits of musical art, or else, as its opponents believe, it is the end of a long *cul-de-sac*, the last stage of degeneration and artistic depravity. For some it is, as its composer has termed it, ' an act of faith '; for others, to whom the original Spanish phrase suggests more appropriate and illuminating associations, it is an *auto da fé* in which music is bound to the stake and sacrificed for refusing to recant her opinions and convictions.

The pure doctrine which this modern musical Torquemada promulgates is that music must appeal to the physical ear alone. Not only are all works which are based upon literary, pictorial, or philosophic conceptions condemned to everlasting hell-fire, but also all works which possess any intellectual or emotional qualities. All these are necessarily bad, even if they should happen to sound well; on the other hand, all music which appeals to the physical ear alone is necessarily good, even if it should sound hellish.

Note how charmingly and characteristically medieval it all is. It is the exact counterpart of that doctrine

136

which denied the possibility of salvation to all who had not been baptized, including all those who had the misfortune to be born before the advent of the Messiah, however Christian and saintly their lives may have been ; with of course the inevitable corollary that whatever crimes or sins a man may have committed, provided he has professed the true faith and been baptized, he will ascend into the Heaven of the old Charlatan of *Pétrouchka* with the *Oiseau de Feu* for a Holy Ghost. Bach, Beethoven, Wagner, almost everyone in fact, are irrevocably damned, even as Plato, Aristotle, and Marcus Aurelius were considered damned by the early Christians. All composers must be immersed in the Jordan (with or without a capital letter, according to one's point of view) of aural values if they would hope to be saved.

Such child-like faith is indeed touching, and worthy of a nobler and more believing age. Yet it is on the face of it distinctly surprising that this doctrine should emanate from a composer who has hardly ever in his life written a work which is not based on some literary or pictorial conception. His apologists, we know, have explained away this awkward fact quite airily, but to those who, like myself, are only ordinary, commonplace people, their arguments seem decidedly obscure and not altogether convincing.

Nevertheless, since they would have it so, let us regard the *Sacre du Printemps* as music pure and simple, without reference to the literary and dramatic conception.

Although it is often convenient for the purposes of criticism and analysis to speak of musical language as if it were made up of three or four separate and independent elements in combination—melody, harmony, rhythm, and possibly a fourth of a vaguer and altogether different nature which, for want of a better term, we call colour—we must be careful not to think

137

of it as such. As long as we make use of these terms in order to define more accurately certain qualities in certain works, they are quite legitimate and sometimes even necessary, but that is all. In actual fact it is impossible to conceive of one without the others. They are interdependent and indissoluble. In the same way it is convenient in argument to speak of body, soul, intellect, instinct, and so forth, yet the human personality remains one and indivisible. We may be conscious of some distinction, but we are unable to say where the one begins and the other ends. They are inextricably bound up with each other. And so in music ; in reality it is as impossible to conceive of melody apart from harmony as it is to imagine a soul apart from the body. Every melody, whether it is of the most primitive or the most subtle order, has its harmonic implications. It may be objected that this is only the outcome of our modern habit of thinking harmonically, but it is not so. Harmony has always existed ; it is a mere absurdity to imagine that it was invented by some nameless medieval monk. The Greeks always recognized its existence without ever employing it in our modern explicit sense, conceiving it rather as a law governing the succession of notes and determining the course of the melody : a kind of guiding principle, everywhere present yet nowhere visible. It was this conception which determined their strict adherence to the mode in which they were writing. Modulation would have disturbed this harmonic equilibrium. Our modern idea of harmony as a simultaneous sounding of different notes is both crude and inadequate, for it is latent in any sequence of unaccompanied notes. Among Busoni's definitions of melody one of the conditions which must be fulfilled is that it shall ' contain a latent harmony ', and also that it must be ' rhythmically articulated and animated '. But no one is likely to deny that there can be no melody, properly speaking, without rhythm.

The contrary can also be shown to be true, namely, that rhythm cannot properly exist apart from melody. The first music, it is often asserted dogmatically, as if it were an incontrovertible and easily ascertainable truth, was pure rhythm—as von Bülow said, ' In the beginning was rhythm '—and the first musical composition was the drumming of a savage's knuckles on the bare earth. This has always seemed to musical theorists to be the most primitive procedure imaginable, and that it must consequently have been the first. It seems to have escaped their attention that there exists an even more primitive and natural way of making music, namely, by means of the human voice. Nevertheless, a moment's thought should be sufficient to show that it is impossible for a musical composition, even of the most primitive order, to consist of rhythm alone. What is rhythm, after all? What conditions its movements, what dictates the subtle tensions and relaxations, what causes the quickening of its pulse here, its wavering there, what makes it a living thing, if not the melodic line? One cannot conceive rhythm apart from melody ; the moment it is divorced from the other constituent elements of musical speech it changes its character ; it stiffens, petrifies, and becomes lifeless—becomes metre. In much the same way that formal design and rhythm when they cease to be representative tend, inevitably, automatically, to become mere geometrical pattern, as in a wallpaper or carpet, so musical rhythm, divorced from melodic implications, also becomes inert, lifeless, mechanical, metrical. Rhythm, in the proper sense of the word, is incalculable, immensurable, infinitely mysterious. We speak of the rhythm of life ; we do not speak of the metre of life. Metres are only of use in speaking of eighteenth-century poetry,

Igor Stravinsky

or measuring distances, or calculating the number of thermal units of gas we have burnt in the last quarter.

In the same way that rhythm, cultivated for its own sake, apart from melodic or harmonic considerations, degenerates into metre, so the exclusive preoccupation with melodic line, at the expense of harmony and rhythm—as in the music of most modern Italian composers, notably Puccini—has not merely had the result of destroying the power to think harmonically, and of emasculating music of all rhythmic vitality, but has actually impaired the melodic faculty itself. In other words, melody has degenerated into tune, has lost its unity and form, has become merely a succession of pleasant phrases bearing no organic relation to each other, and has disintegrated into minute melismatic fragments.

Similarly the characteristic obsession of many modern composers with harmonic considerations to the detriment and impoverishment of melodic and rhythmic interest, has caused the degeneration of harmony itself, as we have seen in the essay on Debussy. His partiality for organum and *faux bourdon* brings us back to Hucbald. Genuine harmonic thought only dates from the moment at which similar motion is abandoned. As I have already said in the essay on Debussy, similar motion of the parts is only what we may call registration, a doubling of the melody at the third and at the fifth, and it makes no difference of principle if seconds, sevenths, and ninths are thrown in as well. Genuine harmonic writing necessarily implies contrary motion among the parts, or, in the case of a sustained pedal, at least oblique motion ; in other words, harmonic writing is at the same time contrapuntal.

Not only, however, are these component elements inseparable from each other, but each is at its highest when they are all in complete equilibrium, when one

Igor Stravinsky

does not predominate over the others. In the music
of the greatest masters, such as Palestrina, Vittoria,
Bach, the later Beethoven, the later Wagner: in the
best modern music, even such as Schönberg's *Pierrot
Lunaire*, and the string quartets of Bartók and van
Dieren—in all these one will find this perfect balance
and equipoise; you cannot say of this music that it is
'harmonic', 'rhythmic', or 'melodic'; it is all and
it is none. But the moment that one element grows
at the expense of the others the perfect concord is
broken or impaired, and even the particular element
thus favoured degenerates, becomes a morbid growth.
It is simply the old Aesopian fable over again, of the
quarrel of the different members of the body. They
are all alike necessary to each other. Polyphony is
musically synonymous with good health.

It was Arius who denied the absolute, co-eternal,
and uncreated equality and unity of the Trinity, and
it is the Arian heresy of music to maintain that rhythm,
melody, or harmony can exist apart from each other,
or that any one preceded the other. Oh, for a musical
Tertullian to castigate the heretics, and restore to
music the pure doctrine, the incomparable style of
the masters, Palestrina, Bach, Beethoven, Mozart, and
Wagner! Contrapuntal or polyphonic writing is the
ideal musical style, the sacred tonal language, the
Sanskrit of music, the tongue of the high priests and
the wise men, handed down from one master to
another throughout the ages, the repository of all that
is most enduring and imperishable in the past, and
destined equally to be the vehicle for the expression
of the greatest conceptions in the future, for in it
alone all conflicting principles, all contradictions, all
oppositions, are reconciled into a unity: melodic
beauty, harmonic strength, and rhythmic vitality.

What has all this ecstatic dithyramb to do with
Stravinsky? In precisely the same way that the

Igor Stravinsky

preoccupation with melodic considerations leads to melodic degeneration; in the same way that an hypnotic concentration on purely harmonic interest involves a corresponding loss of harmonic strength—so Stravinsky's obsession with rhythm in the *Sacre* has led, not only to the impoverishment of both harmony and melody, but to the loss of the very quality to which he sacrificed the other two—rhythmic vitality. The *Sacre du Printemps*, so far from being the triumphant apotheosis of rhythm, the act of restoration to its rightful supremacy of the most important and essential element of musical expression, is the very negation and denial of rhythm. In sacrificing everything to it, Stravinsky has, with admirable poetic justice, lost it, along with its companions, as well. Rhythm has here degenerated into metre.

It must be admitted that very few musicians are aware of any difference between these two things. One has only to maintain a persistent and unflagging metrical figure for some hundred bars, like Rimsky-Korsakov, Stravinsky, or Holst, to be acclaimed vociferously as a master of rhythm; the longer it is continued unbroken, the greater the mastery. Similarly in literature the most outrageous gallops and jingles of Swinburne's later years are by many competent critics spoken of with bated breath as the supreme rhythmical achievement of English poetry. But why not the limerick?

All that Stravinsky achieves in the *Sacre du Printemps* is the musical equivalent of the following line of Swinburne, the bard of Putney Common—not Swinburne the poet—

> The sea is awake and the sound of the song of
> the joy of her waking is rolled,

and even those sections of the *Sacre* which give the impression of complexity, such as the final dance of

142

the Elect, in which every musical interest is sacrificed to rhythmical purposes, are very primitive in construction. The time-signature changes constantly from bar to bar, but the music itself does not ; it is only the eye and not the ear which perceives the changes. There is nothing there but the incessant reiteration of the same insignificant metrical phrase in slightly varying quantities—regular measures with irregularly recurring *caesurae*. Strip the music of the bar-lines and time-signatures, which are only a loincloth concealing its shameful nudity, and it will at once be seen that there is no rhythm at all. Rhythm implies life, some kind of movement or progression at least, but this music stands quite still, in a quite frightening immobility. It is like a top or gyroscope turning ceaselessly and ineffectually on itself, without moving an inch in any direction, until, in the last bars of the work, it suddenly falls over on its side with a lurch, and stops dead.

It is depressing to reflect that such things should be accepted as remarkable rhythmical achievements by a nation which, perhaps more than any other, can justly pride itself on having produced supreme masters of rhythm, both musical and verbal. There is more rhythm in a song of Dowland or in a madrigal of Weelkes or Wilbye than in all the works of Stravinsky put together.

How many people have a true sense of rhythm ? When we speak of melodic beauty we do not mean by it the ceaseless alternation of two or three notes, nor when we wish to give an example of exquisite harmony do we bring forward the earliest examples of organum ; but as soon as one speaks of rhythmic vitality it always seems to be taken for granted that one implies a simple metrical pattern such as we find in the most primitive and uncultured races. On the other hand, the music of certain eastern nations in

143

which the rhythm is extremely subtle and highly
developed is always characterized as monotonous.
Even granting the familiar contention that rhythm is
the element which has been most neglected in European music and should be cultivated to a greater
extent, it is difficult to see why the African tom-tom
should be held aloft as the ultimate and unsurpassable perfection towards which we must all strive.
Why can melody and harmony be subtle and highly
developed, while rhythm must only be primitive? It
is indisputable that the rhythmic interest of the *Sacre*
is on the same level as, and no higher than, the harmonic
interest of the compositions of Hucbald, and the
melodic interest of psalmodic intonation.

Stravinsky's succeeding ballet, *Le Chant du Rossignol*,
a re-hash of the opera already mentioned, is an excur-
sion in the very opposite direction. In place of
primitivism he here exploits decadence; in place of
rhythm, colour. Every possible technical device for
deforming and distorting the tone of instruments is
employed; every little resource picked up in green-
room conversations with orchestral players is brought
forward and made use of. All this colour for colour's
sake becomes devastatingly monotonous after five
minutes, and, like rhythm for rhythm's sake, defeats
its own end. One longs for the sound of an unmuted
trumpet, for the sound of an instrument playing
a phrase which is suited to its character, in a natural
register, as we do for a breath of fresh air in a
Turkish bath. *Le Chant du Rossignol* represents the
ne plus ultra of preciosity and exoticism, as the *Sacre*
represents the ultimate point of primitivism. It is
mere *chinoiserie*, a kind of monstrous after-birth of
the eighteen-nineties. This combination of primitivism and decadence is one of the most curious
features of Stravinsky's mentality. Those who are
interested in studying the connexion between them

are referred to Professor Sigmund Freud's treatise on the ' Resemblances between the Psychic Life of Savages and Neurotics '.

After these two works there is obviously nothing further to be done in either direction ; they both end in a *cul-de-sac*. Consequently, in his succeeding works Stravinsky seeks in desperation for new possibilities to exploit, for it is one of the inexorable penalties attaching to the position in which he has placed himself that he must continue to excite and stimulate his public with something novel and unexpected. Once he stops short or begins to repeat himself he is lost, and will be deserted in favour of a more ingenious rival.

Those who are acquainted with Victor Hugo's novel *Notre-Dame de Paris* may possibly recollect the scene near the beginning, in which the audience, turning aside from the mystery play which they cannot understand or appreciate, divert themselves by holding a Feast of Fools, and decide to elect as *Pape des fous* the man who can make the funniest face and provoke the greatest amount of laughter. Eventually Quasimodo, the deaf and dumb hunchback of Notre-Dame, is unanimously elected, it being only afterwards discovered that he was not trying to make a face at all—he merely happened to look like that. The later works of Stravinsky have always, in performance, evoked roars of laughter and delighted applause from audiences, and have generally been encored vociferously, in spite of the fact that both the composer and his disciples have been at great pains to assure us that he was perfectly serious, and not trying to be funny at all. We quite agree ; it is very unfortunate, but, like Quasimodo, he cannot help it, he cannot help being funny. He is just made like that.

Every generation has its *Pape des fous* who has his one day of homage and is then forgotten, so do not let us grudge our musical Quasimodo his one little day

K

of triumph ; it will soon be over. Let us even join in the procession with the rest of the crowd and sing the *Prosa Fatuorum* used on these occasions, which, curiously enough, sounds like a sibylline prophecy of the coming of this particular example of the type :

> Orientis partibus
> Adventavit asinus,
> Pulcher et fortissimus
> Sarcinis aptissimus,
> (Chorus) *Hez Sire Asne, Hez,* &c.

The works which succeed the *Sacre,* such as the *Pribaoutki,* the *Histoire d'un Soldat, Renard, Les Noces Villageoises,* and so forth, are all more or less tentative experiments in every kind of direction, in the hope of finding something new to say. In all these transformations, new departures, sudden returns on himself, he reminds one of the Cheshire Cat in *Alice in Wonderland* ; the first thing to appear and the last thing to disappear is the grin.

Finally, having successfully annihilated every trace of melodic, harmonic, and rhythmic interest in his work during his frenzied flight from expression, he arrives, in his *Symphonies d'instruments à vent,* at the elimination of colouristic interest as well. He dispenses entirely with stringed instruments as being too expressive ; dynamic changes of *piano* and *forte* might also excite some emotion, consequently, emotion being synonymous with literature, the instruments must only play in their natural *mezzo-forte.* Here at last, one would imagine, he will be safe from the intrusion of the arch-enemy of music, the fiend himself, expression. But no : all his efforts, all his precautions, are useless, as we see from the composer's aggrieved expostulations with M. Koussevitzky, who conducted the first performance, for having made it so horribly expressive. The latter defended himself vigorously and with pardonable indignation against such terrible accusations, and declared that the emotion was already in the music. We ourselves can vouch for the truth of this, having heard a performance at which those of the audience who were not in fits of laughter were bored to the verge of tears. Laughter and tears ; what stronger or intenser emotions can an artist excite? The Greek dramatists who sought to purge the soul by means of pity and terror are quite eclipsed by Stravinsky. Not even aspergations of holy water from the Jordan of aural values, it seems, can protect music from the devil of emotion and expressiveness. Even our Torquemada himself perpetually sins.

Stravinsky reminds one irresistibly of the monk in Anatole France's masterpiece, *Thaïs*, who imagines that all the temptations to which he is subjected are sent to him by the Evil One, whereas they are really sent by God ; it is the Devil, on the other hand, who suggests to him all kinds of absurd feats of austerity, such as remaining on the top of a pillar for months on end. So Stravinsky, in his comic attempt to avoid the temptations of expression and emotion in his music, is denying the very god in music ; in his pursuit of objectivity he is seeking the devil, *der Geist der stets verneint*. The *Symphonies d'instruments à vent* are the denial and rejection of the innermost spirit of music. No more conclusive and convincing demonstration than this work could possibly be found of the truth that expression and emotion are the very core and essence of musical art, without which it cannot exist.

It will be interesting to see what Stravinsky's next step will be. So far he has merely been following the experiments of workers in other fields of art. He may seem to musicians to be a very daring and original figure, but the curves and parabolas which he has executed have been only imitations of similar behaviour on the part of painters such as Picasso, at a few years distance. His antics are like those of a monkey in the Zoo which seems to be behaving in a remarkably human manner, until one discovers that all the time he is only copying the gestures of somebody who is standing behind one. The Cubist, non-representational movement in modern painting which Stravinsky has so far been imitating has come to a sudden close. Its leaders are now in full tilt back to realism, and a similar reaction cannot be long delayed in music. The ebb-tide has already set in, and the high-water line marked by a trail of dead crabs and seaweed will soon become visible. The more indiscriminating enthusiasts for the music of Stravinsky have hardly yet had time to realize their position. They fondly imagine they are still fighting the ' old gang ' of reactionaries and pedants, whereas as a matter of fact their most strenuous opponents are those who were quite amused by and interested in Stravinsky some ten years ago, but who now find him tame, old-fashioned, just a trifle *démodé*. He is what the Germans call an *Überwundenerstandpunkt*. His music is almost as difficult to listen to now as that of Richard Strauss ; it no longer thrills, but only wearies and disgusts.

The chances are, then, that Stravinsky, being little more than an artistic weathercock who turns in whatever direction the wind is blowing, will follow the example of his colleagues in the other arts, and revert to some kind of expressionism, *via* the classical forms. His sudden enthusiasm of a few years ago for the *Sleeping Beauty* music of Tchaikovsky is a significant symptom. But whatever direction he turns in, it will not help him to write good music in the future, any more than it has helped him to do so in the past. The attractive qualities of his works are those which fade most quickly ; they are all on the surface. *Pétrouchka*, for example, is not only empty, but derivative as well. The *Sacre* is more original—it is indeed the only work of Stravinsky which is even worth considering, but this originality is nothing more than a deliberate disregard of the most elementary kind of artistic decency. If a man chooses to walk about the streets with nothing on, he will certainly achieve the reputation of being original, if nothing else. And in this work Stravinsky has actually divested himself of every stitch of artistic clothing. Except for the introduction, which is the best part of the work, perhaps the best thing Stravinsky has written, there is no pretence of construction. His only idea of form, in both this work and in *Pétrouchka*, is the old A B A formula, interspersed with occasional descriptive passages where the stage-action demands it, giving ample opportunity for instrumental display ; his only means of achieving continuity is by repeating whole bars and figures *ad nauseam et infinitum* ; his only harmonic resource is to write simple sequences of thirds in different keys at the same time, or else to move about in blocks of notes according to the recipes of organum. His melodic invention is extraordinarily short and always monotonously pentatonic ; whenever he uses a pleasant little tune one may be sure that it is a folk-song which he has found—such as the opening phrase of the *Sacre* on the bassoon, or the best of the dance tunes in *Pétrouchka*, already used by Balakirev in his *Overture on three Russian themes*, but he never makes them his own by his treatment ; he only repeats them. In short, he has demonstrably none of the qualities of musicianship, except a remarkable orchestral virtuosity, and nothing grows stale so quickly. It is only a condiment which stimulates the appetite without satisfying it. His orchestral colour does not arise out of the music, but is superimposed on it, laid on with a trowel. In short, no composer is less capable than he of writing music which can stand

Igor Stravinsky

on its own legs, unsupported by the complicated paraphernalia of stage scenery, costumes, and dancing. That he of all people should claim to be regarded as a writer of pure music is one of the most remarkable examples of insolence and charlatanism in the history of art ; that he should be accepted as one is only another instance of the melancholy stupidity and gullibility of the musical public.

ALEXANDER NICHOLAS
SCRIABINE

WHILE a fierce storm of controversy has invariably raged round the personalities and the works of almost every other modern composer of note, Scriabine has been proclaimed, by the practically unanimous verdict of critics, representing every conceivable shade of opinion, to be at least the equal of the greatest masters of all time. No sharp breath of critical animosity has hitherto ruffled the calm surface of the pool in which the giant crocodile of modern music reclines, basking contentedly in the sunshine of universal adulation and popular applause. For example, Dr. Eaglefield Hull is of the opinion that ' the sonatas of Scriabine are destined in the future to occupy a niche of their own, together with the forty-eight Preludes of Bach, the thirty-two Sonatas of Beethoven, and the piano works of Chopin ' ; one of the most talented of our younger critics, Mr. W. J. Turner, declares that his music ' represents the chief advance in musical consciousness since Beethoven's time '—whatever that may mean—and similar expressions of enthusiasm and veneration could be found in the writings of almost every critic of note, in this country at least. But the choicest and most characteristic example of all is probably an article which appeared in the *Nation*, on the occasion of the first performance of *Prometheus* in this country, ten years ago. I quote from it at length because, more than any other similar criticism, it represents the considered verdict of the enlightened musical public on the significance of Scriabine's music.

151

Alexander Nicholas Scriabine

'Listening to it solely as music,' we are told, ' only a congenitally unimaginative dullard, or a musician sodden with the futile teaching of the text-books and the conservatoires, could help feeling that here is music that comes as near as is at present possible to being the pure voice of Nature and the soul them-selves '—what, by the way, is the matter with the present, that it should be impossible to get any nearer to the pure voice of Nature and the soul? However, this music, it seems, expresses ' the soul of man, slowly yearning into conscious being out of a primal undifferentiated world, torn by the conflict of emo-tions, violently purging itself of its grossnesses, and ultimately winning its way to the light '. Then, rising to the height of his subject, the writer continues in a passionate *crescendo*, ' The wind that blows through the music is the veritable wind of the cosmos itself ; the cries of desire and passion and ecstasy are a sort of quintessential sublimation of all the yearning, not merely of humanity ' (that in itself would be nothing), ' but of all nature, animate and inanimate. . . . No amount of criticism of the work in details can diminish the wonder of such an achievement as this.' On the contrary, criticism of this kind only serves to increase our wonder. What is there about this music, one asks oneself, that turns a comparatively rational—one might even say rationalistic—musical critic like Mr. Ernest Newman—for it is he and no other who is responsible for this remarkable specimen of what Mr. J. C. Squire calls blank prose—into an ecstatic *yogi*, with visions of the human soul yearning out of chaos into the light, and purging itself violently *en route*? Why is it that no one can talk sense about the music of Scriabine? For if it were simply a momentary aberration on the part of Mr. Newman alone, there would be nothing very surprising in it, and one would merely attribute it to overwork. But

152

Alexander Nicholas Scriabine

unfortunately it is not by any means an isolated phenomenon or even an extreme example of the frenzied and ecstatic dithyrambs which this music inspires in its most devoted admirers, of whom the most exquisite specimens, to use a scientific expression, are to be found among theosophists and occultists. In their eyes Scriabine is not merely the greatest of all musicians, the only musician, but very much more —a prophet, a saint, a teacher, a Messiah, inaugurating a new era in the history of the human race. To argue with such people is merely a waste of time and energy, provoking no other response than the same kind of lofty and pitying smile which the hashish-eater bestows on the miserable and misguided mortal who throws a tumblerful of cold water in his face in the hope of bringing him to reason. One may run a considerable risk of being torn limb from limb, like Pentheus in the *Bacchae*, by infuriated and maenadic worshippers. What is the cause of this divine frenzy on their part? What is the cause of the remarkable degree of interest and attention Scriabine has excited even in circles not as a rule particularly interested in music?

The answer is undoubtedly that, in Scriabine's own words, ' The public is particularly aroused by productions which have philosophic ideas as their basis, and combine the elements of the various arts.' He might have added, in an instructive aside, that it is also more easily taken in by them. Even then the statement needs emendation before it can be said to be entirely true. The public has no great love for philosophic ideas ; indeed it hates philosophers like Kant, Descartes, or Spinoza almost as much as great artists : what it really likes is pseudo-philosophic ideas; artistic philosophers like Rousseau and Nietzsche, philosophic artists with a ' message ' like Watts, Zola, and Scriabine.

Alexander Nicholas Scriabine

It is true, of course, that many great artists have had some philosophic bee or other in their bonnets. Wagner no doubt took himself very seriously as a thinker, but it is fortunately no longer necessary for anyone else to do so. His ideas, such as they are, cannot be said to be integral and essential factors in our appreciation of his music. His second-hand Schopenhauerianism and the hazy ideas of redemption through womanly love which he shares with all typical rakes are only a part, and not a very important part either, of his subject-matter. Wagner's only purpose, after all, was to create a work of art. The philosophic ideas of Scriabine, on the other hand—if indeed one could dignify them by such a flattering designation—have played a large part, not only in the degree of attention he has aroused, but in his own artistic development; they are responsible for the very nature of his music. It was only after he became acquainted with and interested in theosophy that he developed at all. Until then his music was nothing but a pale and attenuated reflection of Chopin, revealing no trace of personality or originality whatsoever. Secondly, his open and avowed purpose is not purely and exclusively artistic. The music is not an end in itself, but only a means to inducing ' the production of an ecstatic state, affording a glimpse of higher spiritual planes '. As the music of Palestrina can only be considered in relation to the rite with which it is associated, so the music of Scriabine can only be understood in connexion with theosophy, the name given by Mme Blavatsky to the religion which she invented, admirably adapted to those weak and dyspeptic spirits who are unable to digest more wholesome and solid religious fare.[1] Theosophy is in fact a kind of peptonized, predigested essence of deity, the Synthesis of Science

[1] As Scriabine is the Palestrina of the Blavatsky religion, so Kandinsky is the Fra Angelico, and Ouspensky the Aquinas.

Alexander Nicholas Scriabine

and Religion, as its founder grandiloquently termed it. Synthetic productions are peculiarly characteristic of our age. First, we had the synthetic philosophy of Herbert Spencer, then synthetic drugs, synthetic pearls, synthetic butter (popularly known as margarine), and synthetic sugar, or saccharine. Now Scriabine has given us synthetic music, *musicine*, a product which bears much the same relation to music as margarine to butter, and saccharine to sugar.

This explains how it is that so many intelligent musicians have been deceived by Scriabine's music, just as experts in precious stones have been deceived by culture pearls. Scriabine's music has all the appearances of great art in the same way that culture pearls have all the appearance of real pearls. As it is only by splitting open the latter that one can determine their genuineness or the reverse, so it is only by careful critical analysis and dissection that one can show the inherent falsity of Scriabine's art. There is in it no core of personality around which, as in a pearl, is formed by accretion a style. It is not a natural spontaneous growth, but is artificially stimulated and provoked. It does not live, but has only a galvanic semblance of life, a false appearance of vitality. Scriabine has carefully and painstakingly analysed and separated out into their constituent elements all the qualities in the art of his great predecessors. By means of the formulas thus arrived at he has tried to construct an art of his own. And certainly all the ingredients are there, but they are not combined ; they do not coalesce into an organic living whole. It satisfies triumphantly all the more mechanical tests of criticism ; it has all the appearance of art. Everything is there except the vital principle. Like a chemist who tries to make life in his laboratory by putting together in a test-tube the carbon, oxygen, hydrogen, and other things which constitute the human body, so Scriabine tries to combine various elements which he has observed to be the primary constituents of all great art, but he has only produced the musical equivalent of a Paracelsian homunculus.

The main ingredients are clearly recognizable. First and foremost, one finds a kind of saccharine derived from the by-products of Chopin's consummate genius. Secondly, we get the element which operates the first fermentation in the music of Scriabine : an extract of diabolism carefully prepared from certain works of Liszt, and first utilized in the *Poème Satanique*. Thirdly, appears a powerful aphrodisiac prepared from the monstrous flowers that grow in Klingsor's magic garden and in the scented caves of the Venusberg. These are the main ingredients, cemented together, not by a strong, central nerve of personality, but by a kind of patent glucose or gelatine—a style with the flaccid, molluscular, invertebrate, viscid consistency of welsh rabbit.

One can understand up to a point that such an art should deceive many people unacquainted with the chemistry of synthetic products, but it does not stand the ultimate, final tests, intuitive rather than analytic. How is it that there has been a general failure to perceive the lack of constructive power which all his work exhibits ? His form, like his thought, is synthetic, a combination of the most timid and conventional procedures of sonata form, and the romantic conception of the vast gradual crescendo from *pianissimo* to *fortissimo*, from misty gloom to luminous ecstasy. His harmonic idiom, for all its appearance of novelty, is fundamentally conventional ; his predilection for the chord which is called the chord of the thirteenth is the same as that of the popular ballad-monger. His harmony is artificially and mechanically arrived at, and is, moreover, monotonous and extraordinarily

Alexander Nicholas Scriabine

restricted in scope. But it is perhaps his melodic poverty which gives the show away most of all, for it is the one element, the pure gold, of musical style which cannot be successfully counterfeited. His thematic material consists of insignificant little snippets, generally only a few notes long and never more than a bar in length. He has no sense of melodic line whatsoever, and he ekes out his poverty by the commonest of all poverty-stricken tricks, namely the device of sequence or *rosalia*—a short phrase of a bar or two repeated several times, each time a tone or semitone higher. He has no rhythmic sense, not even of the primitive kind which Stravinsky possesses. He never ventures outside the limits of the four-bar phrase, and cunningly intricate subdivisions thereof. His music never moves, but merely heaves and undulates like an octopus in the flowing tide. In an age when every minor composer can boast of a reasonably developed colour sense, Scriabine alone shows himself insensitive to instrumental differences. He handles his orchestra as if it were an American organ. Considered as pure sound, his large works are muddy from beginning to end; in blatant coarseness and vulgarity *Prometheus* is only equalled by the *1812 Overture* of Tchaikovsky. His colour, like that of Watts, induces a sensation of acute nausea and actual physical discomfort. That such works as the *Divine Poem*, the *Poem of Ecstasy*, and *Prometheus* should have succeeded in imposing themselves on the public and maintaining their hold on it for so long, is one of the most inexplicable aberrations in the chequered history of art. Fortunately the spell has already been broken to a certain extent within the last year or so; once that has happened, the end is sure to arrive quickly.

It is easier to understand that his smaller piano pieces should be so highly regarded, for he has considerable talent as a miniaturist. Indeed, a number

157

of the short works of his later period have a curious, morbid delicacy and a poisonous charm which are unique in modern music, and they are admirably written for the piano, the only instrument for whose peculiar qualities he has any feeling. In this again Scriabine reminds one strongly of Watts, whose painting, the *Wounded Hero*, shows more feeling for line and colour than any of his more ambitious attempts. They are both artists of a high level of ability in undertakings on a small and unpretentious scale, but they both suffer from the obsession of so many second-rate artists by the ideal of the immense and the colossal. They are not satisfied with the limited range of their own personalities. They are both hag-ridden by the ever-conscious sense of the importance of their mission or purpose, ethical or mystical. They will solemnly tackle the most gigantic conceptions, before which a Beethoven, Aeschylus, or Michel Angelo might legitimately quail. But that is not enough ; we all have gigantic and titanic conceptions every morning in our bath. Only a fool or a charlatan—and occasionally a madman—would endeavour to execute them.

In which of these categories must Scriabine be placed? It is by no means easy to say, for he seems to partake to a certain extent of the characteristics of all three. He was probably one of these unconscious charlatans who are foolish enough to deceive themselves. On the other hand, he undoubtedly suffered from megalomaniac delusions concerning his own importance. He seems to have believed quite firmly and seriously in his divine mission and to have imagined that his projected *Mystery*, which he never lived to complete, was to have been ' the end of the life of our race ', and the beginning of a ' new era in the spiritual evolution of humanity. The only real mystery which he did thoroughly achieve was that of taking in his contemporaries, and possibly also himself, to an unparalleled extent. He initiated an era of charlatanism in music, and it is on this account alone that he will be remembered. His artistic achievement, apart from a few little piano pieces, is virtually nil.

To what extent his music is an effective means of inducing a state of ecstasy, the condition which mystics call a state of illumination, it is not for me to judge, as in performance it has never caused me anything but discomfort. On such occasions one feels like Durtal in Huysmans's novel, *Là-Bas*, when he attended a Black Mass during which the celebrants and audience roll about the floor in delirious convulsions. Seeing that this is the effect that Scriabine apparently sets out to produce he may be said to succeed in his purpose. But it has nothing whatever to do with art. *C'est magnifique, mais ce n'est pas la musique.* As a kind of drug, no doubt Scriabine's music has a certain significance, but it is wholly superfluous. We already have cocaine, morphine, hashish, heroin, anhalonium, and innumerable similar productions, to say nothing of alcohol. Surely that is enough. On the other hand, we have only one music. Why must we degrade an art into a spiritual narcotic? Why is it more artistic to use eight horns and five trumpets than to use eight brandies and five double whiskies?

It is not to be supposed that Scriabine is alone in all this; his music is only the final stage in a tendency which has been steadily growing for the last hundred years. His religion of ecstasy was voiced by Charles Baudelaire, the prophet and precursor of modernity, half a century ago in his *Poèmes en Prose*: ' Il faut être toujours ivre—de vin, de poésie ou de vertu, à votre guise. Mais enivrez vous pour ne pas sentir l'horrible fardeau du Temps qui brise vos épaules.' Terrible words these; the *Credo* of a century which

Alexander Nicholas Scriabine

has seen all its illusions and ideals die unrealized; the illusions of universal liberty, of the perfectibility of man, of universal brotherhood, all the dreams of scientists, sociologists, metaphysicians—all have crumbled away into the dust. All the superb and impossible dreams which have hitherto buoyed up humanity have failed irrevocably. We are dissatisfied with all we have achieved; we are tired of the constant fruitless endeavour; we no longer believe in anything, for nothing is any longer worth believing in. Therefore we only desire oblivion and forgetfulness. *Il faut s'enivrer.* Let us escape from the Reality which has deceived us; let us build up an artificial paradise in which there is nothing to recall the actual; let us, like Prince Prospero in Poe's tale of the *Masque of the Red Death*, shut ourselves off from all commerce with the outside world.

Above all, let us escape from ourselves, the worst enemies of all; do not let us think. Set intuition in the throne of reason, replace will-power by auto-suggestion, and let us kneel before M. Henri Bergson, the Iscariot of philosophy who proclaims the impotence of reason and the superiority of instinct, and proves the futility of intellect by means of the intellect—sinister apostasy!

Let the arts minister to this universal craving for oblivion and stupefaction, and music above all the rest, for it possesses a more direct appeal to the nerves than any other art, in a more sensuous medium. Hence the music of Scriabine and that of Stravinsky as well; they are opposites and are yet alike. The one is a spiritual narcotic, the other a physical and nervous stimulant.

There is no question but that this tendency in art has produced great and enduring masterpieces, like any other tendency; but it is probably more objectionable than any other in the hands of inferior artists.

Alexander Nicholas Scriabine

That which makes the music of Scriabine particularly offensive is his entire lack of self-control. He is never master of himself and of his medium, as Wagner always is, even in the most ecstatic frenzies of *Tristan*. Scriabine's biographers recount that when he was a small boy he used to write plays which he acted before his aunt and grandmother. ' In his excitement he would make his heroes die long before the necessary five acts of the tragedy were over, and would then turn his bewildered look on his audience, saying, "Auntie, there 's no one left!"' In this respect Scriabine never changed; it is the reason why he so often fails to achieve his purpose. Purely from the point of effect, his *Prometheus* fails completely. The climax comes before the end, for he is unable to restrain himself and to husband his resources for the supreme moment. ' Auntie, there 's no one left ', in fact. Neither the heights of spirituality nor the depths of satanism are accessible to an artist so completely at the mercy of his own hysteria. Both God and Devil alike call for a certain measure of austerity and self-control in their worshippers. It is the lack of these qualities, more than anything else, which most effectively, conclusively, and finally damns him.

ARNOLD SCHÖNBERG

IT often happens that the appearance of a powerful and arresting personality evokes the wholly uncritical enthusiasm of a small but energetic body of disciples and devoted camp-followers, and on the other hand the instinctive, unreasoning hostility of the large majority of professional musicians and critics. Both manifestations possess a certain value in so far as they call attention to and awaken interest in the object of their respective admiration and dislike, and, generally speaking, serve to combat the habitual indifference and lethargy of the larger section of the public, but they can hardly claim to be regarded as serious criticism. Their position is rather that of advocates or counsels for the defence and prosecution than of impartial judges, their function rather to present the case for and against, than to pass sentence.

Arnold Schönberg has had the fortune or misfortune to have been the occasion of more indiscriminate adulation and impassioned eulogy on the one hand, of more violent abuse and bitter invective on the other, than any composer since Wagner. Like him, Schönberg seems to possess to a marked degree the propensity of making both friends and enemies in large numbers and of leaving no one wholly indifferent. Yet it is a curious fact that although the storm of controversy which he has aroused has in a large measure subsided, even to the point of a general recognition on the part of thinking musicians of his undoubted significance and importance—a tacit admission to the effect that, whether one likes or dislikes his music, he remains one of the most vital forces and dominant personalities in

Arnold Schönberg

contemporary art—in spite of all this no serious attempt seems hitherto to have been made to determine the precise nature or to assess the ultimate value of his achievement. Judgement has been indefinitely reserved, *sine die*.

Though no apology, then, seems necessary for this modest and tentative effort to break the spell of non-committal silence and discreet reserve with which his work is invariably greeted, and to arrive at some definite conclusion concerning its merits or demerits, it is perhaps as well to state at the outset that I have not the rare privilege of being personally acquainted with Herr Schönberg, more in excuse for the inevitable limitations which this implies than in support of any claim to impartiality it might induce me to make.

For although Schönberg's inexhaustible and almost demoniac energy, contagious enthusiasm, and magnetic personality seem to have reduced everyone who has come into contact with him to a state of beatific coma and hypnotic trance—a state of mind which, however agreeable in itself, is hardly conducive to the exercise of one's critical and discriminating faculties—it is equally undeniable that it is impossible to do him complete justice without reference to his didactic, literary, theoretical, pictorial, propagandist, and other activities, which all, to a greater extent than with any other living composer, play an important part in the great influence which he exerts on contemporary art. With all these aspects of it I am not qualified to deal; they can only be adequately treated by one who has been in close personal contact with him.

For instruction on these points, and for authoritative biographical and other information, the reader is referred to the excellent little monograph recently published by Dr. Egon Wellesz, one of Schönberg's most distinguished pupils and associates, to the little

Arnold Schönberg

book, *Neue Musik und Wien*, by Paul Stefan, and to the pre-war collection of essays by von Webern, Alban Berg, and others. The present study only purports to deal with Schönberg the composer as revealed in his published works.

The most fertile source of the bewilderment and perplexity which Schönberg frequently arouses is the seeming divergency of style which characterizes the successive stages of his artistic development. As one critic has recently observed, ' In 1908, with dramatic suddenness, he produced three piano pieces, showing that not only had he broken with the past, but that he had burned his boats behind him. Between the works that had appeared before that date and those that came after, there was, to all appearances, no continuity of development.'

This is a misconception, although it must be admitted that there is a certain excuse and justification for it in the eccentric system Schönberg has adopted of giving opus numbers to his works, not in accordance with their chronological sequence, but with regard to some idea which he seems to entertain concerning their relative maturity. For not only are all the qualities and defects which can be discerned in his later works already implicit in the early ones, but the stylistic change is on the whole much more logical, continuous, and even gradual, than one might at first be led to suppose. The later works are no more difficult to understand than the early works—easier rather, for though the idiom becomes increasingly unfamiliar and more wholly personal with each successive work, it is at the same time more in accordance with the ideas and conceptions which the composer is attempting to express

In this respect Schönberg is a singularly consistent personality. With many artists, particularly modern

164

ones, the quality of their thought and even their entire artistic direction undergo complete changes at different stages of their development, frequently for no ostensible reason, less in obedience to an imperious inner necessity than to pure caprice and irresponsibility or to mere lack of conviction. Picasso is a good example of this. Schönberg, on the contrary, has always had a strong sense of direction and very definite convictions. His artistic progress reveals a gradual, steady, unwearying, and relentless march towards a fixed and unalterable point, however distant or at first dimly perceptible. Others, again, may realize even their most personal conceptions immediately and without apparent effort. Not so Schönberg. He belongs to that artistic race that begin unpromisingly and only by dint of the most prodigious effort and indomitable tenacity attain to the goal they have set themselves.

Not even between *Die Feen* and *Götterdämmerung* is there such a gulf fixed as between the songs of Schönberg's Op. 1 and those of Op. 22, yet the latter, as with Wagner, are only the complete realization and consummation of qualities which are already latent and imperfectly adumbrated in the former.

Yet it must be admitted that these early works are singularly unattractive and devoid of interest, although they have occasioned that negative and obviously insincere admiration of the see-what-he-can-do-when-he-likes order which is always so profusely lavished upon the immature productions of a master by those who most detest and abominate his later work, simply because they sound more like the music to which they are accustomed. Between the songs which constitute Op. 1, 2, and 3 it is unnecessary to distinguish, except to note that in Op. 2, No. 1, the cloven hoof peeps out for a moment from under the heavy folds of the Wagner-Brahms dressing-gown, and is as quickly withdrawn again. The whole song is constructed on the

165

Arnold Schönberg

somewhat obvious and crude principle already exploited by Wagner, in *Tristan* particularly, which might be defined as the principle of semitonal inflection. Although it is more daring than anything else which succeeds it for some time, the song is highly conventional and almost commonplace at the same time —a not infrequent combination in Schönberg's experimental works, one may observe.

The other songs of these groups are no doubt thoroughly competent technically in so far as one can judge technique as a thing apart, but otherwise it is difficult to find anything even relatively good to say about them. The voice parts are built on the worst kind of German Lied *cantilena* or, rather, cantilever principle; the left hand of the piano part almost invariably stamps up and down the keyboard in octaves with abominable insistence, the right hand never by any chance playing less than three or four notes at a time, the resultant effect being of a dreary turgidity and cumbrousness unexcelled even in the arid deserts of modern German song.

Certainly no one could possibly have guessed that a revolutionary was here in the making. Musical history, however, teaches us that revolutionaries almost always begin timidly and awkwardly; that when they do not, like Berlioz or Schumann, they generally end up as supporters of tradition.

The string sextet, *Verklärte Nacht*, Op. 4, comparatively familiar to English concert audiences, is essentially music of its period and environment, an attempt to transplant into the narrower limits and more intimate atmosphere of chamber music the ideals and methods reflected in the symphonic music of the post-Wagnerian age. Although it undoubtedly compels a certain measure of respect and admiration for its musicianly qualities, its sureness of design, solidity of structure, and consistency of style, it fails entirely

166

to arouse one's sympathy or affection, and leaves one cold and unmoved.

The age is also reflected—though this time in a manner more flattering to it—and magnified to many times its actual stature and importance, in the grandiose *Gurrelieder*, based on poems of Jacobsen. It is beyond question one of the few landmarks in recent German music, i. e. since Wagner. Certain sections of the work, particularly Tove's love song, ' Nun sag' ich dir zum ersten Mal ', and Waldemar's ' Du wunderliche Tove ', are of a most exquisite tenderness and haunting beauty. In the lovely melody of the former can already be observed the wide intervals and the broad sweep of the melodic line which eventually form such a prominent feature of Schönberg's mature style.

In fact, the finest things in the work are at the same time the most characteristic ; its virtues are Schönberg's, its defects are those of the period in which it was written, such as the quite megalomaniac dimensions of the orchestral and choral apparatus which it employs. It is written for five soloists, three four-part male choruses, and one eight-part mixed chorus, four flutes, four piccolos, three oboes and two cors anglais (alternatively five oboes), three clarinets in A or B♭, two E♭ clarinets, and two bass clarinets (alternatively seven clarinets), three bassoons, two double bassoons, ten horns, six trumpets, one bass trumpet, one alto trombone, four tenor trombones, one bass trombone, one double-bass trombone, one bass tuba, six kettledrums, tenor drum, side drum, big drum, cymbals, triangle, tamtam, glockenspiel, xylophone, rattle, some large iron chains, four harps, celesta, and at least twenty first and twenty second violins, sixteen violas, sixteen 'cellos, and twelve basses.

Such excessive and exorbitant requirements, however, are not necessarily a fault in themselves. A

Arnold Schönberg

composer has a perfect right to demand any conceivable number or combination of instruments, provided always that he considers them necessary to the full realization of his ideas. A very much more serious criticism applies to the undue complexity of the musical tissue. This again, it may be objected, is entirely relative to the end in view, but in the case of the *Gurrelieder* much of it is mere paper complexity, appealing more to the eye than the ear, and imperceptible in performance. While even this can be defended if it grows naturally and logically out of an inner logic or organic necessity, as in the work of Bach, it cannot in the present work, in which the complexity is not spontaneous or organic, but consists primarily in the elaboration of a comparatively simple structure, in the superposition of extraneous and purely decorative elements upon a groundwork which does not call for it.

But in spite of these and kindred faults the *Gurrelieder* constitute a quite monumental and impressive work. Although the scoring of the last part was not completed until 1910 or 1911, the actual music with the exception of a few passages at the end, was entirely written in 1900–1, when the composer was only twenty-six years of age. Musical history can show many examples of precocious development, but very few to compare with such supreme and incontestable mastery in the largest forms at such an early age.

The symphonic poem for large orchestra, *Pelleas und Melisande*, Op. 5, written about the same time as the opera of Debussy, with which it affords a striking contrast, is also a work of immense power and vitality, although one sincerely wishes that one could like it better than one does. In sheer polyphonic complexity it rivals and even eclipses the most intricately woven pages of *Die Meistersinger* or *Parsifal*; but not all one's astonishment at and admiration of the achieve-

168

ment can dispel the uneasy but certain conviction of
its inherent sterility, its immense and utter pur-
poselessness—a feeling akin to that aroused by the
contrapuntal excesses of Okeghem and others of the
Netherland school. In spite of many passages of
great beauty and distinction, it remains essentially
an intellectual *tour de force*. It reminds one of
a vast untrodden equatorial forest from which all
daylight is excluded by the thick impenetrable masses
of tropical vegetation, its many treasures hopelessly
buried and hidden from sight by the vast entangle-
ment of giant creepers and luxuriant undergrowth.

It is more than probable that Schönberg felt this
himself and realized that even if it were possible to
go any farther in this direction, it was not the way
which led towards the complete emancipation and
expression of his personality.

However this may be, the succeeding works—the
eight songs with piano accompaniment, Op. 6, and the
six orchestral songs of Op. 8—bear witness to some
momentary hesitancy and vacillation. They are essentially transition works, oscillating tentatively and
uncertainly between the old and the new. They
are written with key-signatures, but are always in
conflict with the principles of tonality ; bold and
novel harmonic progressions alternate with conventional Wagnerian chromaticism, while strange and
tortuous melodic lines betray an increasing dissatisfaction with conventional moulds, and a determined
search after increased plasticity and expressiveness.
Every constituent element of musical style is in a state
of flux and disintegration, of anarchy and upheaval,
offering a strange contrast to the serene and accomplished mastery of the preceding works. There is also
considerable uncertainty of direction. Side by side
with a daring experiment like Op. 6, No. 1, *Traumleben*,
with its characteristic late-Schönbergian voice part,

Arnold Schönberg

we find a comparatively conventional song like *Alles*, recalling the manner of the early ones already mentioned. Yet, however unsatisfactory these songs may be in themselves, they mark a turning-point, a landmark of great significance in the unfolding of Schönberg's genius.

Conscious of the desirability and expediency of imposing upon himself some limitations or restrictions which, like a mould, would impart some measure of logic and consistency to the fluidity and indeterminacy of his thought, Schönberg turns instinctively to the old classical forms. As Dante was succoured by Virgil when he found himself astray in the dark wood, ' dove la diritta via era smarrita', so Schönberg is led by the classic tradition out of the *impasse* in which he had found himself, and ultimately attains to liberation through the exercise of the strictest formal discipline —an instructive parable to all our would-be innovators and callow revolutionaries.

It is certainly a curious and entertaining spectacle, and one which is new to musical history, to observe how Schönberg applies the resources of formal design, conventional structure, and development to the purposes of revolution; how he exploits order and symmetry with a view to their ultimate destruction, and turns the heavy artillery of canons and double-barrelled counterpoints upon the fortresses and strongholds of tradition. As Shakespeare has it, ' 'tis sport to see the engineer hoist with his own petard'.

The first string quartet, Op. 7 in D minor, Dr. Wellesz proudly informs us, lasts forty-five minutes, and from beginning to end there is not a middle part or even a figure of accompaniment that is not of thematic derivation—a pardonable exaggeration, but at least sufficient to show that Schönberg is already *plus royaliste que le roi*. Excess of zeal in monastic discipline was always discouraged by the abbots and fathers superior in the Middle Ages, and regarded by them with grave suspicion, as being symptomatic of spiritual pride or some equally horrid disorder ; and when we find an arch-revolutionary serving as gentleman-in-waiting at the court of classical tradition it is just as well for the custodians of artistic law and order to keep a watchful eye on his movements.

The quartet is a carefully planned and well-proportioned work, besides being a fine example of the best style of string writing, the instruments being treated with great resource and understanding. The part-writing and handling of themes are equally masterful, but the general impression created by the work is curiously disconcerting and unsatisfactory. A comparatively daring or unconventional passage will come to an end with an ordinary dominant tonic cadence, giving one much the same disagreeable sensation that one experiences in falling out of bed on to the floor in the middle of the night ; or a simple diatonic phrase will gradually wander off with an odd kind of inconsequence as one's thoughts are apt to do in those pleasant moments of semi-consciousness when one is neither awake nor asleep. This constant juxtaposition of incongruous elements is more acutely disturbing than the wildest cacophony imaginable. The *Kammersymphonie*, Op. 9, is less disconcerting in this respect, and represents a substantial progress towards homogeneity and cohesion of style. On the other hand, it is formally less satisfying than the quartet. There are plenty of clearly defined themes in it, but their interaction is neither of the symphonic nor contrapuntal order ; that is to say, they are never satisfactorily worked out nor skilfully combined as in the previous work, and their recurrence seems to be dictated less by formal necessity than by the desire to maintain a certain superficial semblance of pattern or

Arnold Schönberg

symmetry. It is, in fact, a somewhat amorphous and loosely constructed string of episodes held together by, but not built out of, certain constantly recurring themes ; they are not the bricks, but the mortar.

While there is much in it that is crude, shapeless, and experimental, it also contains many passages of great power and beauty, and the astonishing command of polyphony revealed in every bar brooks no denial.

Incidentally, it may be pointed out that the characteristically modern predilection for the chamber orchestra of solo.instruments takes its origin in the *Kammersymphonie*. In this, as in so many other things, Schönberg is the pioneer.

Passing over the two ballads, Op. 12, and the *a capella* chorus, *Friede auf Erden*, neither of which calls for special comment, we come to the second string quartet in F minor, Op. 10, at once the highest point to which Schönberg attains during this period of self-imposed discipline and probation and, in the last movement, his final farewell to it, his triumphant liberation from all restrictions.

This work consists of a superbly wrought first movement, full of masterly thematic interplay and development, and a strange and almost sinister *scherzo*, in the middle of which are introduced against wholly irrelevant harmonies the all-too-familiar strains of ' O, du lieber Augustin, alles ist hin ' ; the third and fourth movements are settings of two poems of Stefan Georg, *Litanei* and *Entrückung* respectively, for soprano and quartet—the one a slow movement filled with a glowing ardour and intensity, while in the other, the last movement, Schönberg, as I have said, throws off the last vestige and semblance of compromise with tonality, and at last attains to complete self-realization. In the first words of the poem here set to music there is, one feels, a certain symbolical significance which is not merely accidental—' Ich fühle Luft von

172

anderen Planeten', for never before surely had a new world of possibilities been so unmistakably revealed as in this extraordinary movement. In discarding tonality Schönberg seems to leave the ground for the first time and to soar away into the air like a captive bird when it is liberated. With this work he makes an end and a beginning. The works which immediately succeed it represent him at the summit of his powers and in complete maturity.

The first of these is *Das Buch der hängenden Gärten*, Op. 15, consisting of settings for voice with piano accompaniment of fifteen poems of Stefan Georg. Schönberg has himself written of this work, ' Mit den Liedern nach Georg ist es mir zum erstenmal gelungen, einem Ausdrucks- und Form-ideal näherzukommen, das mir seit Jahren vorschwebt,' and it is certainly one of his most wholly convincing and satisfactory achievements. For the first time since the early works (always excepting the last movement of the second quartet) one is not conscious of any discrepancy or antagonism between his conception and the medium in which they are realized. One does not feel that the forms and methods are being racked and distorted in the endeavour to make them express things which they are fundamentally incapable of expressing, nor, as in the very last works, that the ideas themselves are being subordinated to a growing obsession with purely stylistic considerations.

Perhaps the most admirable qualities of these songs are their directness, simplicity, and restraint—three elements which are most conspicuously lacking in nearly all Schönberg's music. If the vocal part seems at times to be needlessly angular, it is a defect which is to some extent mitigated by the measure of support afforded by the piano part, which is not, as in the latter vocal works, so constructed as to avoid sounding

Arnold Schönberg

any note which might bear any conceivable relation to that which the voice is singing, or rather supposed to be singing, for in many instances this principle is carried beyond the uttermost bounds of human possibility.

The three piano pieces, Op. 11, have attained a greater degree of notoriety than almost any other of Schönberg's works for reasons which it is exceedingly difficult to discover, for they are far more readily comprehensible and accessible than most. The first two are straightforward in thought and almost classical in form and style. The third is more difficult to grasp at first, owing to the sudden violent alternations of mood and to the greater complexity of its harmonic structure.

In general one may say that Schönberg is at his best with limited means at his disposal, when his exuberant imagination and fertility of resource and invention are to some extent held in check. When he is working on a large canvas of unrestricted possibilities his powers seem to waste themselves on the air, to become dispersed and disorganized, while his weaknesses become correspondingly more apparent, more highly accentuated. Consequently the Five Orchestral Pieces, Op. 16, are less convincing than the immediately preceding works, being to a great extent experimental, and, it must be said, not always successfully so. Nevertheless they are immensely stimulating and suggestive of much more than they actually achieve. Indeed it is practically certain that orchestral style in the immediate future will increasingly tend to break away from the Wagner-Strauss tradition, consisting of the treatment of large neutralized masses of tone-colour, and to approximate more and more closely to the ideal set forth in these pieces, namely, the exploitation of the subtler varieties of tone-colour afforded by combinations of solo instruments.

Arnold Schönberg

It is somewhat difficult to determine the precise chronological sequence of the succeeding works. Whether *Pierrot Lunaire* was written at this time, or only after the music-dramas *Erwartung* and *Die Glückliche Hand*, as the opus number (21) would suggest, does not matter very much; stylistic considerations justify one in regarding it as belonging to the period under consideration.

Pierrot Lunaire represents the zenith of Schönberg's powers, the fullest and most perfect expression of his personality. It consists of twenty-one poems (divided into three parts of seven each) by Albert Giraud and translated into German by Eric Hartleben, set for voice and different combinations of the following instruments—piano, flute, clarinet, bass clarinet, violin, viola, and violoncello. In a foreword the composer explains that the voice part is to be what he calls a 'Sprechstimme', neither song nor speech, but something in between; an effect which is very much easier to conceive than to realize. One quite understands the kind of effect intended, but the technical difficulties in the way of its attainment are almost insuperable. To maintain an absolute balance between the singing and speaking voice throughout a long and difficult work such as this, without falling over into either, is a tight-rope feat of which few, if any, singers are capable.

Apart from this purely practical and technical consideration, it is impossible to make any adverse criticism of this superb work. It is one of those few works which possess such power and originality that a musician, one imagines, could hardly fail to be impressed by it —by its formal perfection, its almost diabolical ingenuity and instrumental resource, its astounding wealth of purely musical invention. It is impossible to discriminate between each setting, for there is not a weak number among them from beginning to end.

Arnold Schönberg

They give the impression of having been thrown off one after another with lightning rapidity and absolute sureness of touch in a continuous, unflagging jet of white-hot inspiration.

Out of the unpromising material afforded by these highly artificial, precious, and decadent little poems, Schönberg has created a whole world of strange fascination and enchantment, of nameless horrors and terrible imaginings, of perverse and poisonous beauty and bitter-sweet fragrance, of a searing and withering mockery and malicious, elfish humour, which the poet most assuredly never even contemplated. All the *diablerie* of the Romantics pales beside its demoniac intensity, and the much-vaunted irony and cynicism of Stravinsky appear childish and insipid in comparison with the sardonic and inhuman laughter of Schönberg's sinister and menacing evocation. In all art and literature one can only think of Hoffmann who has anything to compare to it. Even the creations of Poe seem colourless, mechanical, and soulless when placed by the side of *Pierrot Lunaire*. If Schönberg had written nothing else, this work alone would be sufficient to assure him a place apart in musical history.

It will be as well briefly to recapitulate the various successive stages which lead up to this consummation, otherwise it may be difficult to understand the subsequent phase of his development.

First of all, in the early works we find him investigating and exhausting the limited possibilities of the chromatic inflection of conventional harmonic and melodic formulas. Then we have him pushing to the uttermost limits the Wagnerian principles of polyphonic texture, as exemplified in *Die Meistersinger* and *Parsifal*. Thirdly, after a moment of indecision, he reverts to classical models and builds up his works by means of close and logical thematic development

176

and metamorphosis, and by contrapuntal devices of melodic combinations, augmentation, inversion, diminution, *stretto*, and so forth.

In all these phases the principles of tonality are observed, though with little respect, and with increasing impatience and intolerance, until, in the final stage which we have been witnessing, he dispenses with them altogether and with all definite formal restrictions, retaining only the one fundamental principle or factor underlying all musical forms whatsoever, namely, thematic recurrence. Nevertheless there is no deliberate avoidance of traditional methods. He does not scruple to make use of them if and when they serve his purpose. In *Pierrot Lunaire*, for instance, old contrapuntal devices are employed with astonishing virtuosity, and dramatic fitness. No. 8 (*Nacht*) is a Passacaglia ; in the 17th (*Parodie*) can be found a canon in inversion accompanied by an imitation ; in the 18th (*Der Mondfleck*) a double canon of remarkable ingenuity ; yet they are not employed for their own sake, but always with a definite imaginative and poetic purpose.

Finally, in the stage which we are about to examine, Schönberg seeks to dispense with every semblance even of thematic material, and to create a consistent and logical musical structure by means of a mosaic-like method of construction, an infinite accumulation of small and insignificant inorganic details amounting to a kind of musical *pointillage*.

In the music-dramas *Erwartung* and *Die Glückliche Hand*, Op. 17 and 18 respectively, Schönberg has at last succeeded in throwing overboard every vestige and remnant of every element which has hitherto been considered an essential constituent of musical structure and design. Unfortunately in so liberating himself from tradition he becomes a slave to his own mannerisms, the prisoner of his own originality, a very

M   177

much more despotic tyrant and taskmaster than even the strictest traditionalism could ever be.

In these later works can be traced a constantly growing obsession with means as ends in themselves, not as aids to expression. He is as deliberate and pedantic in his avoidance of a concord as any academy professor in his avoidance of a discord. He would no more dream of writing in octaves than the latter would in consecutive 5ths; only consecutive 7ths and 9ths are permitted. Mere 3rds and 6ths should never be used at all, or at any rate not without careful preparation and resolution; voice parts should as far as possible, and even at the risk of monotony, move in leaps of an augmented 4th or some interval larger than an octave, and so on *ad infinitum*—a display of combined pedantry and perversity without parallel in musical history.

The systematic abuse of tone-colour, too, which already assumes disquieting proportions in the *Five Orchestral Pieces*, is here exploited to the utmost limits of insanity. There is hardly a page of these vast scores without a *flatterzunge* for the wind or a *col legno sul ponticello* for strings; mutes for all and sundry are applied and removed every few bars. The kettledrums are generally played with a wooden drumstick, while the cymbals are occasionally directed to be struck with a double-bass bow. The chorus in *Die Glückliche Hand* must not sing or speak their parts, but must employ his patent 'Sprechstimme', which combines the advantages of both these antiquated and obsolete methods.

That such methods defeat themselves and ultimately engender a quite distressing monotony of effect is a truth too self-evident to stand in need of any demonstration, and it is impossible to contemplate these works without a feeling of profound dismay and regret that such genius and talents as Schönberg's should be recklessly and senselessly squandered on such vast and monstrous delusions as these. *Die Glückliche Hand*, in particular, would almost seem to have been created in order to illustrate Rabelais's phrase, *chimera bombinans in vacuo*.

The six short pieces for piano are only aphorisms, notebook jottings for possible future works, and consequently call for no detailed examination. As for that nightmarish production, *Herzgewächse*, Op. 20, a setting of a poem by Maurice Maeterlinck for a superhuman soprano with a compass of nearly three octaves, harmonium, celesta, and harp, the less said of it the better—I cannot trust myself to speak of it ; and the same applies to the four orchestral songs, Op. 22, Schönberg's latest published work. Both are symptomatic of an ever-increasing lack of artistic balance and direction. He seems now to care less about writing good works than about making odd experiments and interesting discoveries with no definite end in view ; the zest lies only in the voyage of discovery, not in the destination or in what awaits him at the journey's end—the characteristic and fatal tendency of nearly all modern composers. To most of them it probably does not very much matter ; they are not capable of anything better, and the little discoveries they are making may quite conceivably be of use some day to someone who will know what to do with them. With Schönberg it is a very different matter. He has shown himself to be an indisputable master, capable of the highest achievements, and, after all, it cannot be too strongly emphasized, particularly at the present time, that one successful work, one perfect achievement, is worth any number of interesting or suggestive experiments.

Schönberg's artistic development is at once an inspiring lesson and a warning example. He attains to his fullest strength and stature under the direct tutelage and guidance of traditional forms and methods. As soon as he discards them altogether he fails disastrously. The fact is that complete artistic freedom is only a theory and cannot exist in practice. It is an illusion, a mirage which recedes before us as we approach it, and vanishes like smoke as soon as we seem to have attained to it.

On the other hand, his correspondingly great achievement shows conclusively that no utterance, however new and vital, is incompatible with the past; that tradition, in the best sense of the word, is a living and eternal principle within whose terms can be reconciled the most conflicting and dissimilar artistic ideals.

That Schönberg should have arrived almost simultaneously at both the zenith and the nadir of his powers is not the least disturbing feature of his extraordinary personality, and constitutes a psychological problem of considerable magnitude. Yet he is not altogether an isolated phenomenon in the history of art. William Blake is another example of a great artist who sought and achieved complete liberation and emancipation from tradition with identically the same disastrous consequences. Within the limits of metre and rhyme he was an accomplished master, perhaps one of the greatest poets England has ever produced; the Prophetic Books, written in defiance of rhyme, rhythm, and reason, are dreary wildernesses and arid deserts of incoherent rhapsody and senseless extravagance, in the midst of which we find here and there passages of extraordinary beauty and power. The same observations hold good of his pictorial art, and one could say that the engravings to the Book of Job bear much the same relation to the Prophetic Books and their illustrations that *Pierrot Lunaire* bears to *Die Glückliche Hand*.

It is interesting to note in this connexion that Blake and Schönberg present many temperamental analogies

Arnold Schönberg

to each other. Both exhibit the same boundless energy and virility, the same deliberate avoidance and disdain of sensuous beauty, though both are capable of it when they choose; both are alternately ascetic and passionate, imaginative and pedantic, utterly lacking in any kind of self-criticism or mental balance, frequently bigoted and insensitive, always inhuman. Both, too, claim to write under the direct dictation of inspiration.

Whether Schönberg will ever extricate himself from the dismal morass into which he has been lured by the will-o'-the-wisp of complete artistic freedom—a gaseous exhalation from stagnant pools of aesthetic theory—remains to be seen. It is perhaps too early yet to despair altogether of an undoubted master who ought still to be at the summit of his artistic powers, but it must be admitted that the symptoms are not reassuring, and the recently published libretto of an oratorio, entitled *Die Jakobsleiter*, only serves to confirm our worst fears. If the music is to be anything like the libretto—and it is only natural to suppose that it will be—we must reluctantly abandon our last hope of his eventual artistic salvation, for a more preposterous farrago of incoherent mysticism, naïve philosophy, and pretentious moralizing it is impossible to imagine. Nietzsche writes somewhere that 'we philosophers are never so pleased as when we are mistaken for artists'. The corollary is frequently true that artists, particularly musicians, are never so pleased as when they are mistaken for philosophers. Judging from this libretto, it would seem that Schönberg, too, would dearly love to be considered a philosopher, a poet, a priest, or a prophet—anything rather than what he is, potentially one of the keenest, most profound musical intelligences of the present day.

Schönberg's disciples and admirers would fain have us see in him only the bold pioneer striking out new paths across trackless continents, the inspired innovator

Arnold Schönberg

opening up new and incalculable vistas of boundless extent, and it is probably in this light that he sees himself. But there is another side to the picture. When one comes to examine his work more closely one discovers that with all its originality and revolutionary daring it is essentially a continuation and extension of the German romantic movement. In musical mentality he is closely related to Schumann, Brahms, and Wagner, and his technique is in large part their technique pushed to the furthest limits of refinement and perversity. In a word, he stands revealed as the last of an old line rather than the first of a new one, and it is certainly to Schönberg the romantic rather than to Schönberg the revolutionary that we owe what is most lasting and vital in his work. Schönberg is the last commanding figure in the history of romanticism; *Pierrot Lunaire* plays the most important part in the harlequinade at the end of the romantic drama in which the romantic spirit satirizes itself, parodies its own heroic attitudes and postures, mocks at its own image reflected in the glass, and scoffs derisively at its own achievement in a last paroxysm of supreme disillusion, with one last impotent gesture of frenzied despair.

It is not easy to estimate the permanent and lasting value of what Schönberg has accomplished. Nearly all his works are merely progressive stages towards the attainment of an end—steps in a Jacob's Ladder which, though it reaches as far as the moon and the *Pierrot Lunaire,* falls short of Heaven, with its topmost rungs leading only into the vast and limitless reaches of the upper air; and it is this fact that the larger part of his work is dissatisfying which will tell most heavily against him in the course of time. But while the prestige of his works with one notable exception will probably wane in the future, his influence will probably steadily increase. Not his direct influence,

Arnold Schönberg

however ; apart from a few pupils and imitators no musician is likely to travel very far along the lonely path Schönberg has trodden, but will content himself with the spoils he has brought back with him.

Besides, there are unmistakable signs in art to-day of a reaction against the more extravagant excesses of recent years, of a reversion to simpler and less sophisticated methods and to saner and more harmonious ideals. The new tendency has already begun in painting, sculpture, and literature ; in music it is only just beginning. The truth is that the ' modern ' movement has exhausted itself. There is nothing left to discover. All the seas have been charted and sounded, all new continents explored, the extreme poles of artistic endeavour have been reached. There are no new worlds left for our Alexanders to conquer. It is time to return from these distant lands and hazardous expeditions and to seek more temperate latitudes and more fruitful soil.

Of all this passing race of heroic pioneers, explorers, navigators, none has been more adventurous or daring, more tireless or indomitable, than Arnold Schönberg, and none has brought back such sumptuous and glittering spoils, such strange and exotic trophies— certainly none is more worthy of our respect and admiration. But Arnold Schönberg, the inspired creator of *Pierrot Lunaire*, commands more than these ; he has our reverent homage, our undying gratitude.

JEAN SIBELIUS

IN the *Kalevala*, the ancient Finnish national epic, there are three heroes : Wainamoinen, a harper and mighty magician, the Orpheus of his race; Ilmarinen, a cunning artificer and smith ; and Lemminkainen, a kind of northern Don Juan. Curiously enough, in the music of Jean Sibelius, the Finnish composer, one is similarly confronted by three wholly distinct and even antagonistic personalities bearing a strikingly apposite relation to those of the three heroic sons of Kaleva, each of whom symbolizes one particular aspect or trait of the national character. In the symphonies it is the great harper, the inspired singer of his race, who speaks ; in many works, such as the *Nightride and Sunrise*, we find only the skilful and accomplished craftsman following timidly and without any originality of outlook in the footsteps of Wagner, Strauss, Tchaikovsky, Grieg, even Brahms ; finally there is the composer of the *Valse Triste*, the *Romance in D flat*, and many similar works of a popular and frequently even vulgar character. It is difficult to realize that they are all the work of the same man ; it is impossible to find a common term which might enable us to reconcile them.

It is not as if one could regard such a work as the Fourth Symphony as being one of those happy accidents which occur at rare intervals in the history of an art, an example of artistic possession, in which a seemingly second-rate artist suddenly produces a masterpiece. There is more than sufficient evidence in many other works to satisfy us that this one is only the full realization and consummation of qualities which had always been present, though frequently dormant, in his art.

Jean Sibelius

Besides, such isolated works as those to which allusion has been made can generally be traced to the influence or inspiration of a greater artist; they are reproductive rather than generative, interpretations rather than creations. At best they are other peoples' masterpieces, even when the original inspirers of the work were themselves incapable of achieving them. This is not so with Sibelius. His finest work is supremely original, owing nothing to any other composer, past or present.

Unhappily the same is equally true of the *Valse Triste*. It cannot be disregarded and dismissed as a single unfortunate lapse from artistic virtue which the world, with its habitual and characteristically unconscious malevolence, will not allow him to forget. Probably no composer of such high distinction has ever written such a large quantity of thoroughly bad works. One cannot even say of them that they were deliberately written with the quite harmless and readily excusable intention of making money. It is a great mistake to imagine that a man of genius can write a popular success whenever he cares to do so; it is a feat which demands a special talent, and the same enthusiasm and conviction which go to the writing of a great masterpiece. There is nothing people hate more whole-heartedly or forgive less easily than the condescension of a superior mind. They possess an uncanny and quite infallible instinct for detecting any attempt to ' talk down to them ', as the saying is; and if the general public has taken to its great soft heart the necrophilistic ardours of the *Valse Triste*, the facile and commonplace nationalism of *Finlandia*, and the elegant banalities of the *Romance in D flat*, one may be sure that it is because it has recognized in them a mind, for the moment at least, completely in tune and in sympathy with its own.

In this respect Sibelius is an almost isolated phenomenon in the history of music. It has been given to very few indeed to have won the esteem of the few and the approbation of the many, and it is probably this disconcerting ambiguity of aspect, this Janus-like faculty of facing both ways, that is primarily responsible for the attitude of non-committal reserve which musical criticism has hitherto maintained toward Sibelius. It is a difficult enough task to understand and rightly appraise a single straightforward personality ; even if there were but two to consider, one might perhaps at least be induced to make some effort ; but when we discover to our horror yet another side to Sibelius, neither a Jekyll nor a Hyde, neither an inspired genius nor a purveyor of ' best sellers ', but a sober, quiet, conscientious, respectable, and undistinguished *Kapellmeister*, it is only natural that we should feel tempted to abandon the problem as being altogether beyond our powers of comprehension. Consequently the general attitude towards Sibelius may be defined as one of curiosity rather than of interest, of suspicion rather than of dislike, of bewilderment generally without either enthusiasm or hostility. He is the dark horse of modern music, and no one is inclined to stake the gold of his critical reputation on him, not even for a place. If I have not the same reluctance and timidity, it is probably because I have so little to lose ; but also because, whatever the merits or defects of his other works, the Fourth Symphony in A minor has always seemed to me one of the greatest things in modern music—an early impression which close and prolonged study has only served to confirm. On the strength of that one work alone I am prepared to maintain that Sibelius is one of the very few great personalities in modern music ; on account of it alone it is well worth while making an effort to understand him.

The key to both the strength and the weakness of

Jean Sibelius

Sibelius is to be found in his essentially primitive mentality—using the word primitive in its truest and best sense, for it is a word which has been used loosely and indiscriminately to denote two quite definite and distinct qualities of mind. First, there is the type to which the English Pre-Raphaelites and Debussy belong, and of which Matisse and Stravinsky are the most characteristic living representatives. The medievalism of the former and the barbarism of the latter two are the result of the attraction which the remote, the exotic, and the strange perpetually exercise over us. They are 'primitives' from being hyper-civilized, super-cultured, over-refined. With them primitivism is simply a form of romanticism, like the cult of orientalism a hundred years ago, and there is as little real relation between the art of Rossetti and that of the Middle Ages, between that of Matisse and African idols, as there was between the East of Victor Hugo's imagining and the East as it really is.

Secondly, there are the true primitives, such as Moussorgsky, Borodin, and Sibelius in music, or Van Gogh and Henri Rousseau in painting. They are primitive not from any theoretic or sentimental yearnings, but simply because their minds are simple, direct, and unsophisticated; they cannot help being so. As a matter of fact they would have been different if they could. For in the same way that the typical modern man has the perpetual craving for the simple, the savage, and the barbaric, so primitive man constantly aspires towards the culture and refinements of civilization. The silk top-hat has vanished from the streets of London and is now almost exclusively worn by naked negroes in the tropical forests and steaming swamps of Central Africa. There are no longer any fetishes to be found on the Congo; they are all in the windows of the Parisian art-dealers in the Rue de la Boétie.

Jean Sibelius

And so in creative art. The true primitive artist is irresistibly attracted to the great traditions and procedures from which the modern decadent endeavours constantly to escape ; and just as a primitive race, on being brought into contact with a civilization in an advanced stage of social and intellectual development, tends inevitably to acquire only its least worthy aspects, so the primitive musician is apt to assimilate only the baser characteristics of our civilized traditions ; the cheap mirrors and glass beads of the salon and the ballad concert, the tawdry, brightly-coloured cotton shift of ' modernity ', and the cheap line of craftsman's tools supplied by German conservatoires and harmony text-books. In other words, he only acquires the vices of traditional musicianship without the virtues which alone are capable of transforming and renewing them. Hence the vein of shallow and conventional operatic Italianism into which Borodin frequently relapsed ; hence the facile and commonplace *clichés* in a great deal of Moussorgsky's music ; hence the amiable banalities and meretricious elegances in the work of Sibelius.

But if I call Sibelius a primitive, I do not intend to suggest that his work is necessarily crude, unfinished, or technically incompetent. All I mean to imply by this misused adjective is a type of mind which works instinctively rather than consciously and intellectually ; and, as the instincts of a primitive race are keener and surer than those of civilized races, so the resultant art has nothing of the clumsiness and uncertainty which we habitually associate with their workings. On the contrary, a great deal of primitive art is extremely subtle, highly finished, and supremely accomplished. When Sibelius's music seems bare and uncouth, it is always with a very definite purpose in view. Finally, it would be a mistake to imagine that I call Sibelius primitive because he happens to come from a country which stands somewhat off the beaten track. There are doubtless as many highly civilized persons in Finland, in proportion to the population, as in any other country. His primitivism is a personal and not a national characteristic, and he would probably have possessed a similar mentality even if he had been born in Paris or in London.

Although primitivism is primarily answerable for all his characteristic shortcomings, it must not be forgotten that it is likewise responsible for his great and outstanding qualities. The famous ' elimination of unessentials ' which the pseudo-primitive artist is constantly striving to achieve with such a conspicuous lack of success, is actually achieved by Sibelius. Despite the comparative simplicity and conventionality of his idiom, he is in spirit one of the most daring of the ' moderns '. It is very important that this should be recognized, for hitherto a new departure in music has always been accompanied by daring idiomatic innovations, with the result that these latter have come to be regarded, not merely as indicative of the presence of an original and daring revolutionary, but as the only kind of originality possible. Sibelius is perhaps the first composer to show conclusively that it is possible to convey a profound and original thought or to embody a striking and novel conception in simple and straightforward language ; just as so many contemporary composers have shown that it is possible to write in a most complex and unfamiliar idiom, and yet reveal a commonplace mind. For although the harmonic and melodic idiom which he uses is for the most part simple and almost conventional, his thought is frequently exceedingly subtle, his purpose often bafflingly elusive and hard to detect. The obscurity of a great deal of his later work, notably the Fifth Symphony in E flat, is not, as in most modern music, the result of employing an unfamiliar means of expression, but is latent in the very conception itself and particularly in his elliptical mode of thought—in his habit of presenting us with his conclusions, without initiating us into the processes or leading us successively through the different stages by which he arrived at them.

Undoubtedly Sibelius's greatest asset lies in his magnificent orchestral resource. For absolute sureness of effect and daring conception it would be difficult to name his equal, even at the present time, when orchestral *virtuosi* abound at every street corner. His distinction in this direction has never been properly recognized, because he does not compete with his contemporaries in producing effects of dazzling brilliance. For most musicians the idea of orchestral colour implies brightness, high tones generally. Sibelius, though he can be as brilliant as any one when occasion demands, is perhaps most characteristic when he is employing a somewhat dark, sombre, and austere, though not necessarily gloomy and tragic, colour scheme, as in *The Swan of Tuonela* and the *Overture En Saga*. The score of his Fourth Symphony, for example, is a revelation of what can be accomplished with small means. In all its four movements the full orchestra is only employed three times, and even then for only a few bars at a time. This austerity and proud restraint stand in striking contrast to the reckless prodigality of means which most modern composers squander on every page. As always, virtue brings its reward, for in grandeur and tragic intensity this work stands unsurpassed in modern music.

While even the most consummate masters of the orchestra have sometimes made great miscalculations of effect—Strauss very often indeed, and even Berlioz occasionally—the scoring of Sibelius is uncannily sure, without ever being timid or unoriginal. He never seems to take risks, like Stravinsky or Schönberg, and consequently never breaks his neck, as they do.

In so far as Sibelius has met with any recognition or appreciation outside his own country (apart, of course, from the *Valse Triste, et hoc genus omne*), it has been as a nationalist composer, and it is undoubtedly true that racial characteristics play a dominating role in a great deal of his work; not merely in such things as *Finlandia* and *Karelia*, examples of that somewhat superficial nationalism which seeks to embody in musical dialect the characteristics of a country which are most likely to appeal to the average casual tourist, such as picturesque costumes and local customs, and are in fact a kind of musical picture postcard, designed primarily for exportation; but also in the symphonies and other works which have their roots in the soil from which these superficial characteristics themselves have sprung, of which they are, as it were, only a secondary and already semi-artistic expression. It is music full of the spirit of the North, music which is one with the sullen lowering rack of storm-clouds and driving whirling snow, with the dense white mists which rise like smoke from the countless lakes of Finland, and it is filled with the breath of the great winds that sweep the desolate plains and roar through the pine forests which clothe the bleak sides of the *asars*, or moraines. It is music full of the loneliness and terror of the long Arctic nights, and, in its happier and more tranquil moments, full of the poignant poetry of the brief season of sunshine and warmth in which the emotions of spring, summer, autumn, are all blended in one fleeting moment of respite between two wintry eternities.

But the nationalism of Sibelius is not merely geographic; it is also ethnographic. It is no mere idle fancy which leads one to trace in his music a striking affinity to that of his younger contemporaries

in Hungary, Bartók and Kodály, for they belong
ultimately to the same race, as their languages clearly
show. Moreover, the close relation between the
Finnish and Magyar races is intensified by the curious
parallel which their history reveals ; not only is the
position of Finland between Russia on the one hand
and Scandinavia on the other strikingly analogous to
that of Hungary between the Balkans and Austria,
but the destinies of both alike have been tragic. In
the art of both Finnish and Hungarian composers
there is the same profound melancholy and despair
which is not that of individuals, but of an exiled and
oppressed race. As the nameless poet of the *Kanteletar*
sang, concerning the magic harp of Wainamoinen :

> From misery the harp is sprung,
> The frame was moulded by distress ;
> The strings by Sorrow's hands were strung,
> And the pegs turned by wretchedness.

But although all these suggestions will undoubtedly
help us to understand something of the spiritual
content of the art of Sibelius, it would be a mistake
to regard him merely as the mouthpiece of a nation,
the artistic representative of a race. In reality he is
very much more than that. Whatever his circumstances and environment had been, he would always
have been a great artist, for his music bears the
imprint of a powerful and independent personality.

In whatever there is of solid and enduring achievement in the work of our contemporaries, the *Pierrot
Lunaire* of Schönberg, for example, or even the very
different *Sacre du Printemps* of Stravinsky, one is
always conscious of a certain strain and effort. They
are all terminal points, not, as so many have supposed, the prodromes of a new art. They are *tours de
force*, exploits upon the tight-rope which is our present
age, stretched across the gulf between past and future.

Moreover, they are feats which can never be repeated, not even by their creators. Sibelius seems to belong to a different race, a different age even; whether to the past or to the unborn future it would be difficult to say. The great A minor Symphony seems effortless, natural, inevitable; it does not give one this terrible sense of strain and tension, this involuntary catching of the breath, this quivering tautness of nerve and muscle. Above all, it does not leave one with the conviction of finality, with the feeling that having created this work, there is nothing more to be expected from the composer. There is no reason to suppose that he will not some day write music equally great; and even if he never does, one supremely great work is surely sufficient cause for gratitude.

BÉLA BARTÓK

IT has almost become an established convention
that composers can only enter the Noah's Ark of
musical history symmetrically arranged in couples
—Bach and Handel, Haydn and Mozart, Beethoven
and Brahms, Strauss and Debussy. The latest example
of this strange tendency of musical criticism is the
coupling together of Stravinsky and Bartók, though
actually there is as little connexion between them as
between any of the other pairs enumerated above. In
many ways, indeed, they are complete antitheses, both
in style and mentality. The reason why this misunderstanding has arisen is probably that, like so many
artists, Bartók is best known and most appreciated on
account of his least important works, and certain short
piano pieces of his might conceivably be regarded as
indicating a sympathy with the general tendency of
Stravinsky's music. But if we wish to understand
Bartók, it will be necessary to dismiss completely from
one's mind any such preconceived notions regarding
him, however dearly cherished they may be.

A comprehensive survey of his entire output reveals
several distinct phases of development. The first,
comprising the *Funeral March*, the two *Rhapsodies*
(for piano and orchestra and piano solo respectively),
and the two orchestral Suites (there is also a Symphony
belonging to this period which I have not had the
fortune to see), is throughout dominated by a specifically national mode of thought which is merely the
outcome of the exploitation of certain melodic or
rhythmic peculiarities of Hungarian folk-music. In
other words, the works of this early period definitely
belong to that movement which took rise towards the

194

end of the last century—itself one of the most important by-products of the Romantic movement—and
sought to base itself upon national sentiment and
racial idioms. It was at best a limited vein and one
which has been quickly worked out; indeed its
possibilities were practically exhausted by the initiators
themselves. Not unnaturally so, when we consider
that the greatest themes of art are common to all
nations. *Rien de plus cosmopolite que l'éternel.*[1]
Nationalism, even considered politically and socially,
is only a stage of evolution, beginning about the
fifteenth century and already giving place to a larger
conception. National sentiment to-day is almost as
artificial as the narrower form of local patriotism
connected with individual cities and districts. We no
longer think nationally, but continentally. Genuine
spontaneous racial sentiment can only exist to-day in
those countries which have held aloof, or have been
compelled to hold aloof for geographical reasons, from
the general trend of European thought and culture,
and it is only justifiable when the nation that pre-
serves its individuality does so with the profound
conviction that its ideal is nobler than that which the
cosmopolitan spirit suggests; otherwise it will be
a sterile and artificial cult as it is in England to-day.
The Hungarian nation, on the other hand, as early as
the fourteenth century under Louis the Great and
Matthias Hunyadi had already attained to a genuine
national consciousness long before any other European
country, and will probably be the last to lose it; and
practically all its art is the expression of a profoundly ingrained racial sentiment. Consequently we
find that these early works of Bartók take rank among
the finest products of the nationalist school, one of
them at least, the first Suite, being an exceptionally

[1] Or as Mr. Leigh Henry prefers to put it: 'The physiological
fundaments of human experience are similar everywhere.'

Béla Bartók

fine work. They are all youthful works in the best sense of the word ; not by reason of any immaturity of thought or hesitancy of expression, but on account of the unflagging exuberance and buoyancy which animate them from first note to last. Consummate musicianship such as that exhibited in the Suite seldom comes to a composer until the peculiar freshness and glow of his youthful conceptions have slightly faded.

As Bartók gains in individuality the national element in his work tends correspondingly to decrease, though it never altogether disappears. In the two *Portraits* for orchestra and the first string quartet the quality of his thought undergoes a profound change, becoming more personal and intimate, yet curiously enough at the same time more abstract and remote in another sense. The rich harmonic fabric and brilliance of orchestral effect which one notes in the Suite give place to a subtle and disembodied polyphonic texture and to delicate tenuous melodic outlines, the strenuous and full-blooded masculinity to a spiritual, almost mystical quality in which austerity and reticence are curiously blent with an exquisite sensitiveness and a grave, wistful tenderness and passion. Bartók may have equalled his first string quartet ; he has yet to surpass it.

Then follows an extraordinarily fertile period consisting of several sets of piano pieces, the only works of Bartók which are even relatively familiar to musicians. These pieces—i. e. the *Bagatelles* (Op. 6), the *Roumanian Dances, Burlesques, Elegies* (Op. 8), the *Esquisses* (Op. 9), the *Ten Easy Pieces*, and the four volumes of *Children's Pieces*, all written in and around the year 1908—are miniatures of exquisite beauty and rare originality. These are the pieces which have been wrongly considered to show a resemblance to Stravinsky. Although they give one the impression of being in large part mere sketches or studies for larger works, they possess, as sketches so often do, a fugitive charm, a delicate, wayward fragility, which elude analysis, and which a fuller development might possibly impair or even destroy altogether. While they are in a sense experiments, it would be a great mistake to regard them in the same light as the experiments of Stravinsky, which are, in the words of an admirer, 'objective investigations of the aural values of sound'. Bartók's pieces are precisely the opposite : are rather subjective investigations of the purely spiritual values of sound. They are not experiments in sonorities and dynamics, but studies in expression, which is a very different thing. Besides, it is as well to point out that they were written at a time when Stravinsky had done nothing worth mentioning, before he had written even the *Oiseau de feu*. If any question of influence arises, it is Bartók who influenced Stravinsky, and not, as most people think, the opposite. One only wishes he had influenced him more—Stravinsky might then have written better music.

In spite of their apparent simplicity and comparative freedom from technical difficulties, these pieces all demand a high level of interpretative ability. It is not sufficient merely to play the written notes ; the exact shade of nuance must be imparted to every note, otherwise the result will not sound convincing. No music is liable to lose so much as Bartók's at the hands of incompetent executants, for no amount of technical proficiency will avail if one does not possess a complete sympathy with and an insight into the composer's intentions. With only very few exceptions they are realizations of definite emotional states and intellectual conceptions, the best of them, such as the *Elegies*, being, for grandeur of conception and tragic intensity, unsurpassed in modern pianoforte music.

Beautiful though these pieces undoubtedly are, it would be a mistake to assume from them that Bartók,

Béla Bartók

like most of his contemporaries, is pre-eminently a miniaturist. He is, on the contrary, one of the few living composers who is capable of constructing works on a large scale ; and if we prefer to emphasize this aspect of his work, even if it should be at the expense of the other, it is partly because the piano pieces are comparatively familiar, but also because, to be perfectly frank, in these days of ' objective aural investigations ' lasting on an average half a minute each, one is apt to develop an alarming disposition to megalomania, even to the extent of supposing that a work lasting thirty minutes in performance, besides being the outcome of at least several months of anxious and constant thought, is *prima facie* of greater intrinsic significance than one lasting thirty seconds, written in the course of an afternoon—a reprehensible attitude, no doubt, but unavoidable. Consequently we prefer to regard the shorter pieces, in the main, as studies preparatory to the larger works which follow them, such as the *Images* for orchestra and the one-act opera, *Bluebeard's Castle*. They are strongly contrasted with each other, the first number of the former work in particular bearing very few traces of the nationalist proclivities of the composer, while the opera is permeated throughout by them, though more by the spirit than by the letter. The second of the *Images*, on the other hand, a *Danse Campagnarde*, is full of the idiomatic peculiarities of Hungarian music.

The opera is one of the most significant works produced by the nationalist spirit, and, like all the best of them, is profoundly tragic, for national art is always greatest when it is the fruit of tyranny and oppression, and when it is watered by blood and tears. Hungary is peculiarly fitted for the production of such an art, for she has the most sombre history of any European nation, except perhaps Ireland. In the European drama she has always been cast for a tragic role ; it

198

seems to be her destiny, from which she cannot escape. She is the Medea of the nations, a beautiful and sinister stranger, in Europe yet not of it, hated and oppressed by all alike, jealous and vindictive in her revenge, but always possessed of a curious attraction.

It is impossible not to see in the figure of Judith in Bartók's opera a kind of symbolic figure of Hungary, and not to feel that in the whole work there is an underlying allegory, however obscure its implications may seem to be. The music is of the most compelling and moving beauty in itself, besides being extraordinarily apt and closely wedded to the dramatic interest. The work is one of the most wholly satisfying solutions of the operatic problem in modern times. It differs from most modern operas, in that the voice parts are an intrinsic part of the musical structure and not merely superadded to the orchestral tissue. On the other hand, this vocal interest does not impoverish the latter, as it is so apt to do.

In this work Bartók would seem to have more or less exhausted the national side of his genius. Although it never entirely disappears, it tends to diminish in each successive work, and to become secondary where it was formerly essential. Looked at broadly, his whole artistic development is a progress from nationalism to complete individuality—or universality, if one prefers it. The most important works of this later period are the second String Quartet (Op. 17) and the two Sonatas for Violin and Piano. They are not in any sense restatements or recapitulations of his previous achievements, but constitute a wholly new departure. On the other hand, they are not mere interesting and stimulating experiments like so much modern music, or studies for future use. Whether one likes them or not, it is at least impossible to deny the absolute sureness and mastery with which they have been conceived and realized. There is nothing tentative, haphazard,

Béla Bartók

or indeterminate about them. Even when one is momentarily unable to grasp or follow his thought, one instinctively feels that the fault lies not in the work but in oneself. But such moments are comparatively few, and decrease in number with each successive hearing or reading. The difficulty with which an intelligent and sympathetic listener has to contend in these works is entirely conditioned by the strangeness or novelty of their harmonic idiom. It is a question of vocabulary, of language ; once we have taken the trouble to make ourselves acquainted with it, the fundamental simplicity and directness of the composer's thought become apparent.

The remarkable treatment of the instruments in the two sonatas is at once novel and wholly logical. It is self-evident that the inherent nature of the violin is so strongly opposed and even antagonistic to that of the pianoforte that the difficulties in the way of reconciling the two are almost insuperable. The combination of tone which they provide is never ideal, and apart from Mozart's there are very few violin and piano sonatas which are really satisfactory to listen to as pure sound, whatever their abstract musical content may be, which is another matter. An ideal unity of tone is generally only achieved through the subordination of one instrument to the other, or through the suppression of the fundamental characteristics of both alike. Recognizing this, Bartók has preferred to go to the opposite extreme. The essentially percussive and harmonic nature of the piano and the lyrical, sustained, singing capacities of the violin are accepted without any attempt at modification or compromise. The composer has preferred to accentuate and emphasize their differences rather than to disguise or partially conceal them. Each instrument is permitted to express its individuality in untrammelled freedom ; the thematic material is not interchanged, but remains distinct and proper to each. And yet, at the same time, strangely enough, from this conflict of two opposing personalities is engendered a fundamental unity and a mutual understanding. They reach the same goal in the end, though by different routes.

It is of Beethoven rather than of any other composer that one is involuntarily reminded in listening to these works. Not that they are in any sense derivative, despite the frequent formal similarity to the later string quartets and piano sonatas of Beethoven—the string quartet in particular so closely resembles the posthumous quartets of the master in form and style generally that it might almost seem to have been modelled on them : it is something more fundamental than that. Indeed, without implying any comparison of relative stature, it can be said that Bartók's mentality throughout all his work is closely akin to that of Beethoven, and the affinity becomes more striking with each successive work.

In a profound and illuminating comparison between Schiller and Shakespeare, Coleridge observes, in his *Table-Talk*, that the former ' has the Material Sublime ; to produce an effect he sets you a whole town on fire, and throws infants with their mothers into the flames, or locks up a father in an old tower. But Shakespeare drops a handkerchief and the same or greater effects follow.' This gift of investing the most unimportant and even trivial actions with a profound dramatic significance has its musical parallel in the art of Beethoven, and to a lesser degree in that of Bartók. In both composers we find the same rigid economy of means, the same intimate and reverent understanding of their material which transforms a quite commonplace phrase into the vehicle of a profound emotion. Both have a predilection for certain melodic figures and harmonic progressions which seem to possess a peculiar, almost esoteric

Béla Bartók

signification. These *motifs* recur constantly throughout Bartók's music, and, by virtue of some secret affinity
or association of ideas, seem to correspond to some
definite ulterior purpose—some preconceived idea
which for lack of any better word has sometimes been
misleadingly termed 'poetic'. An example of this is
to be found in the sequence of notes D, F sharp, A,
C sharp, with which the *Dedication* to the *Ten Easy
Pieces* opens. The same phrase recurs integrally in
both of the *Portraits* for orchestra and also in No. 13
of the *Bagatelles*, bearing the sub-title *Elle est morte*.
Things such as these, and titles like 'En pleine fleur'
(*Images*), 'Un peu gris' (*Burlesques*), must not be regarded as explanatory or indicative of any programmatic
basis of a literary or pictorial nature. Bartók is above
all, to a greater extent perhaps than almost anyone else
at present writing, a pure musician, in whose work,
with only a few rare exceptions, it is impossible to
discern anything which demands or requires any com-
mentary or elucidation, or which even implies the
slightest connexion with anything outside itself.
Such things belong wholly to the domain of music.
It is the programme music of the soul—the record of
subjective psychological experiences. As Gautier said
of Berlioz, it is 'l'art hiéroglyphique, escarpé, où l'on
n'entre pas comme chez soi'. Bartók's very occasional
obscurity, which is heightened rather than diminished
by the almost disconcerting lucidity and directness of
his style, strikes me as being only the result of this
attempt to communicate some fugitive spiritual experience which continues to elude the cold inadequacy
of the written note.

The pre-eminently arresting quality which the
examination of Bartók's works instantly reveals, and
one which distinguishes him sharply from his contemporaries, is that he has no set and invariable method
of procedure, no fixed and determinate style. He

employs no outworn *clichés*, whether of the academies or of the modern Franco-Russian academy, neither is he, as Arnold Schönberg occasionally is, a slave to his own individual mannerisms or idiosyncrasies. It would be more accurate to say that when he does make use of them they cease to be *clichés*. He possesses that rare quality of mind which illuminates everything it touches, transforming it into something rich and strange. At one moment he is writing a melody which no more tolerates harmonic support than a *pur sang* folk-song or plain chant ; at another constructing an harmonic tissue of great subtlety and complexity. He is a master in the art of weaving rich and varied sonorities into an elaborate yet closely-knit orchestral web of dazzling brilliance and grace ; yet when the occasion demands he is equally capable of the most exquisitely wrought polyphonic texture revealing an austerity and restraint as impressive as they are rare. In short, he is a master of expression, yet he has made each method his own. All this catholicity of style results in an utterance quite unusually individual, because it is at the service of a rich and masterful personality. His originality is the outcome of inclusiveness, not of exclusiveness ; it is not one of these delicate hothouse plants, consciously cultivated and jealously sheltered lest the slightest breath of wind from the outside world should wither its precious and anaemic blossoms. Bartók is a fine stylist precisely because he has no style. His utterance is moulded by the particular conception which he desires to realize. He seeks only the exact registration of his thought, nothing more nor less. He is in fact a musical exponent of the *mot juste*—the doctrine taught and practised in literature by Gustave Flaubert, prince of stylists (and of Stylites) half a century ago. ' Le style n'est qu'une manière de penser ; plus une idée est belle, plus la phrase est sonore. La précision de la pensée fait celle du mot—si vous saviez

Béla Bartók

précisément ce que vous voulez dire, vous le diriez bien.'
And if we examine or analyse any work of Bartók we
shall find that a large part of its elusive and wholly
characteristic charm resides in its expressive purpose,
in an indefinable quality of thought behind the notes,
as it were. It would be difficult to find a clearer or
a more convincing demonstration of the truth that in
music, as in any other art, beauty is only relative,
depending upon and resulting from the relativity
between the symbol and its expressive purpose.

It is a very significant fact that the composers who
have contributed most to the extension and development of musical idiom and resources are those whose
sole aim was expression—Monteverde, Beethoven,
Berlioz, Liszt, and Wagner. All ' discoveries ' in
music, all new directions and possibilities, are invariably due to those composers who have had a definite
expressive intention ; they are always the direct
outcome of the need to express some thought or
conception never before expressed, and never by any
chance the result of tonal empiricism, of playing
about with sound for sound's sake. And while it is
the easiest thing in the world to make pleasant sounds
—an occupation unworthy of the attention of an
intelligent man—to think in sounds as clearly, as
faultlessly, as inevitably, as logically as in words,
demands a greater power of concentration and strength
of purpose, a higher degree of purely cerebral power,
than almost any other human activity. To be a
musician one must be either a genius or an idiot—
an unassailable if somewhat depressing truth.

It is equally true that a quite insignificant and
second-rate work will often sound superficially plea-
santer than a great masterpiece. In order to be
expressive a composer must frequently sacrifice sensuous beauty; he cannot have it both ways. He must
be either an Antony or a Saint Anthony. It is no mere

coincidence, but one of those mysterious paradoxes which conceal a profound and living truth, that the greatest of all musicians, the Musician incarnate, should have accomplished his greatest work when he was no longer capable of distinguishing one note from another. Beethoven's deafness is symbolical of what should be the musician's attitude towards his art.

Enough has surely been said to show that in this respect at least, Bartók stands at the very opposite pole from Stravinsky and his school.

By gradually eliminating in the successive stages of his artistic development everything that hinders or does not directly serve his expressive purpose, Bartók has actually arrived at this simplification which we hear so much about but so very seldom encounter in the practice of those who are loudest in its praises. What generally passes for simplification is generally nothing more than conventionalization, which consists in reducing organic forms to a kind of mechanical, lifeless, wall-paper pattern. That there is a danger attendant on the ruthless elimination of unessentials, on this uncompromising attitude towards all the conventions which have governed music, has always been apparent. Art being, after all, something more than Benedetto Croce's ' successful expression ', there is always a danger of boiling down and refining away one's utterance to the point at which the elusive and ethereal element which makes it a work of art has evaporated into thin air, leaving nothing behind it. There certainly is a point, exceedingly difficult to define or to detect in practice, beyond which it is impossible to go without swiftly and suddenly vanishing away like the unfortunate baker in Lewis Carroll's *Hunting of the Snark*. But it is remarkable how seldom Bartók oversteps this limit. On the other hand, Schönberg's set of six piano pieces (Op. 19) is a warning example of a failure of this kind.

Béla Bartók

On a first and superficial acquaintance, accustomed as we all are to the flatulent and plethoric redundance of most modern music, Bartók's music may perhaps appear bare, harsh, and crabbed to some, even to the verge of childishness. It is only after a time that we begin to recognize and to appreciate the subtlety and unobtrusive artistry which inform it. There are indeed few parallels in music, of any period, to this affecting simplicity and directness, frequently more incomprehensible to the average musician than the most apparently complex musical structure, for he has so long had the habit of accepting the symbol for the reality and the image for the god that he is baffled and disconcerted by this deliberate rejection of everything that he had hitherto deemed essential. Bartók is an iconoclast, in the true sense of the word—a breaker of images. He has freed his music from the tyrannic conventions of musicianship which are in reality its negation—all the superfluous counterpoints, meaningless figurations, and other familiar forms of *remplissage* which, like a kind of elephantiasis, have so long inhibited native freedom of expression. He has had the courage to throw off all the vast hampering accretions of musical convention, the parasitic accumulation of centuries—the musician's fatal legacy from the past—and has discovered a fresh enchantment in that ultimate sincerity which is for ever done with eloquence and rhetoric.

Bartók is not afraid to appear crude or uncouth, because he knows well enough the value of what he says. It is only the composer who distrusts himself, and doubts the intrinsic worth of his ideas, who overlays his work with superfluous and irrelevant accessories in the vain attempt to conceal its hollow emptiness. As a generalization one may confidently assert that the better a composer knows what he wants, the simpler his style will be, and *vice versa.*

Béla Bartók

The Greeks used to believe that the man who would not show himself must necessarily have some physical defect. The characteristic maladies of the musician are gymnophobia and agoraphobia ; the fear of nakedness and of empty spaces.

Contrary to the generally accepted belief, the most significant of the younger generation of living composers—Schönberg, van Dieren, and Bartók—are primarily melodists. In the music of older masters, Delius for example, one constantly feels that harmonic considerations are paramount and tend to impoverish the melodic interest. One can conceive the possibility of a work of Delius still retaining the major element of its charm even if every trace of melodic line were omitted. With Bartók it is the very opposite ; it is the harmony which has no independent existence, and the melodic element which predominates. He employs harmony mainly in order to underline and bring into higher relief the salient characteristics of the melodic phrase. In one of the *Ten Easy Pieces* he harmonizes the melody with a single chord on different degrees of the scale ; in another he uses no harmony at all.

Bartók is in a sense a Romantic, though many of the more superficial aspects of romanticism are not to be found in him. His romanticism is purged of the besetting sins of over-emphasis and exaggeration. Expressing it figuratively one could say that his music comes from the heart, which, however, he does not wear on his sleeve, in his boots, or in his mouth. He bears much the same relation to the Romantic school that post-Impressionists bear to Manet, Pissarro, and Monet. In fact one might define him as a post-Expressionist. He has not the same nostalgic yearning or *Weltschmerz* which is perhaps the most characteristic element in all the best art of the past generation, and which has attained such perfect expression in the work of Delius, Verlaine, Yeats, and others too numerous to

Béla Bartók

mention. On the contrary, Bartók possesses at times an heroic strength and virility which had almost lapsed from music altogether of recent years.

However much opinion may differ concerning the relative stature and significance of modern composers, there is one characteristic common to almost all which cannot have escaped the notice of any impartial and discriminating observer, namely, the lack of staying-power, the inability to develop and progress steadily from work to work. By the time they have reached the age at which they ought to be at the summit of their powers, they have no longer anything fresh to say. There are practically no exceptions to this melancholy rule. The later work of Debussy is universally recognized to be markedly inferior to that of his earlier period; Strauss's most fervent admirers are reluctantly compelled to admit that it is impossible to expect anything more from him; Ravel's talent has similarly deteriorated with quite alarming rapidity; Schönberg, for the time being at least, seems to have lost himself completely; and ever since the *Sacre du Printemps* Stravinsky's course of development has been a continual and unrelieved decline. Everywhere it is the same story of premature exhaustion and impotence. Modern musicians like the gods in *Das Rheingold*, deprived of the golden apples of Freya, the life-giving fruits of tradition, seem to have suddenly taken on an aged and withered aspect. It certainly provides food for thought that practically the only composer of the present day who is still progressing —not merely in the narrow sense of idiomatic novelty but in the true sense of spiritual depth and expressive power—should be so akin to the great composer who, more than any other, is despised and rejected by the so-called advanced musicians of to-day—Beethoven.

If I have concentrated, perhaps unduly, on this one particular aspect of Bartók's mentality throughout this

208

essay, it is because it seems to me to be that which is responsible for all that is best in his music. But it would be idle to dispute that he is at the same time a child of his age, and consequently partakes of both its qualities and defects. There is a definite conflict in his art between his simple, profound, and Beethovenian nature and the nervous exasperation and feverish restlessness which are so typical of the modern spirit. Whether the strength of the former will preserve him from the fate which has hitherto overtaken all other sufferers from the latter complaints, it is perhaps too early to say yet, for both elements tend to develop and gain in strength in each successive work. Greatly though one admires the second string quartet and the violin sonatas, one cannot help noticing in them a certain lack of harmonious balance and equipoise—an almost frightening brutality and explosive violence which do not compare favourably with the serenity and self-mastery of the first quartet, which is perhaps the highest point to which Bartók has ever attained. Together with this one observes a tendency towards a hardening and formularization of his harmonic idiom—a characteristically modern fault which, as we have seen, is conspicuously absent from his previous work. His fondness for dissonance of the most aggravated type, as exemplified particularly in the second violin sonata, seems to be in danger of mastering him altogether, and becoming an obsession, as it has with Schönberg. Consequently his immediate future will be watched with sympathy and interest, but not without a certain measure of anxiety. In my opinion he is one of the very few figures of the present time from whom much can still reasonably be expected.

FERRUCCIO BUSONI

THERE is probably no composer living concerning whom there exists a greater diversity of enlightened opinion than Ferruccio Busoni. Outside the limited and exclusive circle of his admirers and disciples it is virtually impossible to find two people of precisely the same mind about him, which is all the more singular for the remarkable unanimity with which he is accepted as a pianist. Some indeed have even suggested that it is precisely his reputation and standing as an executant that has prejudiced his claim to be regarded as a creative artist. But it is difficult to see why this should be so, in view of the fact that Bach, Beethoven, Mozart, Chopin, and indeed almost every composer of the first rank, except Berlioz and Wagner, were among the greatest executants of their times. Besides, is it not universally believed that everyone composes at the piano? Berlioz, it will be remembered, recounts in his *Mémoires* how he was arrested as a spy at Nice by the local gendarmerie because he was always to be seen wandering about the seashore making notes in an album. ‘Je sais très bien, monsieur, qu’on ne compose ainsi de la musique sans piano, seulement avec un album et un crayon, en marchant silencieusement sur les grèves.’

It is, as a matter of fact, much easier to understand how it is that a great composer such as Berlioz should be incapable of playing a note on the piano than to explain how an indisputably great pianist like Busoni should not be an equally great composer. The line which separates creation from interpretation is a very fine one, and difficult to draw. The ability to recreate a great masterpiece, to be able to enter so deeply into the mind of its composer as to play it as he intended it to be played, necessarily presumes the possession of a faculty of comprehension not far short of his, even if it is of a slightly different order, which is by no means certain.

What is certain, however, is that the constant necessity of identifying oneself with the minds of other composers is apt to conflict with the growth of a definite personality of one's own, and to generate a certain eclecticism of outlook, as it did in Liszt. But whereas Liszt's mentality always seems somewhat immature and elementary—a kind of synthesis of Byron, Hugo, de Musset, Delacroix, Paganini, Chopin, Meyerbeer, and others—his style was to a great extent his own. Indeed, it is doubtful if any composer has ever been responsible for more idiomatic innovations with the exception of Monteverde. Liszt is one of the most potent influences for good and bad in the history of music. Busoni, on the contrary, possesses a mentality wholly distinct from that of his age and surroundings and even antagonistic to them ; at the same time he seems to have innovated nothing. In an age in which every composer considers it essential to evolve a personal style unlike that of anyone else, Busoni's work alone presents no individual features whatsoever by which we may recognize it and distinguish it. Liszt in his piano-playing, as far as we can gather from contemporary descriptions, identified himself completely with the composer's intentions, though sometimes magnifying them into something much more impressive than they actually were. Busoni, on the other hand, seems often to make of a work something quite different from what the composer intended. In fact he presents the curiously paradoxical contradiction of being creative in his piano-

Ferruccio Busoni

playing and reproductive in his music ; a personality
is more discernible and recognizable in the executant
than in the composer.

It would be difficult to say whether this impression
which I receive is only the result of his not possessing
a personal style, or whether it is that he has not
so far succeeded in realizing his intentions. I am
inclined to the latter view, for a strong and dominant
personality such as that of Busoni should have no
difficulty in making itself felt even through the
medium of a more or less impersonal style. Besides,
this lack of characteristic features and mannerisms is
only in accordance with his aesthetic aims. Busoni
believes, and probably with reason, that the era of
experimentalism and individualism is rapidly drawing
to a close ; that the near future will witness a renaissance of classicism and the formation of a determinate
and constant style, based upon all that is most fruitful
and enduring in both ancient and modern practice.
In a very significant and instructive passage in an essay
called *Selbst-Rezension*, he thus contrasts his own art
with that of Debussy ; the latter's music ' implies
restriction, as if one were to delete certain letters from
the alphabet, and, in the manner of scholastic diver-
sions, were to construct poems without making use
of the letters A or R ; my aim is the enrichment, the
extension, and the broadening of means of expression.
Debussy's music expresses the most contrasted emotions and situations by means of similar formulas ;
I attempt to find different and contrasted expressions
for the same ideas. Debussy's tone-pictures are
parallel and homophonic ; mine aim at being polyphonic and multiversal. I feel myself to be a beginning ; Debussy is an end.' In order to achieve this
synthetic style he has not only successfully assimilated,
as very few living composers have, the vast legacy of
the past, and reconciled such seemingly contradictory

Ferruccio Busoni

personalities as Bach, Beethoven, Liszt, Chopin, and Brahms in the piano concerto with choral finale which is one of his best works, but he has also set himself to acquire whatever seemed to him of value in the work of his contemporaries ; even from very much younger men than himself he has not been ashamed to learn. In his *Nuit de Noël* we find him at school with Debussy, and in the second sonatina there are manifold traces of the influence of van Dieren and, to a certain extent, of Schönberg also. Finally all these contradictory influences, together with those of Rossini, Verdi, and even Offenbach, are brought together in the gigantic and decidedly monstrous opera, *Die Brautwahl*—one of the most baffling and incoherent works of modern times, though undeniably the production of a remarkably powerful intellect.

But it is not only his catholicity and eclecticism of style which differentiate him from almost all modern composers, but his whole attitude towards his art. While Stravinsky is reported to have said that ' I should like to bring it about that music be performed in street-cars, while people get in and out ', Busoni regards music as something which should be kept apart from daily life. ' Music is the most aloof and secret of the arts. An atmosphere of solemnity and sanctity should surround it. Admission to a musical performance should partake of the ceremonial and mystery of a freemason ritual. The first thing that is necessary is to reduce the opportunities of hearing music.'

His attitude towards the instruments of the orchestra is also diametrically opposed to that of most of his contemporaries. While they aim at writing for them with a definite and almost obsequious regard for their individual capacities and limitations, Busoni aims at their *Entindividualisierung,* i. e. the destruction or at least the minimization of their distinctive charac-

Ferruccio Busoni

teristics by writing for them *gegen ihre Natur*, as means to the expression of abstract musical ideas which are independent of any particular tone-quality. This tendency to abstraction is very marked in Busoni's music and in his aesthetic theorizings. He denies that music can be divided into categories, such as dramatic, religious, concert, or any other similarly specialized form of music (see, for example, his *Entwurf eines Vorwortes zur Partitur des 'Doktor Faust '*). For him there is only music ; if it is good it will be equally appropriate under any circumstances and in any surroundings, and arranged for any instrumental combination. If it is in essence bad, nothing can possibly save it, or disguise its character.

It is largely this antagonistic attitude towards the ideals and aspirations of his age, and the discrepancy between his derivative style and his intensely individual mentality, that are responsible for the greater part of the uneasiness and perplexity which his music almost invariably arouses. It is so very much easier to appreciate a new idiom than a strange personality. The most popular music is always that which says in a novel and arresting manner something to which we are accustomed, which has already been said before, or which only expresses what we ourselves are feeling and thinking. Such is the music of Stravinsky. On the other hand nothing disconcerts an audience more than the art which says something quite new and personal in a familiar idiom. A novel idiom can be readily grasped and appreciated in the course of a few hearings, an unfamiliar and original mind only with great difficulty and sometimes, if it is at all uncongenial to one's own, not at all.

And Busoni's mind, it must be admitted, is not exactly distinguished by its accessibility, or by the easy geniality with which one is there welcomed when one has at last, after many painful efforts, succeeded in entering into it. While the minds of most contemporary artists are like inns into which the host effusively invites all to enter who are passing by, Busoni's mind is like a castle standing in a remote and unfrequented spot, the path to which is hard to find and steep to climb. It is surrounded by a deep moat, and the only means of admission is across a drawbridge, which is reluctantly lowered only to those who succeed in satisfying the owner concerning their credentials, the purpose of their visit, and the probable length of their stay. He himself never comes forward to receive his infrequent and uninvited guests, unless indeed he is the disagreeable and sharp-tongued individual, dressed as a Harlequin and wearing a mask which effectively conceals his features, who accosts us in the entrance hall; otherwise one only meets with people who seem to bear a striking resemblance to others whom we have previously known and met elsewhere. We advance to meet them with out-stretched hand and affable greeting, but are cut short by a haughty and disdainful glance, and realizing our mistake we murmur a confused apology, and pass on. All around the walls are brusque and offensive notices concerning the conduct we must observe if our unsought-for presence is to be tolerated. We are reminded that we must wipe our shoes before enter-ing, that it is ungentlemanly to spit on the floor, together with sundry other admonishments of a similar nature, all testifying to the poor opinion our unwilling host entertains concerning us, and per-petually reminding us that we are on no account to make ourselves comfortable and at home. Finally, we take our departure slightly dispirited, without having seen or even caught a fleeting glimpse of anything which might have made amends for the discomforts we have endured or have justified the inhospit-able treatment we have received. And yet in spite

of it all, at the back of our mind there still
lurks the conviction that there must be something
more there than we have been able to see; that all
this mysterious and impressive exterior must conceal
some rare and precious secret; that possibly we had
chosen an unlucky occasion for our visit. We promise
ourselves to make another call some other time, when
we may be fortunate enough to find the host at home,
affably disposed, and see some of the priceless treasures
of which we have heard so much. But our experience
is always the same. There are a few people here and
there, it is true, who claim to have had quite different
experiences; to have been received courteously and
conducted personally by their host through all his
treasure vaults, and to have seen all manner of strange
and miraculous things. But somehow we are not convinced; their descriptions, though enthusiastic enough,
lack substantiality, definiteness, and reality. We are
inclined to doubt if after all they have really seen any
more than we have ourselves, and to suspect that they
are either more credulous and easily imposed upon, or
else only desire to give us an impression of their
superiority. For they are never by any chance the
sort of people one would most expect to have had the
experiences which they recount, to whom such a *grand
seigneur* would unbend, and in whom he would confide.
They are, to speak quite frankly, generally persons of
a markedly inferior order of mentality. Indeed, the
parasitus busonianus is quite a species apart from all
others, deserving of the closest investigation in the
interests of science. See, for example, the biography
of Frau Gisella Selden-Goth, recently published. The
frenzied adoration with which these good people regard
even the smallest and least important activity of their
cherished idol reminds one of those Zulu courtiers of
the great Cetewayo, who, at their chief's slightest
movement, burst into a rapturous chorus, proclaiming

to the whole world the important information that
' The Great Zulu is eating a coco-nut ', or ' The
Great Zulu has just scratched his left ear '.

Now, there can be little doubt in the mind of any
intelligent musician that Busoni is a great Zulu—
a very great and super-eminent Zulu ; yet the fact
remains that the general feeling concerning his work
is one of respectful bewilderment, not unmixed with
a certain leaven of irritation. What is it then that,
with all its admirable qualities, his art lacks ? That
there is something wanting is certain ; he himself
shows that he is thoroughly conscious of the fact in
both his writings and conversation. But this indefinable something he hopes some day to acquire. He
reminds one strongly of Balthazar Claes, the old
alchemist in *La Recherche de l'Absolu* of Balzac, seeking endlessly, insatiably, indefatigably for some artistic
philosopher's stone ; some formula which will inevitably produce the *magnum opus* of which he dreams.
It seems always within reach, and yet constantly
eludes him. He seeks it in abstract theories regarding
the nature of art, in the analysis of the practice of
those greatest of all alchemists, Bach and Mozart, who
seem indeed to have discovered the great secret
enabling them to transform base metals into pure gold
and commonplace materials into things of eternal
beauty. And always he is certain that he has at last
discovered the formula ; always it is the next work
that will be the masterpiece so long and so eagerly
awaited. And in his new project for a Faust music-
drama, divulged in his recently published pamphlet,
he has so surely discovered the formula for a great
work—if such a formula exists—that one is almost
tempted to believe, and certainly to hope, that this
tireless and indomitable seeker has at last found the
goal for which he has so long been striving.

But up to the present there is no concealing the fact

Ferruccio Busoni

that Busoni's actual tangible achievement is very disappointing. A composer who has not succeeded in finding himself by the time he is fifty years old is very unlikely to do so at all. Everywhere in his music one finds great qualities—striking and original conceptions, gigantic technical resource—yet one is never wholly satisfied by any single work. It is in the mental process which intervenes between the conception and the execution of a work that Busoni would seem to fail—in the embodiment of the abstract idea in musical flesh, as it were. There is a lack of distinction about the musical material of his buildings ; one does not feel that any discrimination has been exercised by the composer in its choice—whether deliberately or through a lack of the critical faculty, it is impossible to say. It is at least certain that his most impressive works, and those which come nearest to being successful, are those which are built out of the musical material of others ; such are the *Fantasia Contrappuntistica*, the *Indianische Fantasie, Variations*, and *Bearbeitungen* generally. He is a master-builder to whom could be confided the execution of the most difficult tasks and gigantic conceptions, provided they have already been put on paper by the architect. He is like one of the genies or efrits in the *Arabian Nights* who are capable of executing the most tremendous and impossible tasks that are given to them, but who are only the slaves of anyone who possesses the magic talisman ; he is like the Cyclops, the workmen of the gods, but not themselves gods, nor yet mere mortals.

What is the essential quality that, up to the present, we miss in all his music ? Is it his total lack of *naïveté* and spontaneity ? It is true that most great artists have possessed them, but there are a few who have not—Leonardo da Vinci and Gustave Flaubert, for example. Is it his lack of sensuous appeal ? There is little sensuous appeal in a great part of Bach, in the later quartets of Beethoven, in the art of Mantegna or in the novels of Stendhal. Is it his lack of directness and charm, the absence of the ingratiating aspect of novelty, is it his somewhat forbidding intellectualism? But these are all defects—if indeed they are necessarily defects—which can be found in the work of many supreme masters.

The correct answer, I think, is that Busoni's music lacks what for want of a better word we may call ecstasy—not using it, however, in the narrower sense, denoting the frenzied and almost sexual emotionalism of Scriabine's *Poème de l'Extase*, but in the widest and most general sense possible. There are many different varieties of ecstasy, ranging from the sensual ecstasy of Rossetti or Swinburne to the purely intellectual ecstasy of Spinoza or John Donne. But in one form or another it is the very stuff of all poesy, of all art, of all fine thought even. There can be no great art without it, whatever other qualities one may possess. Joubert's celebrated dictum that nothing is poetry which does not transport, is equally true of music. And Busoni's music just lacks that indefinable sense of 'lift'. In listening to the music of his *Brautwahl* I was irresistibly reminded of an aviation meeting which took place in the early experimental days of flying. On a bare inspection of the competing machines, the most impressive of all was certainly that of Colonel Cody; a gigantic machine slightly reminiscent of the drawings of Mr. Heath Robinson, beside which the others looked like mere childish toys. But it possessed one serious disadvantage which its unfortunate inventor could never overcome; it could not fly. It ran along the ground beautifully, but never quite succeeded in leaving it. And all Busoni's vast cyclopean constructions never manage to leave the ground, while on the other hand the infinitely less impressive-looking apparatus of a Delius or a Bartók soars away into the

Ferruccio Busoni

air like a bird without any seeming effort or difficulty. At times Busoni would seem to be the Don Quixote of music, and the Pegasus on whose back he fondly imagines he is soaring in the clouds is only the wooden horse with its feet firmly planted all the time on the ground. But such is his earnestness, conviction, and sincerity that there will always be a few Sancho Panzas amongst us who are ready to believe that he has actually flown, and who will even imagine that they themselves have shared in the experience.

BERNARD VAN DIEREN

PROBABLY no experience is more profoundly depressing than a vain attempt to try to convince a musician of the existence of qualities which one clearly perceives and deeply feels in a work of art. As in a dream, all one's shoutings and ravings seem to fall on deaf ears, and the louder one yells, the less one seems to be noticed. In calmer moments one realizes that conversion cannot come from without, that it is impossible to make anyone feel the presence of genius by means of arguments, however irrefutable, or by dialectics however skilful; yet such is the strength of one's appreciation and the force of one's conviction that one inevitably experiences an almost physical need for some kind of proselytizing activity, a quite insane desire to convert others to one's way of thinking. Why this should be so it is impossible to imagine. When we have discovered a pleasant spot in some wood remote from civilization, we do not immediately feel it incumbent upon us to tell every charabanc party we meet about it, or to implore them earnestly to come and join us there the next day, and to be sure on no account to forget to bring a few babies and concertinas with them. Yet why, when we have ' discovered ' some poet, painter, or musician, do we refuse ourselves any rest until we have effectively succeeded in popularizing and vulgarizing him? For there can be no question but that a work of art suffers from the contamination of an ignorant and unsympathetic audience. How much better for every one concerned, how much wiser altogether, simply to say nothing about it, and so far from informing others of the treasure we have found, to guard it jealously

Bernard van Dieren

in a cave, like Fafnir, until it is forcibly taken from us ! Yet for some reason or other this course does not seem to be possible. It seems inevitable that we should continue to shout and rave, knowing all the time that no one will listen who is not disposed to do so.

These philosophic reflections are the outcome of the effort on my part to induce others to recognize and appreciate the admirable qualities which I believe myself to have perceived in the music of Bernard van Dieren. My comparative failure to do so has, however, in no way served to modify my firm conviction that he is not only one of the few composers of the present day whose achievement is intrinsically of great value, but also one who is destined to exercise a profound influence in the future.

In itself it is not at all surprising—rather the reverse, in fact—that his work should have so signally failed to receive the attention which it merits. In the first place, such performances as his works have received, both in England and in Germany, have generally, on account of insufficient rehearsals and imperfect understanding on the part of the executants, been of such a kind as to preclude even the most intelligent and sympathetic listener from making anything of the music. In the second place, practically all his work still remains unpublished, largely on account of the unsatisfactory nature of these performances, but also partly because the composer has never tried to hawk his wares round all the capitals of Europe in the approved modern manner. He has no talent for self-advertisement, and is consequently ignored. Thirdly, and probably most important of all, there can be no question whatever that it is not an art which stands the smallest chance of ever becoming popular. At best it can only hope to attract a very few. Nevertheless, only these few really matter. Let us suppose,

Bernard van Dieren

says Villiers de L'Isle Adam in one of his satiric masterpieces, that 200 people are gathered together in one
room, and that you utter aloud the name of Milton.
' There is good reason to believe that out of this 200,
198 will certainly never have read him, and only the
great Architect of the Universe Himself can say in
what way the other two will imagine they have read
him, seeing that there are not on the whole surface
of the terraqueous globe more than 100 individuals
in a century who are capable of reading anything at
all, even the labels on mustard pots.' Yet they will
all affirm stoutly that Milton was a great poet.

An exaggeration, it may be said. Admittedly, but
the exaggeration is one of language, not of thought.
It is undeniable that the vast proportion of the public
are content to accept unquestioningly the opinions
of those whom they believe, rightly or wrongly, to
possess a higher degree of knowledge and a keener
critical sense than themselves. Actually there is no
such thing as the verdict of posterity ; it is a mere
abstraction. What we are accustomed to call by that
name is simply the standards of good and bad which
are imposed and maintained by a few people in every
age, by dint of their constant and unremitting exer-
tions and the force and sincerity of their convictions.
The only object in writing this essay is to make known
to these few the existence of the music of van Dieren ;
the rest can be safely left to them. Its instantaneous
recognition and eventual popularity are alike out of
the question.

Although van Dieren's output may perhaps seem
small in comparison with that of most other composers, it consists for the most part of large and
significant works which do not merely mark progressive stages in the evolution of a single line of
development or of a restricted circle of conceptions,
but are each the final expression and perfected

223

outcome of a whole train of thought. Once the work is written which best embodies that particular conception, he is finished with it ; he is not content like most to go on repeating in slightly varied terms what he has already said. Each work differs both in aim and conception from every other one ; consequently it is impossible to sum up his art in any comprehensive formula or trite generalization, or to reduce all his works to a common denominator. They must first be considered separately ; only afterwards will it be possible to indicate a few of their more important and clearly definable characteristics or highest common factors.

It is unnecessary to devote much time or space—the two dominant realities of both metaphysics and journalism—to a consideration of the early works, such as the setting of Heine's *Belsazar* for baritone and orchestra, the *Elegy* for violoncello and orchestra, and the *Symphonic Epilogue* to Shelley's *Cenci* for large orchestra, because, whatever their merits or failings, they are not, except for occasional isolated passages, characteristic of the composer's subsequent development. Indeed, the qualities which they exhibit are the exact opposite of those which are dominant in his later works. It is worthy of note, however, that although they are in no sense representative, they are surprisingly different from any other music. Unlike the immature works of most other composers, there is no trace of any outside influence whatever. It would be difficult to think of another instance of this in music except Berlioz, with whose early works these of van Dieren possess a certain affinity, particularly in the manner of handling the orchestra, though in actual substance there is very little resemblance between them. They are certainly not masterpieces such as the *Fantastic Symphony* or even the *Francs Juges* overture.

Bernard van Dieren

The *Sketches* for piano—the only work of van Dieren's which has hitherto been published—are already quite different, although they are separated from the previously mentioned works by only a very brief period of time. They consist of six pieces of strongly contrasted character, which nevertheless bear a definite relation to each other, revealed in the last of the set, an epilogue, in which the principal subject of the initial piece is in turn combined with those of each of its successors—a formal conception as original and striking as it is logically satisfying. It is a device which under varying guises constantly recurs in later works, never failing to impart to them a unity and cohesion, together with a sense of intellectual as opposed to purely emotional and physical climax, which is one of the most noteworthy characteristics of all his music. Incidentally one might observe that anything less 'sketchy' than these pieces cannot be imagined. One is probably not far wrong in ascribing the choice of title to a deliberately misleading ironic intention.

The *Toccata*, also for piano, and belonging approximately to the same period, is a work of a totally different character. To this the name is highly appropriate, for it is in the nature of an improvisation, possessing no form in the accepted sense of the word, i. e. of pattern. It is written entirely without bars ; there are no leading themes, no repetition of melodic or harmonic motives even, each phrase evolving naturally and inevitably out of that which preceded it, as in a piece of well-constructed prose.

The First String Quartet, Op. 5, dedicated to the memory of Niccolo Paganini, is perhaps the most difficult of all van Dieren's works, from the point of view of both the listener and the executants, each of whom must not only be a master of his instrument, but a consummate musician in the wider sense of the word. It also is written throughout without bars, each instrument being treated with the utmost independence and plasticity. It consists of three movements playing without a break, in the course of which are introduced three *capricci* of Paganini; the slow movement in particular is of great melodic beauty.

The next large work, Op. 6, is a Symphony for five solo voices, chorus, and orchestra, based upon Chinese poems translated into German by Hans Bethge. With the exception of a few songs, it is the first work in which van Dieren attains to complete individuality of utterance. In the earlier compositions which we have been discussing, one is certainly conscious of a distinctive personality, but in a slightly more negative way; by the process of elimination one eventually arrives at the conclusion that no one else could ever possibly have written them, although certain phrases taken in isolation might quite conceivably have occurred elsewhere. Harmonically, for example, there is a superficial similarity between the piano pieces and certain works of Arnold Schönberg, although van Dieren was at the time of writing them entirely unacquainted with the music of the Austrian master. In the *Chinese Symphony*, on the other hand, and in all the succeeding works, the individuality is quite positive; not making itself felt by sheer force of personality through the medium of a traditional or derivative style—cumulatively, so to speak—but revealing itself unmistakably even in the smallest and apparently most insignificant details.

The Symphony is incidentally noteworthy for being one of the few works—perhaps the only one—based upon Oriental poems which do not seek to convey the ' barbaric splendour ' or ' languorous sensuality ' of the East by means of large batteries of exotic percussion instruments, whole-tone scales, or monotonous pentatonic melodies—in a word, by means of

all these worn-out orchestral ' properties ' collectively
designated by the name of local colour. The composer has considered it of greater importance to
re-create in the music the essential signification of
the poems, their deep universal and human appeal,
than merely to proclaim their geographical origin.

Although I cannot claim to be able thoroughly to
grasp and appreciate all the subtleties of such a complex and intricate score without having heard it
performed, in spite even of certain passages which,
on paper at least, seem to me to be somewhat obscure,
I have not the slightest hesitation in placing it with
the few consummate achievements of modern music.
Certainly van Dieren himself has done nothing better.

The Overture, Op. 7, was conceived and in large
part executed before the Symphony, but was not
actually finished till some time after. It is written
for a combination of sixteen solo instruments and
constitutes a revelation of what can be accomplished
by so-called limited means. While it is not in any
sense ' programme music ', it may be understood as
the overture to an imaginary comedy playing in Italy
at the time of Carnival. This is sufficient to explain
—for the benefit of those who need explanations—
the frequent alternations of boisterous and irresponsible merriment with a vein of tenderly ironical
amorousness. The entire work is filled with an
entirely Latin gaiety and exuberance like that which
animates the novels of Boccaccio, Bandello, and
Sacchetti, and the ancient *Commedia dell'Arte*.

While the Overture might be said to be written for
a miniature orchestra, the *Diaphony*, Op. 8, built
around settings of three Shakespeare sonnets, is rather
an extension of the principles of chamber-music,
although actually it employs a slightly larger number
of instruments. In other words, it aims primarily
at development and contrast of line, colouristic

Bernard van Dieren

considerations being only of secondary importance. It is probably the first large composition since the time of Bach to be conceived and written almost entirely in the old contrapuntal forms (using the word ' contrapuntal ' strictly, in contradistinction to mere 'polyphony ').

This fact in itself, of course, is not of the least importance. What is more important is that, while most composers since Bach who have essayed the old forms have generally approached them in a spirit of self-conscious archaism, van Dieren employs them as a natural means of expression. So far from being a mere exhibition of perverted ingenuity or a brilliant intellectual *tour de force*, the *Diaphony* is perhaps his most intimate and personal work. It is necessary to emphasize this point in view of the contrapuntal nature of such a large part of van Dieren's music. It is not easy to discover why or how the belief that it is an astounding feat to write a fugue should have gained such universal acceptance. Actually it is not so very difficult, provided one is not particular concerning the quality of the music. In precisely the same way it is easier to write a passable sonnet than fourteen lines of tolerably good blank verse. Formal restrictions are a help in art, not a hindrance, and the most perfect things in music as in any other art will invariably be found to be those in which some convention or restriction has been imposed upon or voluntarily chosen by the composer—a Bach fugue, a Palestrina mass or motet, an aria or concerted number of a Mozart opera.

The fugal forms of the *Diaphony* and other works of van Dieren, then, are not to be regarded as obstacles deliberately created in order to be overcome, but solely as a method of construction, a kind of ideal scaffolding, if anything a help rather than a hindrance. Not merely is it unnecessary for the ordinary listener

228

Bernard van Dieren

to be acquainted with the method according to which the work has been constructed; it is in most cases positively harmful that he should be. It is a matter which concerns the composer alone.

The fact remains that from the point of view of sheer constructive ability there is not one work in modern times, and indeed only the work of Bach and the Netherlanders, that could be compared with the *Diaphony*. This is not a mere statement of opinion, but a fact which can be demonstrated by means of an exhaustive analysis. There is hardly one note in the whole complicated work, lasting the best part of an hour, which does not perform some function with regard to the whole, or reveal some thematic origin. Not one chord, rhythm, or figuration but has a very definite and precise reason for its existence, and for the place and manner of its occurrence. There are in it no merely decorative adjuncts or mechanical, worked-up climaxes and other forms of musical stuffing, for it is an attempt to create a perfectly articulated organism such as nature presents in living organisms of flora and fauna. To those good people who like to imagine artists swimming in inspiration, like flies in treacle, this may seem to imply a lack of that estimable commodity. To them one need only reply that surely the conception of such a plan can itself be called an inspiration.

On the other hand, it might legitimately be urged against the work that its quite staggering complexity necessarily precludes the possibility that anyone but the composer should be able thoroughly to grasp and understand it. To be able to do so would imply the possession of a faculty only little inferior to that of its creator. On the other hand, certain sections, such as the whole of the beginning, and the second sonnet, can be easily understood and appreciated by the average intelligent listener.

Bernard van Dieren

The succeeding period of the composer's activity is almost entirely confined to the simpler medium of the string quartet and represents a marked advance in the direction of greater simplicity, both of thought and style. The second quartet, Op. 9, consists of four movements, each of which is conspicuous on account of the striking originality of conception. In the first movement each instrument has its own subject, which it retains and develops throughout without any interchange. The second, with the exception of a passage for the viola, is played entirely without the bow : not pizzicato exactly, but ' thrummed ' with the finger. The effect in performance, probably not unlike that of the ancient lute, is one of great beauty and originality. The *scherzo* consists of a rapid figure in semiquavers played by the two violins rising gradually, almost imperceptibly, from the lowest to the highest register, and then gradually sinking back again, while the two lower strings are occupied with more sustained and definitely melodic figures. The last movement is an elaborate canon in the course of which every conceivable device of *stretti*, augmentation, diminution, *cancrizans*, and so forth, is employed ; always so naturally and unobtrusively, however, that one would probably not notice their occurrence unless one were told to look for them.

The two recitations with string quartet accompaniment—one a ballade of Villon, the other a sonnet of Baudelaire—are exquisite miniatures remarkable among other things for the manner in which the problem, always a troublesome one, of reconciling the speaking voice with the instruments, is solved. They consist of prologues and epilogues between which the recitation of the poem is skilfully dovetailed. Two songs, also with string quartet, which, together with the foregoing, constitute Op. 10—the first a setting of a passage from de Quincey's prose poem *Levana*, the second a setting of a poem from *The Cenci*—are among van Dieren's most perfect achievements in the smaller forms ; the latter in particular is a lyric of great beauty into which is concentrated all the pathos and tragic intensity of Shelley's sombre drama.

The third quartet for strings, Op. 13, the last of the group, is perhaps the best of all these works for the same medium. In it van Dieren has finally achieved the directness and concision at which he has been consistently aiming ever since the *Diaphony*, particularly in the matter of harmony, which, though surprisingly simple and restrained, is nevertheless wholly personal. The slow movement is especially remarkable for its studied simplicity and directness. In its purity and transparency of style one is irresistibly reminded of the *Madrigali spirituali* of Palestrina, in which the quintessence of the master's art is revealed.

The succeeding works, whatever their intrinsic musical interest, all possess the same absolute perfection of style, the finest example being a setting of a sonnet of Spenser for voice and a chamber combination of instruments. The orchestral *Introit* to a choral work based on the fifth chapter of Rabelais' *Gargantua*, performed a couple of years ago at a promenade concert in London, is not likely to gain any new admirers for van Dieren's music, despite its incontestable contrapuntal mastery. It is one of those works which for no visible reason does not 'come off' in performance. It is probably to be accounted one of van Dieren's few complete failures.

There remains to be noticed an opera in three acts entitled *The Tailor*, to the libretto of Mr. Robert Nichols. It differs entirely from almost all modern operas in being modelled upon the old Italian *opera buffa*, and in being consequently written throughout in set vocal numbers and recitative. It is a veritable

Bernard van Dieren

masterpiece of wit and humour, revealing, as each of his large works does, an entirely fresh aspect of the composer's talents, and one which is doubly welcome to those who may have been baffled and disconcerted by the intricacies and austerities of the *Diaphony*. The caste is small, and the work is intended for a small orchestra; in fact it might be called a chamber opera. From one point of view it might be regarded as a satire on the old operatic conventions; from another it might be considered as a revitalization and re-creation of them. Both points of view would be justified, for it is both at the same time. Like the literary parodies of Max Beerbohm, the musical parodies of van Dieren are so like the originals, and so often superior to them in substance and in musical interest, that it is sometimes exceedingly difficult to say whether there has been a definitely satiric intention or not. This subtlety is perhaps the greatest attraction of the work.

Van Dieren has also written, besides the works already enumerated, a large number of songs with piano accompaniment representing every phase of his artistic development, which it is obviously impossible to deal with here in detail. Many are of great beauty, particularly settings of Heine and Verlaine, two poets for whom the composer seems to have a special affection. His treatment of the voice in these songs, as indeed in all his works, is strikingly contrasted with that of the majority of his contemporaries. He writes for it, not in the instrumental style of Strauss or Schönberg, nor in the colourless *quasi parlando* of Debussy or Ravel, nor in the folk-song style of so many English composers, but always in conformity with the true principles of vocal writing as exemplified in the works of the great Italian masters, Rossini, Donizetti, and Bellini. Needless to say, I am here speaking only of abstract method, not of the quality of the music in itself. The accompaniments are often of the utmost independence and the most extreme difficulty, not so much from the point of view of mere finger technique as from that of interpretation.

If one were asked to say what one considered to be the most striking characteristic common to all of this composer's music, one would without hesitation say that it was his sense of style. Many composers, of whom perhaps Bach is the highest representative, seem to conceive their works more or less abstractly—i. e. without reference to the particular instrumental combination they eventually employ. The genus, or sex (so to speak), remains indeterminate, not only after conception, but even after birth and growth. Sometimes a work will completely change its genus, and change from a piano to a violin concerto, as the young lady in the essay of Montaigne changed into a man. While the medium employed may be thoroughly satisfactory and even felicitous, it remains largely arbitrary; the inner essence of the music is generally unimpaired by transcription or adaptation. One can imagine a work of Bach still retaining the major element of its charm even if it were performed on two combs and an umbrella.

Other composers, of whom Mozart is the archetype, seem to conceive their works from the very start in terms of some definite medium, the idea and the form which it is to receive taking shape simultaneously in the composer's mind. In Mozart's music we are always conscious of a complete and indissoluble identity of form and idea, a perfect fusion of the two elements. It is impossible to dissociate them in our mind. The style varies with the means employed.

For the sake of completeness, it is as well to mention a third category of musicians for whom the choice of medium employed precedes and, as it were, dictates or suggests the idea. To this class belong instrumental

Bernard van Dieren

specialists, generally executants, such as Thalberg, Wieniavski, Vieuxtemps, &c., and orchestral *saltimbanques* and funambulists such as Stravinsky. The artistic value of their productions is practically nil.

Van Dieren belongs to the second group; he is in fact one of the few real stylists since Mozart. One rarely feels that his works are transcriptions of abstract tonal conceptions for more or less fortuitous instrumental or vocal combinations. To rearrange them would be to destroy or at least seriously to impair them. In a few instances where he has rearranged works for a different medium from that in which they were conceived, such as the *Levana* and *Cenci* songs with string quartet accompaniments which were originally written for the piano, the works have been entirely recast, reconceived, as it were, from the beginning. The two versions are entirely different from each other from beginning to end.

While it is perhaps van Dieren's only point of contact with the most representative composers of to-day that his orchestral method consists in accenting the individuality of each instrumental voice, and in permitting it to mould the thematic thought in terms of its own temperament, rather than in doubling and otherwise disposing them all so that they coalesce into a homogeneous and neutralized body of sound like the full swell of an organ, he differs conspicuously from his fellows in relying almost exclusively on the natural characteristics and legitimate capabilities of each instrument, and in avoiding that distressing and almost universal tendency of the present day to exploit every possible device to the artificial deterioration of tone-colour, like the employment of mutes, *col legno*, *sul ponticello*, *flatterzunge*, and so forth.

Van Dieren is first and foremost a melodist; with the exception of Bartók and possibly to a certain extent Schönberg, there is no other composer living

234

Bernard van Dieren

who has such a gift for creating sustained, flowing melodic lines. Do not let this be misunderstood. Melody is of two different types: one that I might call poetic, and the other, prose, melody. The former is constructed for the most part in periods of a definite length, corresponding to the feet and metres of lyric poetry, the whole forming the equivalent of a stanza or group of stanzas. Such are the finest melodies of the older music, perhaps of all music. But there is another kind, which simply evolves out of itself, is not constructed in groups of four or any other number of bars, and makes no symmetrical stanza. Such is the melody of van Dieren. It has not perhaps the same immediate sensuous and emotional appeal of the older variety—and although we call it older or more primitive, there is no implication that it is necessarily inferior, or even superior, any more than one can say that verse is better or worse than prose. On the other hand, this kind of prose melody is a more fitting vehicle for what one might call the more intellectual conceptions and for the development of a logical argument. They serve different purposes, but both have equally their *raison d'être*. The one does not exclude the other. Unfortunately, this kind of prose melody is of comparatively recent development in music, and few musicians have sufficiently developed the faculty for understanding it. The Whitmanesque prosaic poetry of Wagner and the poetic prose style of a large part of the music of Delius is about as far as most people have got. Consequently it is often mistaken for a lack of melody, because it is judged according to the older standard. Nevertheless the faculty for appreciating it is bound to grow rapidly in the course of time. I can only say that while van Dieren's music has been reproached for lacking melody, I find it on the contrary fuller of melody than that of almost any other composer of to-day.

Bernard van Dieren

While his earlier work up to and including the *Chinese Symphony* presents certain difficulties to the listener from the harmonic point of view—one might also include in this category certain passages in the *Diaphony*—the harmonic style of the later works is extremely clear and easy to grasp, even at a single hearing. With all its originality and distinction it is only a development and extension of the procedures of the past. It is essentially the harmony of *Die Meistersinger* and *Parsifal*, and, one might add, of Delius, pushed one step farther. The earlier harmonic style exemplified in the first quartet is definitely atonal; the harmony in the later works, however chromatic, is always felt to be constructed around a tonic, although that tonic may perhaps never be sounded. The characteristic chord which more than any other gives the distinctive harmonic flavour to van Dieren's music is that of the eleventh without the third and with a minor ninth. The secret of the subtle charm of his music is in large part due to the way in which one chromatic chord melts into another without resolution, while one or more of its constituent parts remains stationary, or nearly so.

Finally, his work is distinguished by its amazing rhythmic plasticity. More than any living composer he has emancipated himself from the tyranny of the bar-line and the eight-bar phrase. Other composers who seem to have done so have too often only distorted the conventional metres, as Schönberg and, in a different way, Stravinsky have done. Van Dieren's music is always written without any bars at all, although they have occasionally been inserted afterwards in order to facilitate the execution. Needless to say there is nothing new in all this, or in anything else, for that matter, in van Dieren's mature work, this particular feature of his music being only a reversion to the methods of fifteenth- and sixteenth-century composers.

Bernard van Dieren

As in their music, the rhythmic periods of the different parts in, say, the string quartets of van Dieren, do not synchronize; consequently the employment of regular bars would tend to obscure the sense of one or more of the parts, like a faulty punctuation. This extreme rhythmic plasticity and subtlety have, of course, been regarded as a lack of rhythmical vitality in the same way that his gift for melody has been regarded as a lack of melody. The reader is invited to refer back to the essay on Stravinsky for a development of this point.

All these great qualities in the music of van Dieren —melodic flow, harmonic resource, rhythmic vitality, are the direct consequence and inevitable outcome of the contrapuntal and polyphonic principles upon which his work, like that of the great masters, is based ; for it is the living, eternal principle underlying all great music whatsoever, of any period and in any place. It may now and then be possible for a man of genius like Monteverde or Moussorgsky, or, in our day, Debussy, to create a circumscribed and personal art through the negation of these principles, but their influence will always be pernicious and they are doomed to have no posterity, but only deformed and monstrous abortions. And in any case, what is the achievement of one man, however great, when set against the tradition of a hundred years !

Van Dieren, it seems to me, fulfils Busoni's prediction of the advent of a *Junge Klassizität*, consisting in ' die Meisterung die Sichtung und Ausbeutung aller Errungenschaften vorausgegangener Experimente: ihrer Hineintragung in festen und schönen Formen ' —and his prophecy of the triumph of melody over all other means : ' die universale Polyphonie als letzte Konsequenz der Melodik, als Erzeugerin der Harmonie und als Trägerin der Idee.' Van Dieren, in a word, achieves that which Busoni has always been attempting

Bernard van Dieren

but has never yet achieved. Busoni is to be regarded as a forerunner, one sent to prepare the way for the new Classicism, of which van Dieren is perhaps only the first representative.

The chief characteristics of almost every typical modern composer is the dissatisfaction with traditional means and the love of experiment for its own sake, or the search for new means of expression, leading to stylistic disintegration. Most modern music lacks the organic quality which characterizes the greatest artistic productions ; it is made up for the most part of isolated episodes and fragments cunningly welded together into an artificial semblance of unity. Nietzsche's diagnosis of the symptoms of decadence, ' the decline of organizing power, the abuse of traditional means without the capacity or the aims which would justify it, excessive vitality in small details, refinement as an expression of impoverished life, ever more nerves in the place of muscle '—all this reads as a description of most modern music.

Van Dieren stands in complete opposition to all these characteristic tendencies of the age. In his work one finds a complete avoidance of anything that savours of reckless experiment for its own sake. Despite his originality he reveals a profoundly aristocratic distaste for artistic barricades and *sansculottisme* ; his art is essentially a continuation of the great traditions of the past. It possesses that organic quality, the intellectual grasp and balance of the whole, which nearly all his contemporaries lack.

The underlying spirit which animates this music is a profound serenity and tranquillity which one may seek in vain elsewhere to-day, except perhaps in the music of Delius. In the midst of all the spiritual ferment and restlessness of our time van Dieren stands almost alone, a figure apart, like de Vigny, remote and inaccessible in his *tour d'ivoire*.

238

Bernard van Dieren

It will be readily understood that such an art as this is at the very opposite pole from romanticism, as defined in the first chapter. It would be a mistake, however, to suppose that the music of van Dieren is merely cold, formal, and precise. It is none the less deeply felt for being restrained in its expression ; and even if it were true that he sometimes seems to sacrifice expression to formal perfection, as, after all, even Bach and Mozart often do, the balance between the two elements is never so disproportionate as to deserve the reproach of formalism or pedantry.

The latent antagonism which subsists between him and his age is without doubt the primary cause of his neglect, but the time has arrived when it is at least no longer possible to ignore him. It is safe to say that when the inevitable reaction against the sensationalism and extravagance of most modern music sets in—and there is every indication that the day is not far distant—van Dieren will be recognized, by the elect at any rate, as one of the few living masters of music.

MINOR COMPOSERS

THE following pages are designed merely to fill out, as far as is possible, our survey of contemporary musical activity; to gather into one chapter all these aspects of it which do not require the full exposition accorded to the more important figures. Compared to the foregoing full-length studies it is a series of profiles only, and makes no pretence to completeness or even adequacy.

In Italy, the only country of importance which is not represented in the foregoing essays, the dominating figure, whether for good or bad, is still undoubtedly Puccini. No living composer is more despised and execrated by the leaders of musical opinion to-day in every country, for such very good reasons that the mere attempt to see him in proper perspective and to discuss him dispassionately and without prejudice demands a considerable measure of intrepidity. Yet it is evident that if he were of no significance whatever, he would not have aroused such fury and derision. It is only just both to him and to his detractors to say that this antagonism is not due merely to the natural jealousy which financial success and popular applause inevitably arouse in the breasts of his less fortunate colleagues. There is more in it than that. We do not lash ourselves into paroxysms of rage over the success of Mme Chaminade or Mr. Wilfred Sanderson. What we really resent, if we take the trouble to analyse our feelings, is that, however detestable his music may be, particularly on paper, it is impossible to deny that it generally ' comes off ' exasperatingly well in performance, while other and better music fails as disastrously. Puccini knows what he wants and he gets it.

240

How many composers to-day can say the same? He has probably a surer instinct for the theatre than any composer since Meyerbeer, and that in itself is a quality as much as any other, for the possession of which many better composers would gladly sacrifice a great deal. Moreover, some of his later work is by no means as contemptible as many suppose. For although his operas from *Manon Lescaut* onwards reveal a constantly growing preoccupation with theatrical effect and a correspondingly marked decline in musicianship—a melancholy progression in which *La fanciulla del West* represents the culminating point, or rather the nadir—his recent partial recovery, as exemplified in the so-called *Trittico*, is all the more welcome because it was so wholly unexpected. In this Puccini's artistic development suggests an analogy with that of Verdi. He seems to have set himself to Italianize modern composers in precisely the same way that Verdi, probably less consciously and deliberately, Italicized Wagner. But while the latter's attempt to prolong the existence of the old Italian tradition which was lying gasping and emaciated upon its death-bed, by means of a kind of artificial rejuvenation or transfusion of blood from a younger and more vital organism, resulted in the production of two supreme masterpieces, *Otello* and *Falstaff*—surely sufficient to justify the dangerous and unnatural experiment—the former's operation, performed by a less skilful and steady hand, has hardly turned out so successfully. At best the success has been only partial, though sufficient to prove an abiding possibility.

In Puccini's works the two elements, native and foreign, seem to exist side by side without coalescing as they do with Verdi into a homogeneous and wholly personal style. Like oil and water, they refuse to blend, and only exist together on the basis of mutual toleration and tacit understanding that the one

Q   241 must not intrude upon the domain of the other. When Puccini is in his lyrical vein he writes wholeheartedly in a somewhat dilapidated Italian *cantilena* style; he reserves his modern manner for those moments in which he wishes to be dramatic.

This duality is highly characteristic of modern Italy, of the perpetual antagonism between past and future —to the discomfort of the immediate present—which confronts us in every walk of Italian life, whether political, social, intellectual, or artistic. Every Italian exemplifies in microcosm this constant struggle for supremacy between two hostile and irreconcilable forces, and carries within him at once a Vatican and a Quirinal. Futurism and *passéisme*, d'Annunzio and Marinetti, Puccini and Malipiero, Fascismo and Communismo, are all expressions and products of this dualism. They are essentially the same thing; the one accepts the past, the other tries to revolt against it, but all alike are rooted in the disheartening certainty of their inability to escape it, in some form or another.

Puccini constantly gives one the impression of trying to escape from the past to which he naturally belongs, with which he is in secret sympathy. The neologisms with which he besprinkles his later works so lavishly are not the expression of inward conviction, but seem to be conceived and carried out in a spirit of disagreeable necessity. It is as if he rather dislikes them, really, but feels that it is incumbent on him to keep up to date and move with the times.

In this Puccini resembles Strauss, which he does in other things also, despite many differences. The main strength of each lies in his remarkable gift of musical characterization and psychological penetration. Puccini's gift in this direction is, needless to say, much narrower than that of Strauss, and is practically limited to the delineation of a particular type. As Debussy

wrote of Massenet, his operas are 'documents pour
servir à l'histoire de l'âme féminine'. Manon, Mimi,
Madame Butterfly, la Tosca, and so forth—whether
grande amoureuse, *grisette*, *geisha*, or *demi-mondaine*—
they all belong to the same type, and are all variations
on one theme. Puccini's music itself bears the same
relation to great art on the one hand and to frankly
mercenary art on the other as this feminine type
bears to the virtuous woman and to the prostitute.
Puccini does not write for money, but only takes
pleasure in giving pleasure; he does not ask for the
reverence and admiration of the few, or of that
melancholy abstraction we call Posterity—a very back-
ward and frigid lover—but only asks to be enjoyed
at the moment and for the moment. Moralists
condemn the *cocotte*, aesthetic purists despise Puccini;
no doubt both are right in doing so, and I certainly
would not think of defending either of them on moral
or aesthetic grounds. But when one hears a precious
and willowy aesthete fiercely declaiming against the
iniquities of Puccini, one cannot help being irresistibly
reminded of a Scottish elder shaking a large and badly
rolled gamp at a young lady of doubtful reputation.
In fact one feels that the performance is slightly
ridiculous, in spite of its abstract justification; one
even goes so far as to suspect that indignation is not
the only motive power behind their action. Personally, I must confess to a certain tolerant affection—extremely reprehensible, no doubt—for both
phenomena, and only burning with righteous indignation against the art which pretends to be something
other than it really is, like that of Scriabine or of
Stravinsky. Puccini's music at least does not pretend
to be other than it is, and surely no one ever claimed
for it that it was great art.

While Verdi and Puccini injected Wagner and
Debussy respectively into the veins of the old Italian

tradition, Drs. Malipiero and Casella, greatly daring, have gone one step farther, and have effected a third inoculation, consisting this time of neo-Russian monkey-gland. The alarming result, due, doubtless, to impurities latent in the culture, reminds one strongly of the story of Poe called ' The Facts in the Case of M. Valdemar ', in which the corpse of the said gentleman, galvanized into a factitious semblance of life, continued to reiterate passionately and interminably the word ' Dead ', until it finally collapsed, a ' nearly liquid mass of loathsome—of detestable putridity ', before the eyes of the horrified and bewildered onlookers. The music of Santoliquido, while confirming the deliquescence, does not fulfil the Dionysian promise of the composer's name. As for Pizzetti and his *Pisanella*—this is surely the *pis aller* !

In Spain much the same processes have taken place. Ravel rather than Debussy is the French influence in the music of Albeniz and Granados, and if neither it nor the Russian influence in Da Falla have had quite the same disastrous consequences as those noted above, the reason is to be found in the fact that they were effected, not upon an old and venerable tradition, as in the former case, but upon a young, vigorous, and healthy folk-art which has been able to make some resistance to the more conspicuously evil effects of the process. The manner only is Russian in Da Falla; the substance is the indigenous product of the soil. Apart from these two elements, there is little else in the music. It is always pleasant to listen to, but reveals no distinctive personality. Spanish national music has so far produced no Borodin or Moussorgsky, but only three Rimsky-Korsakovs—which is three too many. To English ears, their work all sounds like endless variations on one Spanish folk-song, provided with an elaborate accompaniment of castanets and similar exotic percussion instruments.

Minor Composers

Crossing the Pyrenees into France one encounters a bewildering quantity of composers but singularly little real achievement, apart from Debussy and Ravel. Among the older generation Vincent d'Indy is a real *maître*, but a thinker and theorist rather than a creative artist. Paul Dukas also commands respect on account of his sturdy independence and his almost Flaubertian probity and restraint, but these admirable qualities seem largely negative—the outcome of sterility rather than of strength. His music is small in quantity, always hard, cold, brilliant, and somewhat arid. It is not what the Italians call *simpatica*. Ladmirault, little known outside France and deliberately ignored inside because he does not subscribe whole-heartedly to the spiritual trade union called *la tradition française*, has written several quite beautiful works, based mainly upon Breton folk-songs. His music is consequently predominantly Celtic in mood, and harmonically he reveals a distinct affinity with Delius. Florent Schmitt, Roger Ducasse, Roussel, de Sévérac, and many others have written a vast quantity of music, mostly in the manner of Debussy and Ravel, which is of no significance whatever.

Eric Satie has been described as the spiritual father of that queer, miscellaneous progeny called Les Six (although now, through the secession of one of their number, they should be called Les Cinq), with considerable justification, for, like him, they combine an undoubted talent for advertisement with a complete lack of artistic ability. Poulenc and Auric most closely resemble their august sire, and expose their mental deficiencies with the cynical bravado and revolting candour of Calabrian beggars exhibiting their sores. Of Mlle Germaine Tailleferre one can only repeat Dr. Johnson's dictum concerning a woman preacher, transposed into terms of music: ' Sir, a woman's composing is like a dog's walking on his hind legs. It is not done well, but you are surprised to find it done at all.' Considered apart from her sex, her music is wholly negligible. Darius Milhaud, for some inscrutable reason known only to himself, sometimes, though not always, takes himself more seriously than any of the preceding, but achieves no more. He lacks both invention and constructive ability. Honegger, a Swiss, is the most talented member of the group, as he is also the most pretentious. Unlike most of his colleagues, who are generally most pleased with themselves when they have made the musical equivalent of a bad pun, he is always very much in earnest. His austerities and self-lacerations, however, seem as pointless as those of a Tibetan monk or dancing dervish, until one makes the momentous discovery that when he ceases to mortify his flesh—and incidentally ours also—he is apt to become merely banal and placidly Wagnerian, as in the *Pastorale d'Été* and other minor works.

The conspicuous defect of every member of the group, without distinction, consists in their complete lack of any sense of style. In a few bars they will pass airily from commonplace to cacophony, for no ostensible musical reason. It is not the cacophony in itself that one minds ; Schönberg is often just as cacophonous, but always with some definite aesthetic purpose, and a very sure sense of style. Call him mad, if you will ; you must at least concede that there is a clearly discernible method and logic in his madness. Les Six have no logic, no method, no aesthetic purpose ; any notes could be taken away or added, without any appreciable loss of effect, without even the composers themselves noticing it, one is fairly certain. They are not even mad—nothing nearly so interesting ; for the most part they are merely fools. They are obviously, demonstrably, pathetically incompetent. Moreover, they have no artistic conscience ; whenever some technical problem arises in the course of their work they refuse to make any effort to solve it: anything will do for them, for they have no convictions.

So much for 'la jeune France'. That the musical community in which such a group of charlatans and mountebanks can achieve a wide reputation must be in a curious state is a point too obvious to need labouring. Their works, however, will probably be of interest to the historian of the future, in that they will afford him an instructive insight into the mentality of post-war France.

Continuing our musical tour across the Rhine, one finds things in an even worse state, if indeed that be possible. Some twenty years ago M. Romain Rolland wrote as follows : ' Do you remember Goethe's ballad of Der Zauberlehrling (l'Apprenti Sorcier) which Dukas so cleverly made into music? There, in the absence of his master, an apprentice set working some magic spells, and so opened sluice gates that no one could shut, and the house was flooded. That is what Germany has done. She has let loose a flood of music and is about to be drowned in it.'

This shrewd prophecy has now been realized. In musical Germany to-day, as far as the ear can reach, nothing is to be heard but a wide ocean of notes in which no landmarks are audible. The only feature of interest, as in the fable, is the swollen and decomposed corpse of the Zauberlehrling himself, Richard Strauss, who, more than anyone else, is responsible for this melancholy state of affairs. (M. Romain Rolland's simile is all the more applicable to him, for in his opera *Feuersnot* he has definitely represented himself as the successor and pupil of the great magician Richard Wagner.) Otherwise nothing else shows above the surface ; the most that can happen to us is to run aground on some nasty snag like Franz Schreker, some

Minor Composers

mud-shoal like Erich Korngold, or a sandbank like Paul Hindemith. We may be thankful if we are able to push off again without having done much injury to our frail craft. If there is any ark of refuge in all this watery waste, wherein a few choice spirits have taken shelter, one can only say that it is very difficult to find. There are no signs of it anywhere.

There is far too much music in Germany; too many composers, too many works published, too many orchestras, too many concerts. In England we are in the habit of complaining of the lack of material facilities for building up a national musical culture like that of the Germans; we do not realize that it is better to have too few than too many. In Germany it is far too easy to get a work published or performed; mediocre music pours from the press in torrents like marks, with the same consequent depreciation of value. Concert succeeds concert with such rapidity and in such profusion that composers have no time to be alone with themselves or to think at all about their work. The English composer may often be compelled for lack of opportunity to put what he considers a good work away, unperformed, in a drawer for a few years. This may be a disadvantage in many ways, but it at least gives him time to consider his work coolly and critically; and when his opportunity arises he will be all the better for it. Besides, this lack of opportunity does at least ensure the working of the necessary though cruel law of the survival of the fittest. In Germany a fine talent is apt to be trodden under foot by a vast and limitless horde of miserable little weaklings and cripples. There is in Germany a terrible dead level of mediocrity that inevitably stifles genius, and there can be little hope for German music in the immediate future unless the financial difficulties of the country bring about some restriction and diminution in the supply, and put an end to this

248

reckless process of spiritual inflation and destruction of true values.

In Austria a similar state of affairs prevails, but instead of the corpse of Strauss, it is the pale and ineffective ghost of Gustav Mahler which dominates the scene. Otherwise there is only Schönberg, whom we have already considered, and a few of his disciples and imitators, such as Alban Berg and Anton von Webern, who outdare their master in his more azure feats. But while Schönberg is driven by instinct and inspiration, possibly perverted and frequently misdirected, they write without spontaneity, through calculation and deduction. They are cerebral without being intellectual, perverse without passion or inner conviction.

Proceeding eastward in our frenzied search for genuine music, like Dr. Syntax in search of a wife, we find in Hungary, apart from Bartók, one sympathetic figure in the person of Zoltán Kodály. He is always spoken of as a follower or imitator of his compatriot and contemporary on account of certain superficial resemblances between them, but this is unjust. Such stylistic similarities as do undoubtedly exist are not the result of the influence of either composer upon the other, but are simply the outcome of wholly impersonal and extraneous influences to which both have equally been subject. Their respective talents have been nurtured under precisely the same conditions, and have reacted to precisely the same artistic stimuli, particularly that afforded by the distinctive idiomatic peculiarities of Hungarian folk-music. But although both speak much the same language, they express a different order of ideas and emotions. Their personalities are quite distinct from each other.

Kodály has written very little—surprisingly little, indeed, but the exiguity of his output is due rather to the deliberate exercise of restraint and self-control than to any lack of invention. He is the possessor of an unsparing critical sense, and a laudable distaste for encumbering the already groaning earth with even one more unnecessary or imperfectly realized work. This aristocratic reserve and sensibility reveals itself in everything he does, and it is this curious and possibly unique combination of a popular and idiomatic mode of expression with refinement and delicacy of feeling which constitutes the peculiar charm and appeal of his music.

His slow movements strike one on the whole as being his best ; they are certainly the most completely personal. He has a vein of wistful meditation, of searching tenderness and melancholy, which is quite his own. With all his simplicity and directness, one is nevertheless always conscious of a curious subtlety and refinement of style, a studious exactness and precision of touch underlying the somewhat deceptive appearance of candour and ingenuousness in his pro- cedure. Bartók undoubtedly touches greater heights than Kodály ; his genius is of a more robust order. Kodály seems rather to avoid extremes, not necessarily because he is fundamentally incapable of them, or because he subscribes to the anti-emotionalist dogmas of certain modern composers, but simply from a natural and instinctive reticence and a habit of emotional reserve. There is a delicate and elusive fragrance about his music which it is impossible to define or analyse ; a subtle aroma not unlike that of his native Tokay, imperceptible, no doubt, to palates vitiated by the vodka of the modern Russians, or by the cocktails of Les Six. We may be indifferent to it at first, but in time we come to appreciate it.

In Poland Szymanovsky seems to be a solitary figure. He began writing strange, rather clotted works, sug- gestive of the Viennese Secessionist art movement, but

seems to have since joined the large French Foreign
Legion of music, which is disappointing, as there were
signs of originality and promise, though hardly of
actual fulfilment, in his early work.

In Russia there is only Prokoviev who deserves
mention—though on second thought one might perhaps question whether even he does. He is quite
clever and accomplished, but without much personality or definite convictions, and is consequently
very uncertain of his direction. He would seem to
bear much the same relation to Stravinsky that
Glazounov bears to the nationalist school of the
previous generation.

And so, without taking the trouble of pursuing our
investigations any further, we return home, weary and
dispirited. Why, indeed, should we go abroad for
things which we can turn out just as well at home?
In the same way that Stanford and Parry provided
us with second-hand Brahms, Cyril Scott provides us
with imitation Debussy; Holbrooke and Bantock
have followed Strauss, and in the music of Goossens,
Bliss, and Berners we find our English Ravel, Stravinsky,
and Satie. In every generation it has been the same
thing; only the models have changed. Like the three
Gorgons of Greek mythology, whose hands, appropriately enough, were of brass, whose bodies were
covered with scales—whether diatonic or chromatic,
we are not told—and who possessed only one eye and
one tooth between them, so these three latter share
a Franco-Russian technique in common. The outcome of their combined efforts, like that of their
forerunners, is precisely nil—not even a minus quantity
—just nothing at all.

The music of Gustav Holst is perhaps the most
characteristic and striking example of this tendency
on the part of British composers generally. While
the others are content with one or two continental

models, his style is a compendium or *pastiche* of the styles of nearly all representative modern composers, which he has equally failed to make his own. He has no more originality of outlook than any of the composers mentioned above; if anything he has less. But while they have no particular convictions, one way or another, Holst has many convictions against him. It is largely on account of his undoubted earnestness and sincerity that his art seems the more definitely pernicious. The faults of the others are negative, his are positive. I observed in the Preface that mediocrities can make even the greatest virtues detestable, and Holst is an example of this. Like so many mediocre minds he is attracted by the largest and most grandiose conceptions; nothing but the greatest themes of all art will satisfy him, such as *The Planets*, the *Hymns from the Rig-Veda*, the *Hymn of Jesus*, and so forth. In Heine's phrase, he perpetually feeds on the fixed stars and drinks the Milky Way.

Two figures, apart from Delius and Elgar, stand *au-dessus de la mêlée* of English composers, namely Vaughan Williams and Arnold Bax. One's first impression of the former is one of complete, almost sublime incompetence. He flounders about in the sea of his ideas like a vast and ungainly porpoise, with great puffing and blowing; yet in the end, after tremendous efforts and an almost heroic tenacity, there emerges, dripping and exhausted from the struggle, a real and lovable personality, unassuming, modest, and almost apologetic. His personality is wholly and without admixture English, and this is at once his virtue and his defect. It accounts for the enormous personal appeal his work has for those who feel in the same way, and for the complete bewilderment and antipathy which it must almost inevitably inspire in those whose racial sympathies and traditions have nothing in common with his. One cannot imagine a typical Frenchman or Italian being able to enter into the spirit of this art; they will only see the apparent clumsiness and incompetence.

The only reproach one could make to Vaughan Williams is that he is too easily satisfied with expressing his peculiar emotion. He is apt to present us with what is after all only the raw material of a work of art, and not the work itself. His works are not what Cézanne called 'realized', but always amorphous and inchoate; they lack solidity and precision. They are mood-pastes rather than works, and are so apt to become monotonous.

Bax is in many ways the exact opposite to Vaughan Williams. He is possessed of immense facility, and has the technique of all the schools, ancient and modern, at his finger-ends. He is consequently prone to write too quickly, and too much, without mature deliberation, with the result that in all his large output there is hardly a single work which is a satisfactory whole; at the same time there is hardly one which does not reveal the presence of a finely sensitive and richly gifted personality. He has potentially every quality, including the rarest of all, genuine creative imagination. If one must conclude by saying that his work is generally disappointing, it is nevertheless an implied compliment of the highest order; one is disappointed because one expects so much.

POSTFACE

IT has often been observed with a certain show of reason that the phase through which music is at present passing, viewed historically, possesses many features in common with the period which followed the death of Palestrina and the subsequent break-up of the old polyphonic tradition in the first decades of the seventeenth century. The symptoms at least are identical. First, the love of experiment for its own sake, and the search for ' new means of expression ' ; secondly, a dissatisfaction with traditional methods without the ability to dispense with them altogether, giving rise to a curious duality and inequality of style. Those composers of to-day who have succeeded in achieving a congruous style have only done so by exclusion, by restricting their vocabulary to a very limited selection of neologisms. In this way, by means of this ' narrowness amounting to a positive gift ', it has been possible for a few composers to achieve a small handful of good works out of the limited resources of their own personalities ; but in the end, as we have seen so often in the course of this book, this narrow circle has generally proved to be nothing but a noosed rope which has in the end strangled their creative faculty altogether.

Nevertheless, despite certain superficial resemblances, the analogy between the two periods is fundamentally false, and consequently misleading. For while the bold and revolutionary innovations of Monteverde and the other pioneers of the *Nuove Musiche* did definitely constitute a new departure, a complete break with the old order, and the beginning of a new era in the art of music, it is impossible to

254

say the same of the secessionists of the present day. The tentative gropings and childish experiments of the former developed in the course of time until a language was formed which was a fitting vehicle for an art at least as great as that of their predecessors; but it is extremely improbable, to say the least, that the experiments of our modern revolutionaries will eventually prove to be the nucleus of a new art, for actually there is very little that is new in them. Monteverde might be called the Christopher Columbus of music, or at least the Amerigo Vespucci who has given his name to the continent which others, as much as he, helped to discover. Modern composers, in spite of their efforts, have conspicuously failed to discover a new continent. At best all they have done has been to circumnavigate the known world, to explore remote and uncivilized territories, and to have reached the extreme poles of musical possibilities. Debussy, as we have seen, only rediscovered the oldest world of all, so old and so completely forgotten that it had all the appearance of novelty—the world of plain-chant and *faux bourdon*. With Stravinsky we find ourselves in barbaric countries under tropic skies, a country of elemental and elementary savage rhythms and simple melodic formulas indefinitely repeated—the very Africa of music. Schönberg has attained to the North Pole of music and to the Antarctic barrier of ice—' a China wall built up from the sea', as Herman Melville has it in *Mardi*, ' and nodding its fronted towers in the dun, clouded sky'. But nowhere has anyone discovered a new world, because there is none left to discover. As in the actual physical world, there are only two worlds in music: the Old Polyphonic World of Palestrina, the New Harmonic World of Monteverde; there is nothing else.

The music of the last twenty years or so, whether that of Debussy, Stravinsky, Schönberg, or anyone else, despite all its appearance of novelty, is in reality only the last expression of expiring Romanticism, which itself discovered no new continent, but only exploited and cultivated the known world to an hitherto unparalleled extent. It was a movement of expansion, enrichment, and colonization, as it were ; the modern movement has been one of adventure and exploration for their own sakes.

It is an easily ascertainable law to which there are no exceptions that the decadence of all artistic movements or tendencies always takes the form of a reaction against its earlier ideals. The chaste symmetry and poise of Renaissance art gave place, towards the end of the sixteenth century, to the curved and undulating lines, the tasteless and overloaded ornamentation, of the baroque. But this change constitutes no new departure in itself ; it remains degenerate Renaissance. Similarly the polished elegance and emotional insensibility which are characteristic of the best art of the eighteenth century dissolve into a flood of tears with Rousseau, Richardson, Saint-Pierre, and others ; yet they unmistakably derive from the same artistic impulse, of which their emotions are only, so to speak, the reflux or backwash. And the modern movement bears precisely the same relation to nineteenth-century or romantic art ; so far from being a new movement or a new tendency, it consists in the reversal of old values, not in the creation of new ones ; in the application of what are fundamentally the same artistic methods and procedures to the exploitation of hitherto neglected or deliberately avoided aspects of the romantic spirit. The modern movement is not a movement at all, but a reflex action, the fag-end and decay of the nineteenth-century tradition, the afterbirth of romanticism, the harlequinade at the end of the play. It would be easy to show by means of musical illustrations that there is not a single technical device or manner of procedure of importance in the modern armoury which cannot be directly traced to its origin in the work of the great romantic masters, and in that of Liszt in particular.

The same holds good of the general ideas and conceptions underlying the music. The great *Faust* Symphony of Liszt contains in embryo, in its three movements, the three separate aspects or phases of the art of the last century. The first, *allegro furioso*, with its characteristic alternations of exultation and despair, admirably symbolizes the art of Byron, Delacroix, Berlioz, and others; the second, impassioned yet serene, represents the more typically English side of the movement, as exemplified in the art of Wordsworth, Keats, Shelley, and Delius; the sinister and demoniac *scherzo*, in which the themes of the preceding movements are derisively parodied and inverted, affords a striking parallel to the art of Rimbaud, Laforgue, Joyce, Stravinsky, and Schönberg in his *Pierrot Lunaire*. Most striking of all, however, is that, in the same way that the last movement of the Symphony ends with the tranquil evocation of the fundamental idea of the whole of the Faust poem, embodied in the lines beginning 'Alles vergängliche ist nur ein Gleichnis', &c., so in the last number of *Pierrot Lunaire* the fantastic and distorted visions clear away, as in *Don Quixote*, and the romantic spirit, lying on its death-bed, looks back with tender longing and regret to the days of its youth, and to its old long-lost illusions, and lives them over again in recollection for the last time. The first motiv of the romantic symphony is invoked at the close of the third movement, the motiv of 'Old, unhappy, far-off things', and thus the romantic cycle is completed, rounded off, consummated, in the after-glow of its departed sunset. Then, the last toneless whisper, 'O alter Duft aus Märchenzeit'—and all is still. The spirit

R

Postface

has departed, the last embers in the sky are quenched. So ends that strange, disquieting, yet profoundly moving work, *Pierrot Lunaire*, and with it ends that magnificent, absurd, chaotic, quixotic adventure called the Romantic Movement.

It is interesting to note that the *Ulysses* of James Joyce also ends in the same way. After the savage and revolting cynicism of the last fifty pages, the final section soars up into the air like a bird, with a lyrical ecstasy unequalled in modern literature. *Ulysses*, too, is a symbol of restless exploration and adventure, of the modern spirit in art. Throughout, it too is a satire and inversion of romantic themes, and creates nothing. Joyce is the Goethean Mephistopheles personified in art, ' der Geist der stets verneint '.

Both these works, and indeed all the typical achievements in modern art, are a *cul-de-sac*, a terminal point beyond which it is manifestly impossible to progress. There is nothing more to be done in this direction ; no new possibilities remain to be exploited, short of a reconstruction of the fundamental physical principles of music by the adoption of third or quarter tones. But why should we go any further ? Why should we emigrate to a new planet or a new solar system ? The sun is not yet burnt out ; there are still infinite potentialities in the world for us to exploit. The fact that there are no new lands to discover does not mean that there is nothing for us to do but sit and twiddle our thumbs—very much the opposite. *Il faut cultiver notre jardin*, all over-run with weeds and become a wilderness while we Candides, Panglosses, and Cunégondes have been careering wildly about the world, seeking for some ulterior wisdom which does not exist.

No doubt it is good to travel, like Ulysses, among strange peoples and to learn their minds ; it is a part, and perhaps a necessary part, of our education, and

the artist who has never travelled in the spirit and
experimented in many and diverse directions is seldom
one of the greatest. But in the end he must give up
his wandering nomadic existence and his adventures
with sirens, Polyphemus, Nausicaa, Circe, and the
rest, and seek again the broad high-roads of artistic
endeavour, the old traditions, his Penelope, faithfully
waiting for the wanderer to return. She has already
been waiting too long.

In art that which is wholly new quickly withers
away or grows stale. Only the eternal commonplaces
are eternally new, though it is true that only a genius
can reveal their novelty. It is the unimaginative who
must travel to strange places in order to find the
beauty which in reality is everywhere and all around
him, if he would only open his eyes. There is as
much mystery in Bloomsbury as in Tibet, if we
know where and how to look for it.[1] People who tell
us that the fugue is exhausted, the symphony exhausted,
the symphonic poem exhausted, the opera or music-
drama exhausted, and so on, are simply showing their
lack of imagination. It is possible that these forms
may for a moment be worked out, in turn, but never
all together. It is only necessary to let them lie fallow
for a time, and they will always renew themselves.
The possible combinations, permutations, transformations of the known are infinite in number. Nothing
can exhaust them. One always has this illusion about
everything. Even a great artist, when he has finished
a work, is apt to feel that there is nothing more left
for him to say, that he has exhausted himself. But
it is only an illusion. No potential source of energy

[1] In the words of the ribald parodist :

> A swear-word in a City slum
> A simple swear-word is to some—
> To Masefield, something more.

Postface

can be exhausted, for it has the capacity for infinite renewal and replenishment out of itself.

The immediate future, it is impossible to doubt, will witness a return to tradition in some form or another, a revitalization of old forms, the reconstitution of an homogeneous musical language by the naturalization and incorporation in the old of whatever has been found to be valuable and enduring in recent experiments. Signs of this have already appeared in the theories of Busoni and in the practice of van Dieren, and in many other similar symptoms. In its turn that phase will also pass, and a new period of storm and stress, a new romantic movement, will ensue. So it always has been, so it always will be. It is the *systole-diastole* of the world of art. They are necessary and complementary to one another. What do all these tendencies and directions matter, ultimately? Only genius matters, whether classic, romantic, or both and neither, like Bach and Beethoven—it is all the same.

It has been truly said that however desperate one's circumstances might be, however hard one's fate, no one would ever willingly divest himself of his *petite personnalité* and become another individual, with different feelings, different associations, and different ideas. The very idea is unthinkable, repellent. And so with our age; we may compare it unfavourably with others, we may sigh for the ' good old days ' of Pheidias, of Bach, of Leonardo, of Shakespeare, but if it were possible would we willingly go back to any one of them irrevocably, never to return, by means of some magic carpet? I hardly think so. Like Oisin, we may in spirit go to the land of the immortals and dwell there for a time, but return we must ; we cannot help it. Our age is a part of us ; we are a part of our age. We cannot live in any other, and we would not if we could.

260

Postface

' Ah, sir,' said the lady, ' this is a sad, degenerate age ! ' ' Ah, madam,' answered the philosopher, ' let us thank Heaven that neither you nor I belong to it ! '[1] A very sound reply, for even the greatest abusers of their age have often been its greatest lovers within their hearts. Was it not Nietzsche who said that in fighting Wagner he was fighting one-half of himself? Poor dear age, you have indeed been sadly abused in many of these pages, but it is a lover's abuse. We all love you in spite of your faults, perhaps even largely on account of them. We cannot help loving you.

[1] Sir Arthur Quiller-Couch, *Essays in Literature.*